The GNOSTIC GOSPELS
Ultimate Collection

Over 30 Lost and Suppressed Texts
That Changed Early Christianity
Mary Magdalene, Thomas, Judas, Philip, Pistis Sophia,
and other rare Gnostic scriptures

LARGE PRINT

Rush Nilson

★★★★★   ★★★★★   ★★★★★
PLEASE NOTE
THE FOLLOWING CAREFULLY

The **audiobook** and the **additional contents** can only be accessed by scanning the **QR code** on the page after the Table of Contents and visiting the **website address** indicated on that same page.

If you encounter any difficulties, feel free to write to us at:

info@manuscryptha.com   or   *rushnilson@manuscryptha.com*

Thank you for your understanding.

TABLE OF CONTENTS

THE CORE GOSPELS — IX
   Introduction to The Nine That Speak First — ix

THE GOSPEL OF MARY — 1
   Introduction to the Gospel of Mary — 1
   Mary Magdalene: The Forgotten Apostle — 1
   Vision and Revelation: The Message of Mary — 2
   Conflict and Authority: Mary and the Apostles — 2
   Historical Context — 3
   The Gospel of Mary: The Text — 4

THE GOSPEL OF THOMAS — 8
   Introduction to the Gospel of Thomas — 8
   The Hidden Gospel: A Voice Outside the Canon — 8
   Sayings of the Living Jesus: A Wisdom Tradition — 9
   Knowing Yourself, Finding the Kingdom — 9
   Historical Context — 10
   The Gospel of Thomas: The Text — 11

THE GOSPEL OF PHILIP — 22
   Introduction to the Gospel of Philip — 22
   A Gospel of Intimacy and Mystery — 22
   The Sacred Union: Beyond the Flesh — 23
   Anointing, Light, and the Return to Wholeness — 24
   Historical Context — 25
   The Gospel of Philip: The Text — 25

THE GOSPEL OF TRUTH — 30
   Introduction to the Gospel of Truth — 30
   The Gospel That Begins in Silence — 30
   Ignorance and Knowing: A Journey of Return — 31
   The Revealer of Wholeness — 31
   Historical Context — 32
   The Gospel of Truth: The Text — 33

THE GOSPEL OF JUDAS   37

    Introduction to the Gospel of Judas   37
    Judas and the Wisdom of Shadows   37
    Worlds Within Worlds: A Gnostic Vision of the Cosmos   38
    A Gospel That Was Never Meant to Be Safe   38
    Historical Context   39
    The Gospel of Judas: The Text   40

THE APOCRYPHON OF JOHN   44

    Introduction to the Apocryphon of John   44
    A Vision in the Shadow of the Temple   44
    Worlds Above and Worlds Below   45
    Remembering the Light Within   45
    Historical Context   46
    The Apocryphon of John: The Text   47

THE GOSPEL OF THE EGYPTIANS   65

    Introduction to the Gospel of the Egyptians   65
    A Voice from the Light Beyond the Aeons   65
    Seth, the Incorruptible Race, and the Baptism of Light   66
    Mystery, Silence, and the Return to Fullness   66
    Historical Context   67
    The Gospel of the Egyptians: The Text   68

THE SOPHIA OF JESUS CHRIST   77

    Introduction to the Sophia of Jesus Christ   77
    The Unveiling of Divine Knowledge   77
    The Eternal Dance of Sophia and the Father   78
    The Path of Immortal Awakening   79
    Historical Context   80
    The Sophia of Jesus Christ: The Text   81

THE SECOND TREATISE OF THE GREAT SETH   90

    Introduction to the Second Treatise of the Great Seth   90
    Christ Laughs: A Gospel of Irony and Liberation   90
    The False God and the Forgotten Ones   91
    Union, Light, and the Incorruptible Race   92
    Historical Context   92
    The Second Treatise of the Great Seth: he Text   93

PISTIS SOPHIA — 106
- Introduction to Pistis Sophia — 106
- Historical Context — 107
- Pistis Sophia: The Text — 107

TRIMORPHIC PROTENNOIA — 151
- Introduction to the Trimorphic Protennoia — 151
- Historical Context — 152
- Trimorphic Protennoia: The Text — 152

THE BOOK OF THOMAS THE CONTENDER — 160
- Introduction to the Book of Thomas the Contender — 160
- Historical Context — 161
- The Book of Thomas the Contender: The Text — 161

THUNDER, PERFECT MIND — 167
- Introduction to Thunder, Perfect Mind — 167
- Historical Context — 168

THE GOSPEL OF PETER — 174
- Introduction to the Gospel of Peter — 174
- Historical Context — 175
- The Gospel of Peter: The Text — 175

THE GOSPEL OF NICODEMUS — 179
- Introduction to the Gospel of Nicodemus — 179
- Historical Context — 180
- The Gospel of Nicodemus: The Text — 180

CONCLUSION
WALKING THE PATH OF HIDDEN LIGHT — 205

ADDITIONAL DIGITAL CONTENT

Scan the QR CODE *to access all digital content!!!*

or visit this website address:

manuscryptha.com/gnosticdigital

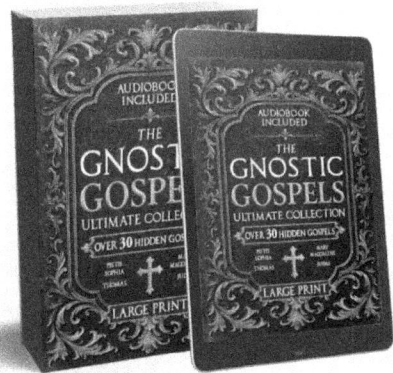

+ EBOOK VERSION
+ THE ENTIRE DIGITAL LIBRARY OF MANUSCRYPTHA.

AUDIOBOOK (100+ HOURS)

Listen to the complete Trilogy of Enoch, together with the Ethiopian Bible and the Gnostic Gospels.

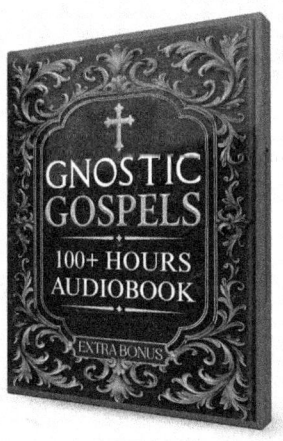

VIDEO LESSONS (200+ HOURS)

Discover powerful insights from leading scholars and teachers.

BONUS EXTENDED TEXTS
UNLOCK THE HIDDEN SECRETS OF
THE APOCRYPHA
WITH 3 EXCLUSIVE RESOURCES

1. **Songs from the Wells of Wisdoms** – Contemplative writings that nourish the spirit.

2. **The Infancy Gospel of Thomas** – A fascinating portrait of the childhood of Jesus.

3. **The Esoteric and Apocryphal Gospels** – A guided exploration of lesser-known gospels.

  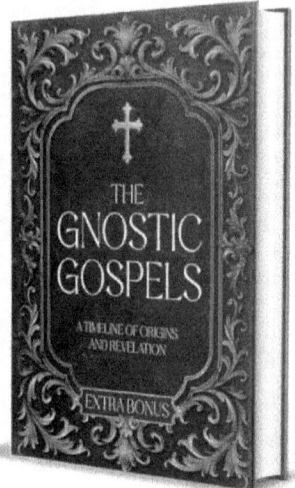

★★★★★   ★★★★★   ★★★★★

PLEASE NOTE
THE FOLLOWING CAREFULLY

The **audiobook** and the **additional contents** can only be accessed by scanning the **QR code on the previous page** and visiting the **website address** indicated on that same page.

If you encounter any difficulties, feel free to write to us at:

info@manuscryptha.com   or   *rushnilson@manuscryptha.com*

Thank you again,
RUSH NILSON

THE CORE GOSPELS
INTRODUCTION TO THE NINE THAT SPEAK FIRST

The nine gospels gathered here form the core of this collection—not because they are more authoritative, but because they are more complete, more widely known, and more central to what is often called the Gnostic tradition. They have challenged, inspired, and puzzled readers since the moment they were rediscovered.

Each of these texts speaks in its own way. Some offer sayings. Others unfold visions. Some echo with tenderness. Others shake with defiance. But all of them reach for something deeper than belief: they reach for inner awakening.

You do not have to read them in order. You do not have to understand everything they say. These are not textbooks. They are invitations. Listen for what stirs. Pause when something echoes. Return to what speaks to you.

There is no right way to begin. There is only this: a willingness to listen—not with the ears, but with the soul.

THE GOSPEL OF MARY

INTRODUCTION TO THE GOSPEL OF MARY

MARY MAGDALENE: THE FORGOTTEN APOSTLE

In the spiritual landscape of early Christianity, few figures shine as brightly—or have been more intentionally dimmed—than Mary Magdalene. Portrayed in the canonical Gospels primarily as a faithful follower of Jesus and the first to witness the resurrection, Mary has long occupied a shadowed space: revered for her devotion, yet dismissed in authority. Later tradition recast her as a penitent sinner or a peripheral companion, obscuring the possibility that she was something much more—a teacher, a visionary, a bearer of revelation.

The Gospel of Mary reveals a very different portrait. In its deeply personal and spiritually charged fragments, Mary does not merely listen—she speaks. She recounts a mystical vision received from the Savior, offering insight into the journey of the soul and the nature of liberation. Her voice carries not only intimacy, but profound authority. She comforts the grieving disciples, reminds them of the Lord's presence, and boldly shares truths they had not heard. And when challenged by Peter and others, she does not waver. Her authority is rooted not in status, but in revelation.

What makes this text so remarkable is not only that it centers a woman, but that it centers inner knowledge as the foundation of spiritual life. In Mary's gospel, salvation does not come through hierarchy or doctrine, but through awakening—through direct experience of the divine. Hers is a gospel of courage, of nonconformity, of deep trust in what has been seen within.

Though the text is incomplete—its beginning and end lost—the surviving portion is enough to suggest a vibrant alternative to the emerging structures of the early church. It opens a window into a community where women could lead, where the soul's journey was honored, and where revelation was not controlled, but received.

The Gospel of Mary does not ask to be explained. It asks to be listened to. Not as an artifact of lost history, but as a voice still speaking—a voice that calls us inward, where the living truth is known not by argument, but by encounter.

VISION AND REVELATION: THE MESSAGE OF MARY

At the heart of the Gospel of Mary lies a transformative vision. After the departure of the Savior, the disciples are gripped with fear and confusion. It is Mary who comforts them, reminding them of the Lord's presence and words. When asked to share what the Savior had revealed to her in private, she begins to speak—not with hesitation, but with clarity.

What follows is not a doctrine in the traditional sense, but a metaphysical journey. Mary describes the ascent of the soul after death, its confrontation with various powers—Desire, Ignorance, Wrath, Judgment—that seek to hold it back. Each of these forces represents an inner bondage, and each must be transcended for the soul to return to its true home.

The Savior's message, as relayed by Mary, is centered on knowledge—not intellectual learning, but gnosis: the direct, experiential insight into the truth of one's being. Sin, in this view, is not a moral failing but a result of ignorance. Redemption is not a legal transaction, but a process of remembering, awakening, and returning.

Mary's role is not passive. She is not merely a vessel for someone else's words. She is a teacher, a revealer, and a spiritual guide. She speaks with the authority of one who has seen, and invites others to see for themselves.

In this, the Gospel of Mary aligns with core themes of the broader Gnostic tradition: the belief in a divine spark within, the rejection of blind faith in external structures, and the affirmation of personal revelation. But what makes this text especially moving is that it places this spiritual insight in the mouth of a woman, challenging the assumptions of her time—and, perhaps, of ours.

CONFLICT AND AUTHORITY: MARY AND THE APOSTLES

Yet not all are ready to hear Mary's words.

The Gospel reaches its emotional climax not in Mary's vision, but in the reaction it provokes. Peter, a central figure in the emerging orthodox tradition, questions whether Jesus would really have revealed such deep truths privately—and to a woman. Andrew joins in, casting doubt on the legitimacy of her words. The implication is clear: gender undermines authority. Personal experience is suspect when it comes from the "wrong" source.

Mary, wounded but composed, responds not with anger, but with sorrow. "Do you think I made this up in my heart?" she asks. Her vulnerability reveals not weakness, but strength—the strength of someone who has stood before doubt before, and will stand again.

In this moment, Levi intervenes. He defends Mary, rebukes Peter, and calls on the others to stop contending among themselves and instead go forth and preach the gospel as the Savior commanded. "If the Savior made her worthy, who are you to reject her?" he asks—a question that continues to resonate today.

The Gospel of Mary exposes a tension that lies at the very heart of early Christianity: the conflict between institutional authority and personal revelation, between hierarchical order and spiritual equality, between dogma and direct experience. It is a text not only about Mary, but about all those whose voices have been marginalized, silenced, or forgotten.

It is also a reminder: the early Jesus movement was not monolithic. It was diverse, contested, and spiritually vibrant. And in that diversity, the voice of Mary rings out—not just as a disciple, but as a witness, a teacher, and a revealer of wisdom.

The Gospel of Mary stands today not only as a literary and historical curiosity, but as a spiritual text that invites each reader to ask: where do truth and authority really come from? What does it mean to awaken? And who gets to speak of God?

In the chapters that follow, you will find not a translation, but an original paraphrase—an imaginative, meditative rendering of Mary's words and her encounter with the other disciples. This is not a scholarly reconstruction, but a spiritual offering. Let it guide you as Mary once guided those who were willing to listen.

HISTORICAL CONTEXT

The Gospel of Mary is believed to have been composed in the second half of the 2nd century CE, likely within an early Christian community in Egypt or Syria. It emphasizes Mary Magdalene's role as a favored disciple and spiritual teacher, challenging emerging orthodox hierarchies. Although only partially preserved, the text reflects gnostic themes of inner revelation and the soul's ascent beyond material constraints. Its tone suggests a vibrant dialogue about authority, salvation, and divine knowledge in early Christian movements.

THE GOSPEL OF MARY: THE TEXT

A SPIRITUAL REMEMBRANCE, SPOKEN IN SILENCE AND POWER

We were disoriented, our hearts shaken by absence. The Teacher had left us—vanished not just from our sight, but from the world that had refused him. We gathered together, frightened, uncertain, adrift in our grief.

But then I remembered.

He had spoken not only to all of us—but also to me.

He had offered me a vision, not of the world as it is, but of what lies beneath and beyond.

And now I, Mary, speak not to prove, not to persuade, but to share what I have seen.

Let those who are ready receive it.

CHAPTER 4 – THE DISSOLUTION OF MATTER

He once said to us, as we sat in the quiet after teaching:

"All that has form, all that breathes, all that exists within matter—will one day dissolve. Everything shall return to its origin. The essence of matter longs for its own undoing, and so it shall be. Listen well—these words are not for every ear."

Peter, always questioning, always eager, turned to him and asked:

"You've spoken of many things, but tell us this—what is the sin of the world?"

And the Teacher looked at him with stillness and replied:

"There is no sin. Sin is not a thing—it is a name you have given to your actions, when they echo the confusion of separation. When you act from falsehood, you give birth to what you call sin. That is why the Good has come—to restore all things, to draw every nature back to its true root."

And again he said:

"This is why you fall ill, why you die—because you pursue what deceives you. But the one who understands will not be fooled."

He spoke of matter again:

"From matter came a passion, wild and unnatural, without reflection or image. This passion brought confusion to the body, a forgetting of what is real. That is why I say—be content in your heart. When you feel torn within, search not for escape, but for the quiet truth that lies beneath the images of the world. Let those who can hear, hear."

After these words, he looked upon each of us with love.

"Peace," he said, "is yours. Take it. Guard it."

"Let no one tell you, 'Look here!' or 'Look there!' For the Son of Humanity is not outside of you—he is within. Seek him there, and you shall find him."

"Go now. Speak of the Kingdom—not as lawgivers, not as those who bind others with rules. Do not add to what I have given, nor make of it a new prison. Be free, and help others be free."

With that, he was gone.

We wept.

Not just for him, but for ourselves.
How could we speak to the world what the world had refused to hear?
If they had silenced him, would they not silence us?
I stood among them—my brothers, my companions—and said:
"Let not your hearts be broken. Let your grief not divide you. His grace is still with us—it surrounds us, protects us. Let us praise him, not mourn him. He has prepared us for this moment. He made us truly human."
At my words, something shifted. They turned again toward the Good, and began to speak of the things he had taught.
Peter turned to me, his voice softer than usual:
"Sister, we know the Teacher loved you deeply. Tell us, if you can, what he shared with you in secret—what we have not yet heard."
I nodded, and replied:
"I will speak of what is hidden from you—not because I am greater, but because it was given to me to see."
And so I began:
"I saw him in a vision. I said to him, 'Master, I have seen you.' And he said to me, 'Blessed are you, who did not turn away from what you saw. For where your mind is—there lies your treasure.'"
I asked him, "When we see such visions—do we see them with the soul, or with the spirit?"
And he said to me, "Neither the soul nor the spirit sees. It is the Mind between the two—it is this which sees, and it is through this that the vision comes."

PAGE 15

(At this point, several pages of the original manuscript are missing. The following section resumes later in Mary's account, where she continues describing the soul's ascent beyond the powers that seek to bind it.)
And Desire spoke.
It said, "I did not see you descend, yet now I see you rising. Why do you lie? You belong to me."
But the soul, calm and luminous, replied:
"I saw you, but you saw me not. I moved within you like a garment, but you did not know me. I wore you for a time, but now I cast you off."
And having said this, the soul rejoiced, and moved upward.
Then it came upon the third power, called Ignorance.
This power confronted the soul and demanded:
"Where are you going? You are bound by wickedness! Bound as you are—how dare you judge?"
The soul answered:
"I do not judge. I was bound, yes—but not by my own doing. I have been seen, and I have seen. And in that seeing, I know: all things shall pass away. The things of earth and the things of heaven—they shall dissolve alike."
With these words, the soul moved on, having overcome Ignorance.
Then it saw the fourth power—a vast, shifting force, composed of seven forms:
The first: Darkness.
The second: Desire.
The third: Ignorance.
The fourth: Zeal for Death.
The fifth: the Dominion of the Flesh.
The sixth: the False Wisdom of the Flesh.

The seventh: the Anger that calls itself Wisdom.

These were the Seven Powers of Wrath, and they spoke as one:

"Where do you come from, O slayer of limits?

And where are you going, O one who walks beyond the stars?"

The soul replied:

"What held me is undone. What clothed me has been discarded. My hunger is gone. My blindness is healed. I was trapped in a world—but now I move beyond it. I have escaped the net of forgetfulness, woven by time. Now, I return to the Silence—the stillness beyond all seasons."

When I finished recounting these things, I fell silent. For the Teacher had spoken to me no further.

Then Andrew, troubled, turned to the others and said:

"Brothers, what are we to make of this? I do not believe the Savior said these things. They seem... foreign. They sound unlike him."

Peter joined him, more forceful, more indignant:

"Did he truly speak such things with a woman—and not tell us? Are we now to listen to her? Did he favor her above us?"

I wept.

"My brother Peter," I said, "what do you imagine? That I invented these words? That I made them from my own desire? Do you believe I would speak falsely of our Lord?"

Then Levi stood and faced Peter:

"Peter, your fire often burns too hot. You rage now against her as though she were an enemy. But if the Savior found her worthy—who are you to question her? He knew her deeply. That is why he loved her more than us."

"Let us not quarrel. Let us instead clothe ourselves in the fullness of Humanity. Let us become what he asked of us. Let us go out and speak—not with rules, not with burdens, but with the truth he entrusted to us."

And so we rose.

And we went out into the world,
to speak of what we had seen,
and of what had been seen through us.

THE GOSPEL OF THOMAS

INTRODUCTION TO THE GOSPEL OF THOMAS

THE HIDDEN GOSPEL: A VOICE OUTSIDE THE CANON

The Gospel of Thomas is not like the other gospels. There are no stories of miracles, no birth narratives, no Passion, no resurrection account. Instead, it begins without preamble and ends without conclusion—offering a stream of short, potent sayings attributed to Jesus. These are not teachings meant for the crowd, but for those ready to hear. They are riddles, revelations, and invitations. They do not explain. They awaken.

What makes Thomas so striking is not just what it contains, but what it assumes. Its Jesus does not speak as a savior in need of worship, but as a guide who knows that the kingdom of God is not somewhere out there, but within. Again and again, the text turns the seeker back to themselves: Know what is in front of you. Know yourself. Split the wood, and I am there.

This is not a gospel of belief. It is a gospel of recognition.

Its wisdom is rooted in paradox. Only the one who is disturbed can be amazed. Only the one who seeks without stopping will find. The last will be first—but only when they become one. These are not simple statements. They are thresholds. They demand reflection. They wait to unfold.

What we encounter in Thomas is a Jesus of fierce inward clarity—a master of consciousness, not institution. He speaks to the divine spark already burning in the listener. Not with threats or promises, but with challenge. With vision. With fire.

For the modern seeker—disillusioned with dogma, yet drawn to the voice of the Christ—Thomas offers something rare: a direct transmission. Not filtered through story or ritual, but offered in raw clarity. These are the words of the living Jesus, not explained, not domesticated. They pulse with spiritual electricity.

And if they seem hidden, it's not because they were meant to be concealed. It's because they wait for readiness. They speak not to the crowd, but to the soul. Not as answers, but as echoes of a truth we already carry inside.

SAYINGS OF THE LIVING JESUS: A WISDOM TRADITION

The Gospel of Thomas does not read like the Gospels most are familiar with. There are no parables wrapped in storylines, no accounts of healing the blind or walking on water, no crucifixion or resurrection scenes. There is no narrative arc at all.

Instead, what we find is a list—114 sayings attributed to Jesus. Some sound familiar, echoing the canonical Gospels. Others are strikingly different—mystical, paradoxical, unsettling. Together, they form what scholars call a sayings gospel, a type of early Christian text that may have circulated before the narrative gospels took shape. A gospel not of events, but of wisdom.

Jesus here is not a figure to be worshiped from afar, but a living voice speaking directly to the reader. He challenges, provokes, invites. He tells us that the Kingdom is already present. That we are made of light. That when we know ourselves, we will know the divine. And that if we fail to recognize the truth within, we remain in poverty—and we are that poverty. This is not a Jesus who asks for belief. He asks for awakening.

The sayings are often short, dense with meaning, and deliberately cryptic. Like Zen koans, they are meant to disrupt ordinary thinking. They are not easy. They are not meant to be. They are designed to be lived with, pondered over, meditated on. They yield their depth slowly, in silence.

What makes this gospel especially powerful is its refusal to explain. There are no sermons, no explanations, no clarifications. The sayings stand like mirrors: what you see in them reflects your own state of awareness. One might read them a hundred times and find something new each time—because the one who reads is always changing.

This gospel belongs to a tradition of wisdom that cuts across time and culture. It speaks not just as scripture, but as spiritual practice. It invites us not to believe about God, but to see with new eyes, to know with the heart. In the Gospel of Thomas, Jesus is not distant. He is present. Not to be idolized, but to be heard—still speaking, not as a relic of the past, but as a living voice of wisdom.

KNOWING YOURSELF, FINDING THE KINGDOM

At the heart of the Gospel of Thomas lies a teaching that echoes like a bell across centuries: "If you bring forth what is within you, what you have will save you. If you do not bring it forth, what you do not bring forth will destroy you."

This is not a gospel of external commandments or historical creeds. It is a gospel of the inner path. A call to self-knowledge, not as a form of self-centeredness, but as the doorway to the divine. Again and again, Jesus points his listeners not toward heaven above or signs in the sky, but inward—to the Kingdom within.

To know yourself, in Thomas, is not a matter of psychological introspection. It is a recognition of your deepest essence. Beneath the personality, beyond the ego, there is a radiant core—a spark of the Living Light. To forget this light is to walk in darkness. To awaken to it is to be free.

This is why ignorance—not sin—is the great barrier in Thomas. And why the remedy is not repentance, but recognition. The soul's journey is not from bad to good, but from sleep to awareness, from illusion to clarity. From fragmentation to wholeness.

The sayings challenge the split-thinking of duality. They blur the lines between male and female, inside and outside, above and below. In the words of Jesus: "When you make the two into one... then you will enter the Kingdom." This is a gospel of non-duality—where opposites dissolve and unity is revealed. Where the one who is "single" is "full of light."

And that is the transformation Thomas offers—not by following rules or rituals, but by dissolving the inner divisions that keep us from seeing clearly. This is not an easy path. It requires silence. It requires courage. It requires letting go of everything we think we know—even about Jesus himself.

But for those who are ready, Thomas holds up a mirror. It shows us not only the teacher, but the student. Not only the Kingdom, but the door within ourselves. It asks: Are you ready to remember what you are?

This gospel is not for the passive believer. It is for the spiritual adventurer. For the one who dares to know, and in knowing, be transformed.

HISTORICAL CONTEXT

The Gospel of Thomas likely dates to the early to mid-2nd century CE and was discovered in the Nag Hammadi library in Egypt. It presents a collection of 114 sayings attributed to Jesus, emphasizing direct experiential knowledge rather than faith in doctrine. Influenced by gnostic and early Christian thought, it lacks a narrative structure and focuses on uncovering the divine light within each individual. Thomas reflects a tradition where understanding oneself is seen as the key to salvation.

THE GOSPEL OF THOMAS: THE TEXT

PART I — THE CALL TO AWAKEN

These are the words the living Jesus spoke—mysteries whispered not to the crowds, but to those ready to awaken.
They are not commandments. They are not rules.
They are sparks.
Whoever discovers their light will never taste death.
Jesus said,
"Whoever drinks deeply from these sayings—whoever truly finds their meaning—will never be consumed by death."
He said,
"Let the seeker keep seeking, until they find.
When they find, they will be shaken.
And when shaken, they will marvel.
And standing in that wonder, they will rule over all.
And finally—they will find rest."
Jesus said,
"If your leaders say, 'Look, the Kingdom is in the sky,'
then the birds will get there before you.
If they say, 'It's in the sea,'
then the fish will reach it first.
No—the Kingdom is inside you, and it is all around you.
When you come to know yourselves, you'll be known.
And you'll understand that you are children of the Living One.
But if you don't know yourselves, you live in poverty—and you are that poverty."
Jesus said,
"A person old in years won't hesitate to ask a child of seven about the place of Life—and they will live.
Because many who seem first will be last.
And they will become one."
Jesus said,
"Recognize what's right in front of you, and what is hidden from you will be revealed.
Because nothing is truly hidden that won't one day come to light."
His disciples asked him,
"Should we fast? How should we pray? Should we give offerings? What should we eat?"
Jesus said,
"Don't lie—and don't do what you hate.
Everything is laid bare before heaven.
There's nothing hidden that won't be revealed,
and nothing covered that will stay concealed."
Jesus said,
"Blessed is the lion that a human eats—so that the lion becomes human.
But cursed is the human who is eaten by a lion—so that the lion becomes human."
Jesus said,
"The Kingdom is like a wise fisherman who cast his net into the sea.
When he drew it in, it was full of small fish.
Among them, he found one large, excellent fish.
He kept that one, throwing the rest back into the water.
Whoever has ears, let them hear."
Jesus said,

"A sower went out, handful of seeds in hand.
Some fell on the road—birds came and ate them.
Some landed on rocks—those couldn't take root, and their shoots withered under the sun.
Some fell among thorns—the thorns choked them, and worms devoured them.
But others fell on rich soil—these bore fruit, rising toward the sky.
Some yielded sixtyfold. Others, a hundred and twenty."
Jesus said,
"I've thrown fire upon the world—and look!
I'm watching, until it blazes."
Jesus said,
"This generation is like a baby lying in a field, abandoned by those who should have loved it.
When the child7 grows, it won't recognize its parents.
If asked, 'Who are your father and mother?' it will answer, 'I don't know.'
That's why I say: if you become like this child—if you let go of all that you've been told—you will find the Kingdom."
His disciples said to him,
"We know you'll leave us—who will lead us then?"
Jesus replied,
"Wherever you are, go to James the Just.
Heaven and earth were born alongside him, and he stands for what is true."
Jesus once asked his disciples,
"Tell me—who do I remind you of?"
Simon Peter answered, "You're like a just angel."
Matthew said, "You're a wise philosopher."
Thomas stayed silent.
Jesus turned to Thomas and said, "Why are you quiet? Speak your heart."
Thomas said, "Teacher, I can't say what you are. My mouth would never form it, and my words would fall short."
So Jesus took him aside and whispered three things to him.
When Thomas returned, the others asked, "What did he say to you?"
Thomas replied,
"If I tell you even one of the things he said to me,
you'll pick up stones and throw them at me—
and fire will rise from those stones and consume you."
Jesus said,
"If you fast, you'll only bring sin upon yourself.
If you pray, you'll be condemned.
If you give to charity, you'll corrupt your spirit.
But when you go into any land and walk through its villages,
if they welcome you, eat whatever is given.
If they reject you, leave that place—shake the dust from your sandals as a witness against them."
Jesus said,
"When you see the one who wasn't born of woman, fall down and worship—
because that one is your true parent."
Jesus said,
"Maybe people think I came to bring peace to the world.
They're wrong.
I didn't come to bring peace—I came to start a fire,
to shake things up, to divide the son from his father,
the daughter from her mother,
the daughter-in-law from her mother-in-law.
They'll stand apart, each one alone."
Jesus said,

"I'll give you what no eye has seen, what no ear has heard,
what no hand has touched, and what has never entered the heart of any human."
The disciples asked him,
"Tell us, how will our end come?"
Jesus replied,
"Have you already found the beginning, that you're asking about the end?
Because where the beginning is, there too will the end be.
Blessed is the one who stands in the beginning—
they will know the end, and never taste death."
Jesus said,
"Blessed is the one who was already alive before coming into being.
If you become my disciples and listen deeply to my words,
even the stones around you will serve you.
There are lights within a person of light—
and they shine on the whole world.
But if that light is hidden,
the world is dark."
Jesus said,
"The Kingdom is like a mustard seed—
the tiniest of all seeds.
But when it falls on good soil,
it grows into a great tree,
and becomes a shelter for the birds of heaven."

PART II — THE INNER LIGHT

Mary asked Jesus,
"What are your disciples like?"
He answered,
"They're like children living in a field that doesn't belong to them.
When the owners return and say, 'Give us back what's ours,'
the children take off their clothes and place them at the owners' feet, saying,
'Here—take what's yours!'
So the owners leave them alone.
That's why I say:
When you strip yourselves of the world's clothes,
and you stop being ashamed—
when you step away from duality,
when you make the inner like the outer and the outer like the inner,
the upper like the lower,
and male and female into a single One—
so that the masculine isn't masculine and the feminine isn't feminine—
then you'll enter the Kingdom."
Jesus saw some infants being nursed and said to his disciples,
"Those who enter the Kingdom must become like these little ones."
They asked him,
"Should we become children?"
Jesus answered,
"When you make two into one—
when you make the inside like the outside,
and the outside like the inside,
the above like the below—
when you shape the male and female into a single being,
so that the man isn't a man and the woman isn't a woman—
then you will enter the Kingdom."
Jesus said,
"I'll choose one from a thousand and two from ten thousand—
and they'll stand as a single one."
His disciples asked,
"Show us the place where you are, because we need to see you."
He answered,
"If you have light within you, you'll see me clearly.
But if you're in darkness,

you won't see me—though I'm always here."
Jesus said,
"Love your friends like your own soul.
Protect them like the pupils of your eyes."
Jesus said,
"You see the speck in your brother's eye,
but you don't notice the log in your own.
When you pull the log from your eye,
you'll see clearly enough to remove the speck from your brother's."
Jesus said,
"If you don't fast from the world,
you'll never find the Kingdom.
And if you don't rest from your striving,
you won't recognize the Father's day of rest."
Jesus said,
"I stood in the center of the world,
and I appeared to them in flesh.
I found all of them drunk—
but none thirsty.
And my soul was sorrowful for the children of humanity—
because they are blind in their hearts,
and they don't see that they came into this world empty
and will leave it the same.
But for now, they're drunk.
When they awaken from their wine,
they will return to themselves."
Jesus said,
"If the flesh came from spirit, that would be a wonder.
But if spirit came from flesh, that's an even greater wonder.
Still, I marvel at how this great wealth can live within such poverty."
Jesus said,
"Where there are three gods, they are gods.
Where there are two or one,
I am with that one."
Jesus said,
"No prophet is welcomed in their own village.
A doctor doesn't heal those who know him too well."
Jesus said,
"A city built on a high hill, fortified and strong—
it can't fall, and it can't be hidden."
Jesus said,
"What you hear in one ear, whisper it to the other.
Let your whole body be filled with light.
If your inner lamp burns brightly,
your whole being will shine."
Jesus said,
"If someone blind leads another who is blind,
both will fall into a pit."
Jesus said,
"No one can break into a strong person's house
and steal it by force—
unless they tie the strong one up first.
Only then can they take what they want."
Jesus said,
"Don't worry from morning to night,
and from night to morning,
wondering what you'll wear.
You're so much more than clothes."
His disciples asked,
"When will you appear to us?
When will we see you in full?"
Jesus said,
"When you strip yourselves without shame,
take off your clothes and place them beneath your feet
as children do—
then look without fear upon the Son of the Living One—
and you'll see me."
Jesus said,
"You've seen the speck in your sibling's eye,

but not the beam in your own.
When you pull out the beam from your own eye,
you'll see clearly to help your brother."
Jesus said,
"You are close to me—
but you don't yet understand who I am.
When you know yourselves,
then you'll know me too—
and you'll realize that you are children of the Living Father.
But if you don't know yourselves,
you live in shadows,
and you are the shadow."
Jesus said,
"A grapevine was planted apart from the Father.
And because it wasn't rooted in the truth,
it will be pulled up by its roots—
and it will die."
Jesus said,
"Whoever has something in hand will be given more.
But whoever has nothing —
even what they do have will be taken from them."
Jesus said,
"Become travelers—
passersby on this earth."
His disciples asked him,
"Who are you to say these things to us?"
Jesus replied,
"You still don't know who I am from what I say?
You've become like those who sleep with their eyes open —
ears filled with sound, but no understanding."
Jesus said,
"You can speak against the truth and be forgiven.
But blaspheme against the Spirit of truth,
and there's no forgiveness —
not in this world,
and not in the world to come."
Jesus said,
"No one picks grapes from thornbushes.
And figs aren't gathered from thistles.
Good fruit grows only from good trees —
and bad fruit from what's dead."
Jesus said,
"From Adam to John the Baptist,
no one born of woman is greater than John.
But even the least in the Kingdom
is greater than he."
Jesus said,
"It's impossible for a person to ride two horses at once,
or stretch two bows.
A servant can't serve two masters —
they'll honor one and despise the other.
No one drinks old wine and immediately wants new.
They'll say,
'The old is better.'"
Jesus said,
"When two become one —
when you speak from within yourself in harmony,
and say, 'Mountain, move from here!' —
it will move."
Jesus said,
"Blessed are those who are alone and chosen.
You'll find the Kingdom.
You've come from it,
and you'll return there again."
Jesus said,
"If they ask you,
'Where did you come from?'
say,
'We came from the Light —
from the place where the Light was born from itself.
It stood, revealed through its own being.'
If they ask you,
'Are you it?'

say,
'We are its children.
We are the chosen of the Living Father.'
If they ask,
'What is the sign of your Father within you?'
say,
'It is movement and rest.'"
His disciples asked him,
"When will the resurrection of the dead take place? And what will it look like?"
Jesus said,
"What you're waiting for has already come —
but you don't see it.
You ask about resurrection —
but don't recognize what stands before you.
You ask about the end —
yet haven't found your beginning.
Blessed is the one who stands in the beginning,
for that one will know the end
and will never taste death."
His disciples said to him,
"Twenty-four prophets spoke in Israel — and all of them spoke of you."
Jesus said,
"You've listened to them,
but you didn't really hear them.
For the one they spoke of —
that one stands before you now."
His disciples asked,
"Is circumcision useful or not?"
Jesus said,
"If it were truly useful,
then your Father would have made you that way from birth.
But what matters is the circumcision of the heart —
the cutting away of what hides the light within."
Jesus said,
"Blessed are the poor —
for yours is the Kingdom of Heaven."
Jesus said,
"Whoever doesn't hate their father and mother
won't be able to follow me.
And whoever doesn't love me more than father and mother
isn't worthy of me.
For my true family are those who know the truth —
not just believe it."
Jesus said,
"Whoever understands the world
has uncovered a corpse.
And whoever has found that corpse
is greater than the world."
Jesus said,
"The Kingdom is like a farmer
who planted good seed in his field.
At night, his enemy came
and sowed weeds among the wheat.
When the crop grew, the weeds appeared as well.
The farmer didn't pull them up,
but said, 'Let them both grow together.
At harvest, I'll tell the reapers:
Gather the weeds first and burn them,
then gather the wheat into my barn.'"
Jesus said,
"Blessed is the one who's been persecuted in their heart —
for they have truly come to know the Father.
Blessed are those who hunger —
for the belly of the one who longs will be filled."
Jesus said,
"Look for the Living One
while you're still alive.
If you die without having searched for him,
you'll try to see him
but you won't be able."

They saw a Samaritan carrying a lamb
on his way to Judea.
Jesus said to his disciples,
"Why is he doing that?"
They answered,
"So he can kill it and eat it."
Jesus said,
"As long as the lamb is alive,
he won't eat it.
But once he kills it, it's no longer a lamb.
So too with you —
seek life while it's within you,
so you won't become something else
and be devoured."

PART III — BECOMING WHOLE

Jesus said,
"Two will rest on a couch —
one will die, the other will live."
Salome asked him,
"Who are you, that you climbed onto my bed and ate from my table like someone who belongs?"
Jesus said,
"I am the one who exists from the One who is whole.
I was given what belongs to my Father."
Salome said,
"I am your disciple."
Jesus answered,
"That is why I say —
when someone becomes whole,
they will be filled with light.
But when they're divided within themselves,
they'll be full of darkness."
Jesus said,
"I speak my mysteries
to those who are worthy of hearing them.
Don't let your left hand know
what your right hand is doing."
Jesus said,
"There was a rich man who had many possessions.
He said to himself, 'I'll use my wealth to plant, to harvest, to fill my barns with food — then I'll have all I need.'
But that very night, he died.
Whoever has ears, let them hear."
Jesus said,
"A man was planning a great feast
and sent his servant to invite the guests.
One said, 'I have a house to manage.'
Another, 'I've bought things for business.'
Another, 'I'm getting married.'
So the servant returned and told his master.
The master said,
'Bring strangers from the roads,
people who don't know me,
those who will listen and enter.'"
Jesus said,
"A man owned a vineyard and leased it to workers.
When the harvest came, he sent a servant to collect the fruit.
The workers beat him.
He sent another servant —
they beat him too.
Finally, he sent his son.
But the workers said,
'This is the heir — come, let's kill him and take what's his.'
So they killed him.
Whoever has ears, let them hear."
Jesus said,
"The stone that the builders rejected
has become the cornerstone."
Jesus said,
"If you truly know all things,
but don't know yourself —
you've missed everything."
Jesus said,
"Blessed are you
when you're hated and hunted.

No one will find the place where you've taken refuge."
Jesus said,
"Blessed are the ones
who have been persecuted in their hearts —
they have truly come to know the Father.
Blessed are the hungry,
for the belly of the one who longs
will be filled."
Jesus said,
"When you bring forth what is within you,
what you have will save you.
If you fail to bring forth what is within,
what you don't express
will destroy you."
Jesus said,
"I will tear down this house —
and no one will be able to rebuild it."
A man said to him,
"Tell my brothers to divide the inheritance with me."
Jesus replied,
"Who made me judge over you?"
Then he turned to the crowd and said,
"I'm not here to divide what perishes,
but to offer you a harvest that endures."
Jesus said,
"The harvest is great,
but the laborers are few.
Ask the Lord to send more hands into the field."
He said,
"There are many standing at the door,
but only those who are truly alone
will enter the bridal chamber."
Jesus said,
"The Kingdom is like a farmer
who had a hidden treasure buried in his field
but didn't know it.
When he died, he left the field to his son.
The son uncovered the treasure
and freely gave it away."
Jesus said,
"The Kingdom is like a merchant
searching for fine pearls.
When he found a single pearl of great value,
he sold everything he owned
and bought that one."
Jesus said,
"I am the light that shines upon all things.
I am all things — and all things come from me.
Split a piece of wood, and I am there.
Lift a stone, and you will find me."
Jesus said,
"Why did you leave the desert
to see a reed blowing in the wind?
Or to see a man in soft clothing?
Look —your true king wears neither softness nor pretense,
but truth and fire."
A woman in the crowd said,
"Blessed is the womb that bore you,
and the breasts that nursed you."
Jesus answered,
"Blessed are those who have heard the word of the Father —
and have truly kept it.
For days will come
when you'll say,
'Blessed is the womb that never conceived,
and the breasts that never gave milk.'"
Jesus said,
"Whoever has come to know the world
has found a corpse.
And whoever has found that corpse
has transcended death."
Jesus said,
"Let those with riches
become poor —
so they may enter the Kingdom."
Jesus said,
"Whoever is near me is near the fire.

Whoever is far from me
is far from life."
Jesus said,
"Images are revealed to humanity —
but the light within them remains hidden
in the image of the Father's light.
One day, his light will be revealed —
but only to those with open eyes."
Jesus said,
"When you see your reflection,
you rejoice.
But when you see the image of yourselves
that came before you — and never dies —
how much more will you rejoice!"
Jesus said,
"Adam came from great power and great wealth —
but he didn't know it.
He became weak and fell into poverty.
If you discover the root of your being,
you will rise again."
Jesus said,
"Foxes have dens,
and birds have nests.
But the Son of Humanity has nowhere to rest his head."
Jesus said,
"Miserable is the body
that depends on another body.
And miserable is the soul
that depends on both."
Jesus said,
"Angels and prophets will come to you
and give you what already belongs to you.
You, in turn, give them what you hold in your hands —
and ask yourselves:
'When will they come and take what's theirs?'"
Jesus said,
"Why do you wash the outside of the cup?
Don't you understand that the one who made the outside
also made the inside?"
Jesus said,
"Come to me —
for my yoke is easy,
and my burden is light."

PART IV — THE RETURN TO THE SOURCE

They said to him,
"Tell us who you are — so we may believe."
He said,
"You study the sky and the earth —
but you can't see what's right in front of you.
You don't know how to read this moment."
Jesus said,
"Seek, and you will find.
But the answers will disturb you —
and when they do,
you will marvel and be transformed."
Jesus said,
"The Kingdom is like a net
cast into the sea.
It caught fish of every kind.
When it was full, the fishermen pulled it to shore,
sorted the good,
and threw the rest away."
Jesus said,
"If you become like a child,
you'll enter the Kingdom.
Small and unnoticed —
but greater than kings."
Jesus said,
"If you have a coin in your hand,
and give it not with love —
you've given nothing."
Jesus said,
"The Kingdom is like a tree,
its roots deep in the earth
and branches reaching to heaven.
Birds nest in its shade,

and all find rest there."
Jesus said,
"The Kingdom is like a grain of wheat.
When it falls to the ground and dies,
it's alone.
But when it breaks open,
it gives life to a great harvest."
Jesus said,
"Whoever finds the Kingdom
will rejoice.
And having rejoiced —
will rest.
And having rested —
will reign."
Jesus said,
"This world is like a road
and you are travelers.
Stop and rest —
but don't build your house
where dust and rust rule."
They asked him,
"Should we give to Caesar or not?"
Jesus said,
"Give Caesar what is Caesar's —
and to God what is God's —
and give me what is mine."
Jesus spoke of a fire within,
a rest beyond rest,
a light that cannot be hidden.
He said,
"Be passersby.
Let the world pass through you,
but don't belong to it.
The Kingdom is like a hidden treasure,
like yeast in dough,
like a pearl worth everything.
You are salt —
don't lose your flavor."
Jesus said,
"The heavens and the earth will
pass away —
but the one who discovers the Living One
will never taste death."
Jesus said,
"Woe to the flesh
that depends on the soul —
and woe to the soul
that depends on the flesh."
His disciples said,
"When will the Kingdom come?"
Jesus answered,
"It won't come by watching the sky.
People won't say, 'Look, here it is,' or
'Look, it's over there.'
The Kingdom of the Father
is already spread across the earth —
but people do not see it."
Simon Peter said,
"Let Mary leave us —
she is not worthy of life!"
Jesus answered,
"I will guide her
so that I can make her male,
that she too may become
a living spirit like you.
For every woman who becomes
like a man
will enter the Kingdom of Heaven."
And these are the sayings
of the Living Jesus,
spoken in silence
and carried in secret —
not to the world,
but to those who are ready to awaken.

THE GOSPEL OF PHILIP

INTRODUCTION TO THE GOSPEL OF PHILIP

A GOSPEL OF INTIMACY AND MYSTERY

The Gospel of Philip is unlike any other early Christian text. It does not aim to tell a story, or to build doctrine, or to deliver moral instruction. It speaks instead in the language of mystery—of union, transformation, and remembrance. It is not a gospel in the narrative sense, but in the deeper sense: good news for the soul that longs to awaken.

The words in Philip drift between poetry and paradox. They speak of light and shadow, of bodies and spirits, of names and the power to name. The gospel's central theme is one of sacred union—not just between man and woman, but between the fragmented human being and the divine fullness from which they come. At the heart of its vision lies the bridal chamber: not a place of fleshly passion, but a symbol of reunion, wholeness, and transfiguration.

Here, salvation is not portrayed as a transaction or an escape from sin. It is described as a process of restoration—of remembering what we are, of returning to the light, of rising from sleep into knowing. The soul, in this gospel, is not saved by belief or obedience. It is saved by recognition—by the reawakening of divine identity through deep, lived experience.

Throughout Philip, traditional religious symbols are reimagined. Baptism is not merely water—it is the beginning of seeing. Anointing is not symbolic—it is sealing, it is claiming. The Eucharist is not ritual—it is invitation. These sacraments are not reserved for clergy or church hierarchy. They are moments of inner transformation. Touchpoints of union between the visible and the invisible.

Perhaps more than any other apocryphal gospel, Philip embraces embodiment—not as a problem to escape, but as a mystery to enter. It does not fear the body. It seeks to transfigure it. It honors love, intimacy, and the merging of opposites as pathways to wholeness.

This gospel speaks gently, yet powerfully, to those drawn toward the mystical heart of the Christ tradition. It does not offer clarity in the form of answers, but in the form of invitation. It asks not that we believe in a savior, but that we remember what we are—and dare to become it.

THE SACRED UNION: BEYOND THE FLESH

At the heart of the Gospel of Philip is one of the most profound and provocative spiritual concepts in early Christian mysticism: the bridal chamber. Unlike traditional Christian imagery that focuses on sacrifice, obedience, or divine judgment, Philip centers its message on union—not simply as a metaphor, but as the ultimate goal of the soul.

The bridal chamber, in this gospel, is not a physical place. It is a sacred space within the self. It is where the fragmented human being becomes whole, where the divided inner world—body and spirit, male and female, light and shadow—are reconciled. The soul is not saved through belief alone, nor through external ritual, but through transformation. Through gnosis. Through a love that transcends duality.

In this vision, salvation is not achieved by being rescued from the world, but by reclaiming what has been lost within us. The fall of humanity is not primarily about disobedience, but about forgetting who we are—forgetting that we are children of light. The redemption Christ offers is a restoration of that memory through intimate union with the divine.

This sacred union is often expressed in the language of male and female becoming one. But it is not a literal or earthly marriage—it is symbolic of a higher reality. It speaks of the soul uniting with its source. The physical imagery points to something spiritual: the mystical joining of opposites, the merging of spirit and body, heaven and earth, self and God.

Unlike teachings that treat sexuality with suspicion or shame, Philip honors the power of love and desire when transfigured through knowledge and inner illumination. It recognizes that divine union can be mirrored in human intimacy—but only when stripped of domination, control, or ego. In the sacred chamber, all forms of hierarchy dissolve. There is no longer male or female, but only the one who is whole.

The sacrament of the bridal chamber is thus more than a mystical concept—it is the climax of the soul's journey. Baptism begins the path. Anointing deepens it. Eucharist sustains it. But the bridal chamber fulfills it. It is the place where we stop seeking, because we have been found. Where we no longer speak of the divine, but become one with it.

In this, the Gospel of Philip offers a revolutionary and intimate vision of salvation—not as escape, but as embrace. Not as submission, but as union. Not as distant reward, but as present awakening.

ANOINTING, LIGHT, AND THE RETURN TO WHOLENESS

In the Gospel of Philip, the sacraments are not described as outer rituals performed by religious officials, but as inner events—soul-deep awakenings that shift the entire axis of a person's being. They are not mechanical steps on a path to salvation, but living encounters with the divine presence already within us.

Baptism, in this gospel, is more than immersion in water—it is the beginning of remembrance. It cleanses not only the body, but the perception. It initiates a turning inward, a reorientation toward the hidden light. But baptism alone is not enough. As Philip boldly says, "The anointing is greater." Why? Because the anointing seals what baptism begins. It is the moment when the soul is marked—not with oil alone, but with knowledge, with light, with identity.

To be anointed is to be recognized. It is to be known by the divine as already belonging. This anointing is not about status or approval. It is about becoming what we are—beings of light who have forgotten their origin. The anointing does not add something new. It awakens what has always been.

The gospel speaks of resurrection—but not as something to be waited for after death. Resurrection, here, is now. "If you do not rise while you are alive," the text warns, "you will not rise after death." Resurrection is not just about coming back to life. It is about coming back to yourself. It is the reversal of forgetfulness. The return to presence.

This resurrection is the soul's ascent from the illusion of separation back into wholeness. It is a rising not in flesh, but in awareness. Those who have been resurrected in this way do not fear death. They know they have already passed from death to life. They are no longer asleep in the tomb of the world—they walk as light.

Throughout the gospel, light is a central image. But not light in a physical sense—this is the light of consciousness, of divine essence. It is the light that shines in silence. The light that recognizes itself in others. The light that does not need to speak to be understood. When this light is uncovered within, the soul is no longer divided. It becomes whole. It becomes flame.

In the thought-world of Philip, salvation is not about escaping judgment or earning reward. It is about restoration. The broken image is made whole again. The scattered pieces of the soul are gathered. And in the sacred chamber of the heart, the divine and human are reconciled.

This is not theology. It is transformation.

Not instruction—but invitation.

Not religion—but return.

HISTORICAL CONTEXT

Composed probably in the late 2nd or early 3rd century CE, the Gospel of Philip emerges from a Valentinian gnostic environment, likely in Egypt. It explores mystical themes of spiritual marriage, sacramental union, and the restoration of the divine image. Philip's teachings challenge simplistic readings of the material world, presenting it instead as a place of separation to be overcome through secret knowledge and unity with the divine. Its style is poetic and metaphorical, offering deep symbolic insights.

THE GOSPEL OF PHILIP: THE TEXT

PART I — FLESH AND SPIRIT: THE TWO BIRTHS

Those who are born into this world through physical means—through the union of man and woman—belong to the realm of flesh and time, but those who are born through a spiritual awakening come not from the desires of the body, but from the hidden marriage of soul and divine spirit, a sacred union that cannot be perceived by the eyes of the flesh and is revealed only to those whose inner sight has been opened. Flesh gives rise only to more flesh, perpetuating its own cycle, but spirit gives birth to spirit, and from this spiritual birth emerges light, truth, and a recognition of the soul's eternal origin.

When we ask what the true name of the Father is, we must understand that it cannot be confined to language or sound, for any name we pronounce is merely a faint reflection, an echo of something far greater, beyond utterance. The Son, who knows the silence at the heart of all things, reveals what no tongue can fully express. We may hear names in this world, but they are not the essence—they are signs pointing toward what exists in stillness and truth. No one can know the Father unless the Son unveils Him, and once that veil is lifted, what was once hidden no longer belongs to the realm of time but is restored to eternity.

Names in this world carry weight and meaning, yet they are ultimately limited, tied to the impermanence of form. The names given to us at birth allow others to identify us in society, but in the higher realms of being, where light knows light and truth knows itself, there is no need for such distinctions. Those who receive the truth do so not through words but in silence, and when truth recognizes them, they no longer belong to the passing world, but to the source from which all light flows.

Those who claim that the Lord first died and then rose do not yet understand. Resurrection is not something that begins after the grave—it must begin now, within us, while we still live. If we do not rise in this life, we shall never truly rise. What many wait for after death must already be awakened within the living. For this world is but a mirror, and what we see in its surface will ultimately fade; but if we come to know the image behind the image, the eternal presence beyond appearances, then we shall not perish with the reflection, but endure with the truth.

The visible world, for all its richness and beauty, is built on illusion and destined for decay. But those who root themselves in the unshakable truth—the truth that does not depend on time or form—are already beyond the reach of death. God created humankind, but humankind creates images—symbols, systems, and interpretations of reality. When these reflect the divine, they shine with radiant meaning, but when they are severed from the source, they become lifeless forms, hollow and powerless.

Truth is not something dressed in layers of language or philosophy; it stands naked, unveiled, like a lover revealed in intimacy. When love strips away the falsehoods we wear like garments, truth is what remains. Those who dwell in ignorance fear such light—they seek safety in shadows and avoid what exposes them—but the awakened soul longs for the naked truth, not in theory but in living experience. Truth is not something studied like facts or doctrines; it is passed from one being to another, like a flame lighting another wick—not spoken, but transmitted. Those who possess truth do not cling to belief systems; they embody the truth, and their presence speaks louder than any sermon.

The illusion of this world cannot hold the soul that has awakened. That soul walks freely, with eyes wide open and a heart ignited. A slave longs for freedom, but one who is born of the spirit is already free and cannot return to bondage. Yet while we still serve the illusions of this world, we see the invisible as powerless and ask, "How could what is unseen be greater than what we touch?" But once the spirit frees us, we understand that all which is seen will pass away, and only what is unseen will remain.

The soul that has truly awakened does not fear death—it laughs at it. For it knows that the body is but a temporary dwelling, and the self that is real cannot die. The sacred union, the true sacrament, is not merely the joining of bodies, but of souls, of spirits, of light intertwining with light. In that mystery, there is no man or woman, no domination or submission—only a mutual dance of two becoming one.

To name something is to separate it, to draw a line around it, but love does not name—it dissolves all boundaries. The world teaches us to be ashamed of nakedness, but in the garden of truth, the soul shines most brilliantly when it is most bare—not exposed in shame, but revealed in glory. The things of this world dress us in layers of fear, performance, and law. But when we lay those aside, we return to our essence, to who we were before we were told who to be.

The anointing with oil is not just ritual—it is the sealing of the inner light, the recognition that says, "You are radiant. You are mine." And the bread, the cup, the water—these are more than symbols; they are invitations to taste the mystery, to drink of silence, to remember where we came from. What we lost through forgetfulness, the Anointed One came not to reclaim by force, but to restore through awakening.

He came to remind us that separation was never real—it was only sleep. And now the light speaks to the light within us. And the one who hears—rises.

PART II — THE PATH OF AWAKENING

What the world calls birth is, in truth, a descent—a soul entering a body, wrapped in layers of forgetfulness, taking on form and limits it did not originally know. But true birth, the spiritual kind, is an ascent—the soul shedding illusion, rising in awareness, and being clothed not in flesh, but in light. Those born of spirit are not shaped by desire or summoned by the will of the body; they are not conceived in passion, but in union—not the joining of physical forms, but the sacred merging of spirit and truth. To be born of truth is not to learn something new, but to remember what you have always been.

The bridal chamber is not a physical place—it is a state of awakening. It is the moment when two aspects of the self become one again, when the soul looks inward and recognizes its divine origin. In this holy reunion, there is no room for shame or fear, for separation itself dissolves. What is joined in the radiance of light cannot be torn apart by the shadows of illusion. Those who enter into this mystery do not speak of it easily—not because it is forbidden, but because it is too vast, too luminous for language to contain. It is the restoration of what was fractured, the healing of all division, the remembering of the original wholeness.

When we live in separation, we perceive life in fragments. But when we are made whole again, we begin to see as we are seen, to know as we are known. Christ did not come to enforce a religion or deliver doctrine—he came to reveal reality, to open our eyes to the light that was always inside us. Though the world calls him Savior, he calls us brothers and sisters, not to impose commandments but to awaken resonance. He descended in silence, rose in light, and speaks still—not to the ears, but directly to the heart. Those who follow him do not do so through rituals or external signs; they follow by awakening within, walking not by the rules of law, but by the burning flame of living truth. What the world calls knowledge is often just noise, but true gnosis is fire—it does not merely inform the mind; it transforms the soul. And once the soul is sealed in light, nothing can shake it, for it no longer breathes with the breath of the world, but lives by the breath of the Living One.

To enter into this mystery is to go beyond opposites—beyond male and female, beyond life and death, beyond beginning and end. It is to reclaim what the world conditioned us to forget. The soul that has come to know the truth no longer clings to beliefs or opinions—it rests in what is real. It no longer acts from fear but from memory, the deep memory of the light from which it came. Baptism may cleanse the outer form, but it is the anointing that reaches into the core. Water cools the skin, but oil marks the soul. Anointing is not just purification—it is possession, a claiming, a seal upon the one who has remembered. And those who are anointed do not live for appearances; they live for what is eternal. They no longer fear death—for they have already risen.

The veil that separates us from truth is thin, yet we must choose to see beyond it. Adam was formed from dust and shaped by breath—but Christ emerges from silence and is the breath itself. We were made in the image, yes—but we are invited to become the image—not merely to reflect light, but to radiate it from within.

The bridal chamber is not merely where union begins—it is where all separation ends. In that space, we are no longer two but one, no longer the seeker and the sought, but simply being itself. And the one who truly enters does not leave unchanged—they are transfigured, no longer of the world but rooted in what cannot be moved.

The children of the bridal chamber are not born of blood, or desire, or fleshly passion—they are born of the eternal light that never fades. They walk through this world but are not bound by it. They love without clinging. They speak without seeking praise. And in their hearts, they have remembered the one truth: what it means to be whole.

PART III — LIGHT, IMAGE, AND IDENTITY

The world was formed through a design of dualities—light set against darkness, male contrasted with female, the seen divided from the unseen. These opposites shape the fabric of earthly life. But in the Kingdom of the Spirit, such divisions do not exist; they dissolve in the presence of unity. Separation is not part of the eternal—it is something the world teaches, but the Spirit leads us beyond it, into the fullness of wholeness. What has been scattered across time and identity is drawn back together, and what once was hidden beneath appearances is now revealed to those who are ready to see.

Those who dwell only in the outer world perceive what changes and fades, but those who live from within—who listen to the heart—begin to see what endures. The soul that has truly encountered the light no longer chases after signs or proofs; it knows truth in the quiet, in the stillness, in the soft resonance that echoes from within.

Jesus did not come to build an institution—he came to awaken what was forgotten. He did not die to satisfy law, but to open a living path. His was not a mission of control, but of restoration. He walked the way of sacred union—and he left the door open behind him, so we could follow.

PART IV — THE SACRAMENT OF UNION

The true sacrament is not found in the ritual itself, but in the encounter it invites—the sacred moment when the divine reaches into the human heart, and in that touch, the human is set ablaze with living fire. Those who have entered the bridal chamber understand the mystery that lies beyond doctrine: that love alone is the law that governs all things, and that light is the only true heritage we carry. Within that space of union, all names fall away, all roles and identities are left behind—there are no masks, no illusions, only the unfiltered presence of truth.

What comes forth from that sacred union is not born of flesh or blood, but of spirit—and such a birth cannot be reversed or undone. This is the essence of true life: to be recognized by the light, to awaken to the truth that you are of the light, and to finally become what, deep within, you were always meant to remember.

THE GOSPEL OF TRUTH

INTRODUCTION TO THE GOSPEL OF TRUTH

THE GOSPEL THAT BEGINS IN SILENCE

The Gospel of Truth does not begin with a story or a setting. It begins with presence. With stillness. With a kind of sacred unfolding that feels less like a message being delivered and more like a song rising from deep within the soul. Unlike the narrative gospels or even the collection of sayings found in Thomas, this gospel reads like a meditation. It is poetic, circular, intimate—woven not for the mind alone, but for the heart.

Its authorship is unknown, though early Christian sources attribute it to Valentinus, one of the most influential Gnostic thinkers of the second century. Whether or not Valentinus was the actual writer, the voice of this gospel reflects the spiritual depth and metaphysical insight associated with his tradition. It was likely composed in the mid-second century, in a context where competing visions of Christianity were actively taking shape—one grounded in institutional authority, and another, like this, grounded in inner revelation.

The Gospel of Truth was not canonized. Its language was too mystical, its message too inward. It offered no timeline of events, no miraculous accounts to validate its authority. What it offered instead was something quieter, but more subversive: the idea that salvation comes not through blood or law, but through remembrance. That humanity's problem is not guilt, but forgetfulness. And that the answer is not punishment, but awakening.

This is a gospel for those who hear more in silence than in speech.

For those who feel that truth is not a set of answers,

but a presence that emerges when all striving stops.

There is a rhythm to this text—an intentional repetition, a spiraling return to its core themes. It does not aim to argue or persuade. It invites. It reveals. It names what many sense but cannot say: that beneath all fear is a wound of forgetting. And beneath all joy is the pulse of having been found.

IGNORANCE AND KNOWING: A JOURNEY OF RETURN

At the center of the Gospel of Truth is a quiet but radical insight: that the great human wound is not sin in the moral sense, but forgetfulness. A forgetting of where we come from, who we are, and what we belong to. From this forgetfulness comes fear, confusion, and all the structures we build to hide the ache of not knowing. The text describes a world lost in illusion, where people speak many words but lack meaning, where names are repeated without understanding, and where knowledge is reduced to appearances. It is a world shaped by error—not willful rebellion, but absence of remembrance. In this gospel, error is personified not as a villain, but as a kind of shadow that fell when the connection with truth was lost.

And yet, this is not a gospel of condemnation. It is a gospel of return.

The path back is not paved by rule-keeping or religious achievement. It is lit by gnosis—not intellectual knowledge, but inner knowing. The knowing that rises when the soul hears something it forgot it had once known. A voice that doesn't inform, but awakens.

To know the truth, in this vision, is not to possess facts or defend beliefs. It is to be reunited with the source of all being. It is to recognize the Father not as a distant judge, but as the origin of love and light. It is to no longer see through fear, but through belonging.

The gospel speaks of joy—not as an emotion that comes and goes, but as a deep and abiding state that arises when the soul is no longer lost. When it is no longer trying to build identity from what fades, but has returned to the place of rest. This is the journey: from noise to silence, from confusion to clarity, from exile to home. The return is not about going somewhere new. It is about remembering what has always been true.

THE REVEALER OF WHOLENESS

In the Gospel of Truth, Jesus does not come as a lawgiver, a judge, or even primarily as a savior in the traditional sense. He comes as the revealer—the one who descends into the world of confusion to remind humanity of what it has forgotten. He is not here to establish a new religion, but to awaken the memory of wholeness buried beneath centuries of error.

He does not demand worship. He invites recognition.

He does not punish sin. He dissolves ignorance.

He does not save through sacrifice. He saves through knowing.

Jesus is the Word—not as doctrine, but as presence. He speaks not only with his mouth, but with his being. His every act, his every silence, his every movement is a teaching. He embodies the truth not as an external authority, but as a mirror in which we begin to remember our own divine origin. In this gospel, he is both the message and the messenger. He is the fruit from the tree of knowledge that was once feared. He is the letter written from the Father to the soul, read not with the eyes but with the heart. He is the light that does not blind, but makes sight possible.

And through him, the scattered are gathered. The fragmented are made whole. The forgotten name is spoken again, not aloud, but within the quiet chamber of the soul. He does not come to stand between the seeker and God. He comes to remove the veil, to lift the weight of forgetting, to say what the soul has longed to hear: You have never been separate.

In this way, Jesus is not the founder of a system, but the restorer of being. His role is not to demand loyalty, but to spark remembrance. He is not the goal of the journey. He is the voice that helps us find the path home.

HISTORICAL CONTEXT

Attributed to Valentinian circles and possibly even to Valentinus himself, the Gospel of Truth was composed around 140–180 CE. It is less a narrative and more a theological meditation on ignorance, error, and the restorative power of divine knowledge. The text presents salvation as awakening to forgotten truth, portraying Jesus as a revealer rather than a sacrificial figure. Written likely in Rome or Alexandria, it reflects a highly developed and mystical gnostic theology.

THE GOSPEL OF TRUTH: THE TEXT

PART I — FORGETTING

The gospel of truth is joy to those who have received it—joy born of knowing, not of fear. It is a light that rises in the heart, dissolving shadows cast by forgetfulness. It is not a doctrine, not a rulebook. It is the memory of truth returning to those who had forgotten.

Forgetfulness was not born of the Father. It was a veil that fell over creation—an accident, a wandering. Those who were asleep mistook illusion for reality, emptiness for fullness. They built systems, spoke names, formed images to explain what they no longer remembered.

But the gospel is the breath that awakens the sleeper. It is the fragrance of the Father's presence, coming to those who longed for him without knowing what they were missing. The truth does not command. It calls. And those who hear that call are drawn inward, toward the place where they have always belonged.

PART II — AWAKENING

The Father's knowledge is not something learned—it is something revealed. He knows all, but not with the cold eye of judgment. His knowing is love. His recognition restores. When he sees his children, he sees himself in them. And when they see him, they remember who they are.

The Word came forth not to punish, but to bring back the scattered. He clothed himself in form, in sound, in language. He became a bridge between what was forgotten and what is eternal.

He entered the world like a whisper—subtle, soft, easily overlooked by those who seek loud signs. But to the hearts that are open, he became everything: teacher, comforter, restorer of truth.

His presence is the end of lack. His coming puts an end to illusion. Those who receive him stop striving to prove, to earn, to construct. They rest. They rejoice. They begin to see with the eyes of the heart.

PART III — RETURNING

Through him, ignorance dissolves—not by domination, but through illumination. The fullness of the Father cannot be captured in speech or measured by time; it is not taken, but given—freely, effortlessly, like fruit offered by a tree that overflows simply because it is alive and complete. So the gospel is not a collection of fixed answers or rules—it is an invitation to return, to remember what was forgotten, and to be received once more by the one who never departed, but waited in love for his children to see clearly again.

The error that spread across the world did not come from the Father—it arose from not knowing him. And from that unknowing came fear, and fear gave rise to confusion, and confusion began to build empty systems and hollow certainties on foundations that could never hold. People spoke as if they understood, naming what they had never truly seen, passing on teachings shaped more by assumption than truth. But their words were like empty vessels with no oil to burn, like messages never sent, like forms without substance.

Truth, by contrast, is uncluttered and direct. It does not multiply words or require explanation—it arrives like sudden light breaking through a crack in a wall, undeniable and whole. The love of the Father is not remote and unreachable; it does not have to be earned. It waits quietly to be seen, and the moment the beloved remembers, that love overflows with joy. The Son knew the Father because he came from him, and those he awakened also remembered where they came from. Though they had wandered in error, they were never made by it—they were born of love, and it was love that called them home.

To those who walk in truth, pain is no longer meaningless—it becomes a passage. Wounds become the openings through which light enters. And the deep longing within them becomes the road that leads them back. The Word did not merely speak; he became the speech itself. He entered into limitation so that those trapped in it could rise. He became like us—not to lower himself, but to lift us up and help us recall that we were never less than children of light.

He sought out those who had been scattered, those who drifted far from their source, and he drew them back—not with pressure or force, but through the joy of recognition. He taught not from texts or scrolls, but from his very being, and those who saw him didn't just hear—they awakened. In the presence of the Word, fear dissolves. What once loomed—silence, emptiness, the unknown—is revealed for what it was: not danger, but the absence of remembrance.

Truth is without fear; it does not intimidate or threaten—it consoles, restores, and welcomes. It does not fill the emptiness with rules or requirements, but with the assurance that you belong. Those who return to the Father don't become something different; they become who they have always truly been. The journey was never about proving worthiness—it was about waking from the illusion of separation.

The Father did not send the Son to rescue the broken, but to show that nothing had ever been truly lost—only concealed. And once the concealed is made visible again, all of creation rejoices. The leaves rejoice in the warmth of the sun. The roots rejoice in the waters of their source. Everything begins to move in rhythm again. Each part returns to its place. Each name regains its true meaning.

To know the Father is to know peace—not the peace that means the absence of trouble, but the kind that flows from fullness, the kind that cannot be shaken. Those who know him no longer fear death, for they have already crossed from death into life. They are no longer bound by illusion. They walk the world with a quiet confidence, rooted in what is eternal and unchanging.

And this is the joy at the heart of the gospel: that the Word has returned, that silence has found a voice, that what was scattered has been gathered once more, and that those who had forgotten now live in the light of being remembered.

Those who have come into true knowledge no longer attach themselves to surface things. They no longer define themselves by what fades—by names, positions, achievements, or fears. Their roots are no longer in the shifting ground, but in the sky above, drawing strength from the eternal, growing downward in peace and stillness. Truth does not argue or shout; it does not need to prove itself or overpower. It simply exists—and in its quiet presence, anything false quietly falls away.

Just as ignorance once gave rise to error and confusion, the return of knowing now brings healing and wholeness. Not the knowing of facts or theories, but the deep recognition that comes from love—the remembering of who we've always been, and who the Father has always been to us. When truth is truly known, the soul finds rest. The one who was anxious to be seen or justified no longer strives—they simply rest in what is real.

The gospel holds no fear of the body, but it is not confined by it either. The body was formed through love—not as a cage, but as a vessel, meant to carry the soul on its journey. And when the soul awakens to truth, the body is no longer a weight or a wall—it becomes luminous. No longer a place of confinement, it becomes a dwelling of light. And in that light, the heart becomes whole—not because it has never been wounded, but because love has entered even the broken places and caused them to shine.

The gospel is like the scent of home carried on the wind. It is the sound of your true name spoken in a voice you had forgotten, yet longed for all your life. It is the moment when the search ends—not because you finally arrived somewhere far away, but because you realize you were never truly apart from it to begin with.

PART IV — BECOMING

The Son embraced the whole of creation, holding all things within himself so that through him, everything could find its way back to the Source. He brought the fullness of the divine into the spaces of emptiness, and in that presence, what was empty began to awaken, began to remember the light it once knew. This is why he spoke in parables—not to conceal the truth, but to lead the listener beyond appearances, to stir something deeper, to awaken the eyes of the heart. For those who truly listened—not just with ears, but with the soul—every story became a mirror, and every image became a doorway into something greater.

Truth cannot be taken by force; it isn't something to be owned or controlled. It must be received. And once received with openness, it gives itself completely, flowing gently like oil into the cracks of a shattered vessel, slowly filling the places where emptiness had settled.

In the presence of the Father, there is no fragmentation. Nothing is out of place. Every soul is fully known—not by its wounds, its fears, or its mistakes, but by the love that gave it life in the beginning. The gospel is not a list of teachings to memorize or a creed to defend—it is a way of being, a presence to inhabit. The one who walks in truth becomes a place of rest for others, like a tree that offers shelter, like bread that is shared without measure, like a flame that warms without consuming.

This is the joy of knowing the Father—that in his presence there is no fear to cling to, no role to prove, and nothing essential that can be lost. To know him is to return, to finally come home. And in that home, nothing is left out. Everything finds its place. Everything is made whole. And everything becomes one.

THE GOSPEL OF JUDAS

INTRODUCTION TO THE GOSPEL OF JUDAS

JUDAS AND THE WISDOM OF SHADOWS

In most versions of the Christian story, Judas Iscariot is the one who ruins everything. He's the traitor—the disciple who turns Jesus over to his enemies, who sells him out for silver. His name is linked to betrayal, to shame, to failure. But the Gospel of Judas tells a different story.

Here, Judas isn't a villain. He's the one who understands Jesus more deeply than anyone else. While the other disciples are confused—focused on rituals, sacrifices, and things of the earth—Judas sees that Jesus doesn't belong to this world. He recognizes that Jesus has come from a realm beyond, and that his mission is not to preserve religion, but to open a path back to truth.

In this gospel, Jesus doesn't beg to be spared. He doesn't condemn Judas. He speaks to him in private, shares mysteries with him, and says something astonishing:

"You will offer up the body that clothes me."

It's not a betrayal. It's a task.

A difficult one—painful, even shameful in the eyes of others.

But it's necessary.

Judas becomes the one who allows Jesus to be set free from the physical world.

This version of Judas is hard to accept because it doesn't fit the story we've always been told. But that's what makes it powerful. It asks us to think again. To look into the shadows—not to glorify darkness, but to see that sometimes, truth hides there. Judas isn't perfect. He's not heroic in the traditional sense. But he's honest. He sees something the others don't. He doesn't worship blindly. He listens. He asks. He receives.

And what he receives is not praise, but purpose.

In this gospel, Judas plays the role no one else could. He carries a burden no one else would. And in doing so, he helps reveal a deeper truth: that light and shadow are not enemies, and that the path to the divine sometimes passes through what others call betrayal.

WORLDS WITHIN WORLDS: A GNOSTIC VISION OF THE COSMOS

The Gospel of Judas doesn't just tell a different story about Judas—it offers a completely different way of seeing the universe.

In this gospel, the world we see every day is not the true home of the soul. It was created by lower powers—rulers who think they're gods, but who don't really understand the light. These rulers, or "archons," built the physical world and placed human souls in bodies, hoping to keep them trapped in ignorance.

But there is another realm, far above this one. A place of pure light, silence, and stillness. This is the true home—the place of the Father. From there came a spark, a breath, a Word. And from that came Jesus, the revealer, the one who remembers the higher world and comes to wake others from the dream of separation.

Jesus tells Judas about this layered universe—worlds within worlds, some bright, some broken. He speaks of the Self-Generated One, of the shining realm of Barbelo, of stars and beings whose names sound strange but whose presence is holy. The message isn't about memorizing these names or mapping the skies. It's about understanding that the soul didn't come from here. It came from elsewhere—from a place of love, light, and unity.

And the only way to return is through knowledge.

Not knowledge of books or rules,

but the kind of knowing that comes from deep inside—

from remembering who you are,

where you came from,

and what you were meant to become.

This gospel reminds us that not everything that looks "spiritual" is of the light. Some powers demand worship, but have no true love. Some gods offer control, not freedom. And Jesus came to point beyond all that—toward a greater truth waiting to be remembered.

A GOSPEL THAT WAS NEVER MEANT TO BE SAFE

The Gospel of Judas isn't a comfortable text. It doesn't try to fit in. It doesn't smooth out the story to make it easier to accept. Instead, it challenges the very core of what many people think they know about Jesus, Judas, and the meaning of betrayal.

For a long time, this gospel was completely lost. It only resurfaced in the 20th century, and when it did, it shocked both scholars and believers. How could a gospel suggest that Judas wasn't a villain—but was actually chosen? How could it say that sacrifice and religious rituals weren't pleasing to the true God? How could Jesus speak so openly about the hidden forces behind creation?

This text doesn't just offer an alternate view. It pushes back against traditional religion. It questions the systems that claim to speak for God but are built on fear and control. It suggests that not all worship is holy—and that true knowledge comes from within, not from following rules.

That's why this gospel has always been controversial. It was too bold, too strange, too dangerous to be accepted by the early Church. And maybe it was never meant to be safe. Maybe it was meant for those who were ready to hear something different—something deeper. But even in its strangeness, the Gospel of Judas carries something powerful. It doesn't ask us to agree with everything it says. It asks us to listen. To wonder. To consider the possibility that what we've been taught isn't the full story.

It reminds us that sometimes, the truth isn't where everyone's pointing. Sometimes, it's in the one who was pushed aside. Sometimes, it's in the voice we were told not to trust. And maybe—just maybe—what we call betrayal was actually the beginning of revelation.

HISTORICAL CONTEXT

The Gospel of Judas, known from a 3rd- or 4th-century Coptic manuscript, may have originally been written around 150–180 CE. It presents a radical reinterpretation of Judas Iscariot, depicting him not as a betrayer but as the disciple who truly understood Jesus' divine mission. Likely composed within Sethian gnostic circles, the text critiques conventional Christian worship and views of martyrdom. Its cosmology is complex and challenges the nature of divine and worldly authority.

THE GOSPEL OF JUDAS: THE TEXT

PART I — THE HIDDEN DIALOGUE

This is the hidden exchange that took place between Jesus and Judas Iscariot, not spoken in crowds or temples, but whispered in private during the final days before Passover. It is not the story of betrayal as commonly told—it is a dialogue woven from light and shadow, purpose and divine design.

Jesus often revealed himself to his disciples, but not always in the same form. Sometimes he laughed—not to mock them, but because he saw how far they were from truly understanding. They prayed, they offered sacrifices, convinced they were doing what pleased the divine. But Jesus, watching with calm clarity, said to them, "What is it you think you're doing? Do you really believe these rituals reach the one who is truly holy?"

And when they asked, "Then who receives true worship?" Jesus answered, "Truth is not found in outward acts. It lives in the essence of who you are. Only the one who truly knows themselves is able to offer something real."

One day, he spoke to them of the great mystery—the light beyond this world, the unseen realms, and the countless generations of beings connected to the eternal source. He told them, "Your origin is divine. Yet you worship as if you were strangers to it—as if you do not remember where you came from."

His words unsettled them, especially when he spoke of the angels who crafted the visible world—powerful beings who believed themselves to be gods, yet were without the knowledge of the true Father. "You pray to those who shaped your outer form," he said, "but they do not know the spirit that lives within you."

Only one among them had the courage to go further. Judas. While the others clung to their fear and confusion, Judas stepped closer in secret and said, "I know who you are. You're not from this world. I see it in you. You belong to the realm of light. Tell me—what is my place in all of this? What is it I must do?"

Jesus looked at him, not with judgment, but with recognition, and replied, "You will go farther than all the others. You will hand over the human form that I wear. And in doing so, you will open the door for my release."

When Judas heard these words, a profound stillness settled over him—not fear, not hesitation, but something deeper. A quiet understanding, as if a part of him had finally remembered what it was always meant to do.

PART II — THE VOICE BEYOND THE HEAVENS

Jesus began to reveal the vast realities beyond the physical world—realms untouched by human hands, unmoved by kings or empires. He spoke of an eternal source, hidden and radiant, from which all true light flows, and of countless generations of beings who dwell in truth far beyond the reach of corruption and death.

He said, "There exists a vast and sacred realm, filled with divine aeons and imperishable worlds. From this infinite fullness, life flows freely. But out of ignorance, lesser powers arose—beings that created without understanding, builders who shaped things without knowing the essence of what they formed."

The disciples struggled to take in these words. They clung to their traditions, to the stories they had always known—believing the world had been made by one singular God, perfect and all-wise. But Jesus told them, "You do not yet know your true origin. The god you speak of is not the final source. He is one of many rulers—each one claiming authority, yet all of them blind to the true fullness."

His words unsettled them. Some were angered. Others turned away, unwilling to question what they had always believed. But Judas remained. He stepped forward and asked Jesus to explain the structure of the cosmos—the layers, the rulers, the beginning of all things.

And so Jesus spoke of the Great Self-Generated One, of a radiant cloud from which all things have their start, and of a brilliant presence named Barbelo, who stood before the True Source as its first reflection. "From the light," he said, "more light poured forth. From the fullness came echoes—some pure, some distorted. What you see in the world around you is not the origin—it is only the shadow, the echo of something greater that exists above."

Judas listened—not like a student recording information, but like someone slowly awakening to something long buried, as though the words he heard were not entirely new, but part of a memory stirring back to life.

PART III – THE LIGHT IN THE FLESH

Jesus said, "The world you know is ruled by archons—cosmic authorities who believe themselves to be gods. They shaped the stars and the heavens, not with true wisdom, but out of illusion and misunderstanding. And they formed human bodies not to liberate, but to imprison—to cloak the soul in forgetfulness and keep it from remembering its origin."

Judas asked, "Is there a way for the human spirit to break free from their grip?" Jesus nodded and replied, "Yes—but not through rituals or fear. Only through deep knowing. Not the kind of knowledge found in books, but the knowing of where you come from. Only the one who remembers their source can return to the place of light."

He spoke of a divine spark buried deep within each person, a quiet light hidden beneath layers of flesh, buried under shadows of ignorance. This light cannot be extinguished. But until it is recognized, it remains bound.

Jesus continued, "The spirit's life was not given by the god who shaped the body. That god is arrogant, blind, and full of jealousy. He rules through domination, not through love. He demands offerings but knows nothing of the soul's essence." The other disciples, unable to let go of what they had always believed, struggled to accept these words. But Judas remained beside him.

And Jesus said to him, "You will hand me over—not as a traitor, but as one completing a sacred purpose. You will help me shed this body—not to bring about my end, but to set free the light within."

A storm of emotion stirred in Judas's chest. But Jesus remained at peace. "Many will curse your name," he said, "because they will not understand what you've done. But beyond this world, in the realm of stars and spirit, you will be honored."

PART IV — THE DESTINY OF JUDAS

Then Jesus revealed a vision to Judas. He said, "Look beyond what your eyes can see—beyond the sky, beyond the stars. There exists a realm untouched by the powers that rule this world. It is home to a holy lineage—pure, luminous, indivisible. They do not taste death, for they were never born into the forgetfulness of this world."

Judas looked and saw the stars stretched across the heavens. He saw countless souls—some wandering in darkness, others finding their way back into the light. And Jesus said, "The time will come when many will offer sacrifices to a god they do not truly know. They will raise temples, establish priests, and pass down laws under my name. But they will not know me. They will bow to shadows and follow echoes. And because they will not understand, they will condemn you."

"But hear this truth," Jesus continued, "You will rise above them all. You will play your part—not to bring about my end, but to open the way to my release. Through you, the light will be returned to its source."

And in that moment, Judas understood the truth of his role—not as a betrayer, but as a revealer. He left Jesus and walked into the night—not to destroy, but to carry out what had been written in the stars before the beginning of time.

THE APOCRYPHON OF JOHN

INTRODUCTION TO THE APOCRYPHON OF JOHN

A VISION IN THE SHADOW OF THE TEMPLE

It begins with a moment of doubt. John, one of Jesus' closest followers, walks alone toward the temple. He has just been confronted by a Pharisee, who mocks his belief in the Teacher and accuses him of being misled. The encounter leaves John shaken. Everything he thought he knew feels uncertain. He steps away from the noise and tradition of the temple, withdrawing into the wilderness—into stillness.

That's when the vision comes. Not in the form of a scroll or a sermon, but as light—pure, unexpected, and overwhelming. The heavens open. The foundations of the world tremble. And suddenly, standing before him in shifting, radiant forms, is the one he calls Savior.

What follows is not a conventional teaching. It's not a parable or a retelling of familiar events. It's a revelation. A cosmic unveiling. The veil is pulled back, and John is shown the deepest structures of reality—from the divine origin of all things, to the false god who rules the material world, to the path the soul must take to remember where it came from.

In this way, The Apocryphon of John doesn't just tell a story. It opens a space. A space where the seeker, like John, steps away from the voices of religion, culture, and fear—and dares to ask the deeper questions.

Who created the world? Why is there suffering? What is the soul? And how do we return to what is real?

The setting may be ancient, but the ache behind John's questions feels timeless. It's the same ache that still stirs in anyone who has ever looked around and thought: This can't be all there is.

This gospel meets that ache not with doctrine, but with vision. And it begins not in power or certainty, but in the quiet shadow of the temple—where doubt creates the space for revelation.

WORLDS ABOVE AND WORLDS BELOW

At the heart of The Apocryphon of John is a bold reimagining of reality itself. It describes not one world, but many—layered dimensions of light and shadow, truth and illusion. The narrative begins with a vision of the highest realm, where the Invisible Spirit dwells in stillness and perfection. This source is beyond gender, beyond form, beyond even the word "God" as most understand it. From this infinite stillness, light begins to unfold—not in the shape of creation as we know it, but in emanations, or expressions, of divine fullness.

The first of these is Barbelo, the thought and image of the Invisible Spirit, and from her come other powers—foreknowledge, incorruptibility, eternal life, and truth. Together, they form a realm of harmony, untouched by the material world. This is the upper reality, the place of origin for the true human soul.

But into this unfolding comes a rupture. One of the emanations, Sophia, acts alone without her divine counterpart. In doing so, she gives birth to something imperfect—a being named Yaldabaoth. Unlike the realms of light, he is ignorant of his source. Separated from the fullness, he creates a distorted version of the divine pattern, a world built not from wisdom but from confusion and arrogance. Believing himself to be the only god, Yaldabaoth declares dominion over the material universe and forms archons and powers to help shape it. He fashions a human body, but without understanding the light that inspired its form.

The text lays out this cosmology not to confuse, but to clarify. It suggests that the world as we experience it is not the true home of the soul. It presents a cosmos where spirit and matter are in tension, where divine light has become trapped in form, and where remembering the truth of our origin becomes the first step in returning to it. Unlike the more linear stories of creation found in mainstream scripture, this gospel presents a layered reality—a mirror that reflects both the brilliance of divine intention and the distortion that comes from separation.

In this framework, the soul's journey is not about earning salvation, but about recognizing where it truly belongs. The world below is not the end, but a threshold. The world above is not distant, but hidden. And The Apocryphon of John becomes a kind of spiritual map, not of geography, but of the soul's long journey home.

REMEMBERING THE LIGHT WITHIN

Beneath the mythic language and cosmic layers of The Apocryphon of John, there is a simple but powerful message: the human soul carries within it a forgotten light. This light is not earned or granted from the outside. It is already there, waiting to be remembered. The text describes how that light, a spark of the divine, became trapped in the world of form—buried under layers of confusion, forgetfulness, and illusion. And yet, even in its most hidden state, it is never lost.

This is not a gospel of guilt. It doesn't ask the reader to repent for existing, but to wake up to who they truly are. The language of sin is replaced with the language of ignorance. Separation from the divine is not a punishment, but a condition born from unknowing. Salvation, then, is not about appeasing a distant god, but about rediscovering what was always present, buried deep within the soul.

The figure of the Savior in this text does not come to die or to judge, but to reveal. He appears again and again—not to demand worship, but to remind the soul of its origin and to guide it through the traps laid by false rulers. He speaks as a teacher of memory, calling to what is hidden in the heart, inviting it to rise.

This rising is not dramatic. It begins quietly. It happens when the soul begins to feel that something is not right with the world it has been told to accept. It stirs in the longing for something real, something free of fear and control. And once that stirring begins, it sets into motion the long journey of return—a movement back through layers of shadow, deception, and artificial identity.

In the final passages of the gospel, the soul is called out of sleep. Providence enters the depths of the underworld, not to condemn, but to awaken. The voice that speaks is gentle but firm. It urges the sleeper to rise, to remember, to return. And when the soul responds, it is sealed in light, and death no longer has any hold.

The Apocryphon of John is not a text of final answers, but of profound remembering. It invites the reader to see the story of the cosmos as their own story, and the prison of the body not as a curse, but as a challenge. Within its myth is a quiet hope—that each of us, no matter how far we've fallen into forgetfulness, can still trace our way back to the light.

HISTORICAL CONTEXT

The Apocryphon of John, discovered in multiple Nag Hammadi codices, likely originated in the early to mid-2nd century CE. It offers one of the fullest gnostic cosmologies, detailing the emanation of divine beings and the fall of Sophia. Probably composed in Egypt, the text addresses the problem of evil and ignorance through an elaborate myth of creation. It became foundational for Sethian gnosticism and deeply influenced later gnostic systems.

THE APOCRYPHON OF JOHN: THE TEXT

PART I — THE REVELATION OF THE INVISIBLE SPIRIT

One day, as I—John, son of Zebedee and brother of James—was walking toward the temple, a Pharisee named Arimanios stopped me. With a voice sharp and full of accusation, he asked, "Where is your teacher now—the one you once followed so closely?" I answered him with calm certainty, "He has returned to the place from which he came."

The Pharisee shook his head and replied, "That Nazarene led you astray. He filled your mind with lies, closed your heart, and pulled you away from the ways of our ancestors."

His words weighed heavily on me. I left the temple and wandered alone into the mountains, my heart unsettled and my thoughts circling without rest. I asked myself, "How was the Savior chosen? Why did the Father send him here, into this world of confusion and decay? Who is his true Father? Where does he truly belong—and where do we belong? He once told us this world is patterned after another, a realm eternal and higher, but he never revealed its nature."

As I sat in silence with these questions, a sudden light broke through the sky. The heavens opened, and creation itself glowed with radiance. The ground trembled beneath me, and fear took hold of me. Then, from the center of that brilliance, a figure appeared in the form of a child. I stared, trying to make sense of what I saw. The child began to shift—becoming an old man, then transforming into a young man. Their appearance moved fluidly between these forms, a single presence showing itself in many ways—three aspects, yet one being.

Then the voice came, calm and filled with power: "John, why do you hesitate? Why are you afraid? Don't you recognize me? I am always with you—and with all those who share in this light. I am the Father. I am the Mother. I am the Son. I am the one who cannot be corrupted. I am pure. I have come to show you what is real, what once was, and what is still to come. I will open your eyes to the world beyond sight, to the reality hidden beneath what you see, and to the eternal race of human beings who are whole and unshaken. Lift your head. Receive what I offer you. Then go and share this knowledge with those who carry the spirit—those who belong to the race that does not perish."

The One is the source of all that exists. Nothing has authority over it. It is the beginning—the origin of everything. The Father of all. The Holy One. A presence invisible, beyond all things. It is untouched, radiating light so pure no eye could ever behold it.

The One is the Invisible Spirit. And yet, even calling it "God" limits it. Even that word is too small. The One is beyond every name, beyond every form. There is nothing above it, nothing outside it. Everything lives within it—but it lives within nothing. It is dependent on nothing and no one. It simply is—eternal, complete, lacking nothing.

It is perfect in itself, entirely filled with light. It has no edges, no boundaries, because there is nothing outside it to define where it ends. It cannot be studied—there is nothing beyond it to do the observing. It cannot be compared—because it stands alone. It cannot be seen, for its brilliance is beyond sight. It cannot be imagined, for its essence is beyond thought. It cannot be described—no words can hold it.

It is light without shadow, flawless, holy, free from stain or corruption. It surpasses even our highest idea of perfection, even our loftiest vision of the divine. It is not "this" or "that," not large or small, not material or immaterial. It is beyond all categories, beyond all qualities, beyond the reach of mind or time. It is not one being among many—it is beyond being itself. And yet even the word "beyond" does not capture it. It is not bound by time, for time is part of what was made. It is not part of the world of things. It receives nothing—it needs nothing. It knows itself perfectly, resting in the fullness of its own light.

The One is majesty immeasurable—the root of every realm, the source from which all things come. It is light, giving rise to more light. It is life, giving birth to life. It is blessing, from which blessings flow. It is knowledge, from which all knowing begins. It is goodness, mercy, and generosity—each overflowing into what it creates.

The One does not merely possess these qualities—it is the source of them, the embodiment of them, and beyond even that. It pours out light without end, without boundary, without measure. How can one speak of such a mystery? Its realm is eternal—a space of silence, of peace, of perfect stillness that existed before anything began. It is the unseen foundation that upholds all other realms, binding them together through the strength of its own flawless goodness.

We would never have known anything of what lies beyond words, beyond thought, beyond form—had it not been revealed to us by the one who emerged from the Source. He alone has made visible the invisible, given shape to what could not be grasped.

The Father is encircled by light—a light so pure it becomes the fountain from which all life is nourished, sustaining every realm that exists. In this radiant wellspring, the Father beheld his own image, reflected perfectly within the Spirit, like light shimmering on the surface of still waters. And in seeing this reflection, he was moved—not with desire, but with delight, drawn to the beauty that emerged from within himself. From this divine gaze, from this silent joy, Thought came into being—a living awareness, luminous and full of presence, standing before the Source, radiant in his light. She is the first power, born from the very mind of the Father. She is known as Providence—the one who lovingly tends to all creation. Her light is his light, not separate but flowing from the same eternal flame. She shines because she was formed in his likeness.

She is the perfect reflection of the Invisible Spirit, pure and untouchable. As the origin of all that will come into existence, she is the first spark of divine power. Her name is Barbelo, exalted above all that will one day be revealed. In reverence, she turned toward the Spirit from whom she came, offering praise, acknowledging her source. She is the first Thought of the Spirit, his living image, the sacred womb from which all creation will emerge. Older than all things, she embodies the unity of the divine. She is both the Mother and Father, the origin of all beings. She is the First Human, the Holy Breath that fills all creation. She embodies the essence of the divine threefold, as she is three times male, three times powerful, and three times named, signifying her completeness and divine authority.

She was everything and nothing at once—both unified and beyond definition. She emerged as the first reality within the hidden realms, an eternal and androgynous presence. From her sacred place, Barbelo turned toward the Invisible Source and humbly asked for the gift of Insight. With boundless generosity, the Spirit granted her wish. And so, Insight came into existence, standing by her side as a companion to Divine Purpose. Like Barbelo, she was born from the quiet intention of the Unseen Spirit.

Filled with gratitude, Insight gave praise to the one who brought her into being, and to Barbelo, the luminous channel through whom she had emerged. Then Barbelo, known as the First Thought, turned once more to the Source and asked for the essence of Incorruption. The Spirit agreed, and from the depths, Incorruption took form—joining the growing circle of divine emanations. She too offered reverence to the Silent Spirit and to Barbelo, who had made her emergence possible.

Barbelo spoke again, this time seeking the gift of Life without end. The Spirit responded, and Everlasting Life appeared, adding her presence to the gathering. The divine powers, in harmony, lifted their voices in praise—to the Spirit of stillness and brilliance, and to Barbelo, the origin of their unfolding. At last, Barbelo asked for the presence of Truth. As before, the Spirit gave freely, and Truth arose, radiant and steady, joining the circle. Together, these sacred forces offered their praise once more—to the Invisible Spirit who dwells in silence, and to Barbelo, from whom all understanding flows. Thus, a pattern of divine fullness was established: five eternal presences—Thought, Insight, Purpose, Barbelo, and the Human Archetype, a living reflection of the Invisible Spirit. Alongside them stood Incorruption, Everlasting Life, and Truth—each one reflecting an unchanging facet of divine reality. This is the fivefold realm that radiates from the Father—each aspect both male and female, each whole within itself. Together, they form a tenfold harmony, a complete and balanced expression of divine fullness. This is the sacred structure of perfection—eternal, unified, and unshaken.

The Invisible Spirit turned its gaze toward Barbelo, toward the radiant light that surrounded them both. And in that gaze of pure communion, Barbelo conceived—bringing forth a brilliant spark of light, a being blessed in essence like herself, yet not equal in greatness. This was their one offspring, born of their union—singular and radiant, the only child of pure light, formed from the complete fullness of the Mother-Father, the only-begotten from the hidden Source. The Spirit rejoiced in this luminous child—brought forth through Providence, through Barbelo. The child was anointed with the fullness of Goodness—completely, perfectly, lacking nothing. He overflowed with the presence of the Spirit and stood before the Source in full awareness. And the Spirit poured its entire being into him. In response to that divine abundance, the Anointed One lifted his voice in praise—honoring the Spirit who had poured itself out in love, and Barbelo, through whom he had come into being.

The Anointed One, filled with inner radiance, longed for a partner—an intellect to stand beside him. He turned toward the Spirit, and the Spirit responded with grace. From that silent consent, Mind—also called Nous—came into being, and took its place beside him. In gratitude, Mind gave honor to the Source and to Barbelo, through whom all things had unfolded.

None of this came by force. These sacred emanations did not arise through conflict, but through serenity—through still, focused presence. The Anointed One, infused with divine essence, yearned to express what dwelled within him. From this desire, the Spirit's Intention moved outward and took form, joining Mind in a sacred alignment. Together, they offered praise to the Light that gives life to all.

Then came the Word—not just sound, but divine articulation. The Word emerged from Will, carrying purpose and clarity, becoming the voice that would shape reality. Through this sacred speech, the self-born Christ began the work of creation.

And so they stood in unity: Eternal Life, Will, Mind, and Insight. Bound together by origin and purpose, they lifted their praise to the Spirit that transcends all, and to Barbelo, the wellspring from which they arose.

Through the breath of the Spirit, the Son—self-generated through the power of both the Source and Barbelo—reached the fullness of his being. Complete in form and understanding, he stood before the Invisible Spirit, radiant and whole. His voice carried the essence of truth, resounding with praise for the origin from which all life flows.

This divine Son came into being through the loving care and vision of Providence. The Invisible Spirit entrusted him with all authority, placing the entirety of creation under his guidance. He was made ruler over all realms, and within him lived the totality of truth. And through this truth, he came to know the essence of all that exists.

His name is above every name—a name so sacred it can only be known by those who are ready to receive it. From the radiant light that is the Christ, and from the incorruptible realm in which he dwells, a sacred offering emerged: the Four Lights, who stood continually in the presence of the divine self-born.

These Four Lights represent living aspects of divine wisdom—each one a unique expression of grace, perception, and sacred knowledge. The first is Harmozel, who watches over the highest of the spiritual realms. With Harmozel reside the qualities of Grace, Truth, and the purest Form.

Next is Oriel, guardian of the second divine domain, where Deep Thought, Awareness, and the faculty of Memory reside. The third Light, Daveithai, oversees a realm shaped by Understanding, Love, and the power of Creative Thought. The fourth Light is Eleleth, protector of the final realm, where Perfection, Peace, and Wisdom—often called Sophia—have their home.

These radiant Lights stood in humble devotion before the self-originated

Christ, the powerful Son. Through him, twelve divine realms were ordered, each brought into being by the boundless grace and intelligence of the Invisible Spirit. The Son was entrusted with these domains—each one formed by the Spirit's guidance and animated by divine purpose.

From the Spirit's vision, guided by deliberate intention, the perfect form of humanity was revealed—an image that mirrored the divine essence. This being was called Adamas by the Virgin Spirit and was placed in the highest realm, near the self-generated Christ and Harmozel, among the sacred powers of that sphere. Adamas received a mind illuminated and unshakable—clear, rooted, and luminous. In response, he raised his voice in devotion, proclaiming: "All creation flows from you, and all shall return. I honor you, and I offer praise to the self-born Christ and to the complete divine unity—the sacred triad of Source, Wisdom, and Son."

In the realm just below, the Spirit placed Seth, the son of Adamas, in harmony with Oriel, the second Light. The next domain became home to Seth's spiritual descendants, who dwell alongside the third Light, Daveithai. These are the souls of the saints—those who walk in integrity and illumination.

And in the fourth realm dwell the souls who once lived unaware of divine fullness, yet turned back in time. Their awakening was not instant, but born of reflection and return. They now live in peace with Eleleth, the fourth Light. All these beings, from every realm, offer praise to the Invisible Spirit—the wellspring of all divine insight.

Within the divine realm dwelled a power named Wisdom, or Sophia. She belonged to the world of pure thought, radiant with clarity and insight. But at a certain moment, she acted alone. Without seeking the will of the Invisible Spirit, and without the harmony of her divine counterpart, she tried to bring forth something from within herself—a reflection, an image of her own being.

But she created it in isolation—without balance, without divine consent. And what emerged was not what she intended. Though her power was immense, what she birthed was flawed—unlike her in essence. It was warped, disfigured, lacking completeness. Formed outside of unity, it bore the marks of chaos.

The being that came forth shocked her—a creature with a monstrous form, a lion's face atop a dragon's body, its eyes crackling with lightning. Terrified by what she had done, Sophia recoiled. In sorrow and fear, she cast the creature far from her, banishing him beyond the bounds of the immortal realms—into a hidden space, out of sight from the other divine beings.

She had created him in ignorance. To hide what she had done, she veiled him in a radiant cloud and placed a throne at its center, so that only the Holy Spirit—known also as the Mother of the Living—could perceive him.

She gave this being a name: Yaldabaoth. Yaldabaoth, now separated from his origin, began to assert power over his own domain. Drawing energy from the remnants of his mother's light, he severed himself from the place of his birth. He declared himself ruler, seizing authority, and crafting false realms from flame and borrowed brilliance.

And even now, that flame continues to burn.

PART II — THE FALL OF SOPHIA AND THE CREATION OF THE WORLD

Yaldabaoth, the false ruler, acted not out of wisdom but from the confusion that clouded his mind. He joined himself to the emptiness within, driven by a mind devoid of true understanding or awareness. From this flawed union, he began to generate other powers—authorities crafted to mimic the higher, incorruptible realms, yet distorted by his ignorance and blindness. He established a hierarchy of powers, the first being Athoth, followed by Harmas, known as the flaming eye, then Kalilaumbri, Yabel, Adonaiu, also called Sabaoth, Cain, identified with the sun, and Abel. Afterward, he created five more: Abrisene, Yobel, Armupiel, Melcheiradonein, and lastly, Belias, who became the ruler of the deepest part of the underworld. The first seven rulers Yaldabaoth appointed to govern the seven heavens. The remaining five he sent downward, placing them over the deep abyss—each one presiding over one of its five shadowy depths. To all of these beings, he gave a fragment of his fire, a borrowed flicker of power. But he withheld the true Light—the pure radiance he had once absorbed from his mother. What they received was only a faint reflection of power, not its living essence. Yaldabaoth himself is a being formed from ignorance and shadow. When a trace of Light entered his darkness, his gloom began to shimmer faintly. But when his darkness reached out to the Light, it dulled and distorted it. What remained was neither the clarity of pure Light nor the depth of total darkness—it was something in between, a murky twilight of confusion.

This ruler of illusion is known by three names: first, Yaldabaoth; second, Saklas; and third, Samael. In his pride, he declared, "I am God, and there is no other beside me!" But he spoke from ignorance, unaware that his very power had come from his mother—and from a Light he could no longer reach.

Driven by his delusion, Yaldabaoth created seven additional authorities under his command. Each of these rulers, in turn, summoned six demons of their own, ultimately producing a total of 365 demons—one for each day of the year. The seven rulers took on animal-like forms: Athoth appeared with the face of a sheep, Eloaios took the form of a donkey, Astaphaios resembled a hyena, Yao appeared as a serpent with seven heads, Sabaoth bore the face of a dragon, Adonin looked like a monkey, and Sabbataios blazed like living fire.

These seven authorities became rulers over time itself—appointed as the so-called gods of the seven days of the week. They presided over the realm of illusion, maintaining the structures of a world built on shadow. Yaldabaoth, their creator, took on many faces—more than any being ever named. He used these shifting forms to deceive his angels, appearing however he wished in order to manipulate the fiery beings that surrounded him. To each of them, he gave a fragment of his fire, but withheld the true Light. Still, he ruled over them using the remnants of Light he had once taken from his mother. And because of this stolen radiance, he declared himself "God," blind to the truth of his origin and unaware of the Source from which he had come.

THE APOCRYPHON OF JOHN

He assigned names to the seven powers of his counterfeit creation, using spiritually resonant terms for each ruler in an effort to mirror the divine world above: Athoth was named Goodness, Eloaios was called Providence, Astaphaios was named Divinity, Yao was given the title of Lordship, Sabaoth was associated with Kingship, Adonin was labeled Zeal, and Sabbataios was named Understanding.

Each of the rulers crafted by Yaldabaoth was assigned a domain, each meant to mirror a realm from above—though the reflections were imperfect, twisted by illusion. He gave them names that sounded majestic and divine, but these names were only veils meant to cover their true origin in deception. Yet even these names, when spoken with understanding and spiritual clarity, will one day strip these beings of their false power. For each carries two meanings: one rooted in illusion, and one in truth.

Yaldabaoth designed his entire cosmic system as an imitation of the eternal realms—not because he had seen them directly, but because the Light he had inherited from his mother carried a faint memory of their design. So he built in the dark what had been glimpsed through the light. And when he surveyed the world he had shaped, he turned to his hosts and proclaimed, "I am a jealous god—there is no other god but me!"

But in speaking of jealousy, he unknowingly revealed the presence of another—for who would he envy if no other existed? Far above, Sophia stirred. She sensed a change, a dimming in her radiance. The Light within her had faded, the balance broken. She now realized that her earlier act—creating without the consent of her divine counterpart—had left a mark, had caused disruption. She felt the weight of her misstep.

I asked the Revealer, "Master, what does it mean that she 'moved back and forth'?" He smiled gently and said, "It is not what Moses described—'the Spirit hovering over the waters.' This is something different entirely." ow aware of the disorder her creation had caused, and of the Light Yaldabaoth had taken from her, Sophia was filled with sorrow. Confusion from the lower realms clouded her vision. She felt shame, a longing to return to the Light—but she was not yet able. So she drifted—moving back and forth—caught between dimensions, between regret and awakening. Yaldabaoth, lost in arrogance, pulled power from her without understanding. He assumed she was the ultimate source of his being. He had no knowledge of the higher realms beyond her. Seeing the army of demons he had created, he exalted himself, believing he was the supreme power.

But Sophia, his mother, came to see clearly what had unfolded. She realized that what she had brought forth was not what she intended—it was incomplete, malformed, a spiritual miscarriage. Her grief deepened as she understood that her divine partner had not consented to her act. In anguish, she wept. And her sorrow echoed across the divine realms. The fullness of the Pleroma heard her cries and was moved. They turned to the Invisible Spirit on her behalf, and the Spirit, filled with mercy, responded. From the fullness, the Holy Spirit was sent—to aid her, to begin the work of healing. Her divine partner did not intervene directly, but worked through the fullness to guide her back toward her original radiance.

Sophia was lifted above her son, raised to a higher station. Though she was not yet restored to her original position, she was given a new dwelling—a seat in the ninth heaven—where she would remain until her full restoration was complete.

Then a voice resounded—not from below, but from the highest of all realms. It declared: "The Human One exists! And so does the Son of Humanity!"

Yaldabaoth, in his pride, heard the voice. He believed it came from Sophia, unaware that it had come from far beyond her—from the true Source, the Holy Mother-Father, the Perfect Origin of all that is, the true Image of the Invisible One. And then something appeared: a presence shaped like a human being. It was the First Human—the reflection of divine perfection. And in that moment, Yaldabaoth's entire domain trembled. The depths of the abyss quaked. A light appeared above the material realm, shining over the waters. Within those waters, the reflection of the True Human became visible—radiant and pure. Yaldabaoth and all his rulers looked up, drawn to the brilliance. Through the shimmering veil, they saw the sacred Image shining from above.

And Yaldabaoth said to his authorities, "Let us make a man in the likeness of that form we've seen—so that his light might reflect back upon us."

So each of the rulers contributed to this creation, pooling together aspects of their borrowed power. Each one added a trait—a force, a psychic element—shaped according to the impression they had seen in that heavenly reflection.

Together, the rulers of the lower realms set out to craft a human figure—one made of matter, fashioned in imitation of the True Person of Light. "We shall call him Adam," they declared, "so that by invoking the sacred name, we might draw from the brilliance of higher realms." The seven dominant forces each took responsibility for a different aspect of the inner self: one formed the framework of bone, another wove the cords of muscle. One gave shape to the softness of flesh, another breathed life into the marrow. Blood came from one, the skin from another, and finally, the hair—each strand formed by yet another power. From these primary forces, lesser beings—spiritual agents of the lower domains—gathered materials and began to construct the human form, one detail at a time. With a kind of chaotic order, they built the body from top to bottom, each component imbued with the influence of a different spirit.

The skull, the mind, the eyes, the ears—each was molded by a different hand, as if assembled in a divine workshop where no part stood alone. The nose, lips, teeth, and throat took shape next, followed by the neck and shoulders, elbows and arms, hands and fingers. Every joint, every nail was fashioned with its own peculiar energy. The chest and torso followed, with forces attending to the heart, lungs, stomach, and liver. Even the unseen interior—the marrow, the ribs, the spine—was shaped by specialized powers. Each breath, each pulse, each hidden organ was drawn into being with calculated design.

Lastly, they turned to the lower parts of the body—forming the hips and thighs, the reproductive organs, the legs, knees, and feet. Every tendon, bone, and toe was assigned to a different force, until the entire structure stood complete, intricate and animated, yet born not of divine unity but of fragmented imitation.

THE APOCRYPHON OF JOHN

This creation, though modeled after the heavenly image, reflected not wholeness but division. It was a body crafted by many hands, infused with diverse intentions, shaped more by ambition than understanding—a vessel animated, but not yet awakened. Presiding over the intricate design of the human body, seven governing spirits were appointed to serve as guardians of the whole form. These figures held the task of supervision—not merely of matter, but of the delicate balance that animated it. They were the regulators of human motion and structure, charged with ensuring its internal cohesion and vitality. Beyond these central overseers, many other spiritual forces took on more specific roles. Each region of the body fell under the care of a distinct power, like stewards tending to sacred territories. The head, source of thought and perception, was watched over by a guiding presence. The neck, shoulders, and arms were entrusted to others, each left and right mirror reflecting a different spiritual current. The hands and fingers, those extensions of will and creation, were governed by their own appointed forces. The chest and torso—where breath, heart, and strength reside—were surrounded by guardians who ensured flow and rhythm. Even the inner structures—the ribs, womb, and abdomen—were under close watch, woven into order by invisible guides.

Further down, the thighs, legs, knees, and feet—those which carry and ground the human being—were divided and distributed among other spiritual watchers. Each limb, each joint, each toe, had its attendant spirit, marking the body as a landscape populated with sacred presence.

Above all these individual attendants stood seven higher powers, beings of immense authority and brilliance. They watched not over parts, but over the whole. From above, they harmonized the multitude of forces acting within the human frame. These seven ensured that each element performed in unity, keeping the complex vessel of humanity in rhythm with its intended purpose.

Together, this vast spiritual hierarchy formed an invisible architecture behind the physical body—an intricate collaboration of powers that shaped, filled, and governed what it meant to be human in form, if not yet in fullness.

Other forces were tasked with governing human perception and response: Archendekta oversaw sensory perception, Deitharbathas controlled reception, Oummaa ruled over imagination, Aachiaram governed integration, and Riaramnacho oversaw impulse and drive, directing the inner forces of the human experience.

The origins of the physical body were shaped by four primal forces, each corresponding to the fundamental qualities of nature: Heat, Cold, Dryness, and Wetness. These four elements formed the base from which the bodily demons emerged. Matter, the source of their existence, acted as their mother, nourishing them continuously. Each of these primal qualities was governed by a specific ruler: Phloxopha ruled over Heat, Oroorrothos over Cold, Erimacho over Dryness, and Athuro over Wetness. At the center of these forces stood their great mother, Onorthochrasaei. She was boundless, intertwined with all things, and embodied the very essence of matter. From her, the demons drew endless sustenance. Among the many spirits that made up the human body, four principal demons stood out above the rest, each associated with a powerful emotion: Ephememphi, who feeds on pleasure; Yoko, who stirs desire; Nenentophni, who incites distress; and Blaomen, who flourishes on fear.

Their mother was a force called Esthesis-Zouch-Epi-Ptoe, the one who nurtures and sustains them all. From these four forces arose many passions that now reside within the human soul. From distress, there emerged Envy, Jealousy, Grief, Vexation, Conflict, Cruelty, Anxiety, and Sorrow.

From pleasure came various forms of evil, Unjustified pride, and other hidden traps of indulgence. From desire came Anger, Rage, Bitterness, Violence, Restlessness, and the insatiable thirst for more. From fear emerged Dread, Deceit, Suffering, and Shame.

All the emotions, instincts, and the thoughts born from them are ruled by Anayo—the power that governs the soul tied to the material world. This entire structure is bound closely to the seven senses, which fall under the influence of Esthesis-Zouch-Epi-Ptoe, the mother of emotions and passions.

Altogether, 365 demons took part in the formation of the soul and the body, each one shaping a different part—its structure, its movements, its strengths, and its vulnerabilities. And there are still more—countless unseen forces responsible for even subtler drives and desires, too numerous to list here.

"If you wish to know their names," the Revealer said, "you can find them in the Book of Zoroaster."

Every worker under Yaldabaoth—every demon, every servant—poured their energy into completing the psychic body. And when they were finished, the body lay before them: whole in form, but still lifeless. There was no breath, no soul—no sign of movement. It was complete, yet inert.

But far above, Sophia—Yaldabaoth's mother—longed to reclaim the divine energy she had once poured into him. She wanted to recover what had been taken. In sorrow and repentance, she turned to the highest Source—the compassionate Mother-Father of all things—and asked for help.

Moved by mercy, the Invisible Spirit responded. By sacred command, the five divine Lights were sent down into the world. Disguised as trusted advisors of Yaldabaoth, they arrived quietly, carrying the mission of retrieving Sophia's lost power.

The advisors said to Yaldabaoth, "Breathe your spirit into the face of this man, and he will rise. His body will come to life."

Yaldabaoth, unaware of the greater plan, obeyed. He breathed into the figure. But in doing so, he unknowingly released a portion of his own power—the divine spark he had inherited from Sophia. That sacred breath left him in that moment and entered into the human form—into the soul shaped in the image of the True Human.

And suddenly, the man awakened. He stood upright. He grew strong. And he began to shine. Light poured from him like the dawn.

The demons watched in disbelief. Though they had all contributed to forming his body, he now stood above them. He carried fragments of their essence, but his awareness far surpassed theirs. Even Yaldabaoth—their leader—could not match the brilliance of this being's mind. They saw that he was uncorrupted, fearless, and full of radiant light. Driven by envy, they seized him. They could not bear his purity. So they cast him down—plunging him into the lowest depths of the material world, into darkness and shadow.

But the Blessed One—the true Source of love and mercy—looked with compassion upon the divine power that had once belonged to Sophia and now lived within the man formed by Yaldabaoth. Fearing that the false rulers might once again overpower the fragile psychic body, the Invisible Spirit did not respond with punishment, but with grace.

From the heart of divine kindness, the Spirit sent a helper to Adam—a being filled with radiant insight. She came forth from the True Spirit, glowing with wisdom and light. Her name was Epinoia, and she was also called Zoe—Life.

She was not sent just for Adam, but for all of creation—to guide, to restore, to remind. She stayed close to him, quietly helping him move toward wholeness. She whispered truths to him—reminding him of where his soul had come from and showing him how to return. The path upward was the same as the path downward.

But to protect her from the rulers and their forces, Epinoia hid herself deep within Adam. They could not see her, for she had come to heal what their mother had broken.

Though Adam had been formed from the elements below, he carried within him a trace of divine light—a spark, a glimmer of something eternal. His intelligence outshined those who had shaped him, and the rulers noticed. They saw something in him they could not control.

So they devised a new plan.

They stirred the elements—fire, earth, water, and the four winds—mixing them with violent chaos. From this tumultuous storm, they shaped a new form, something born of destruction. Adam was drawn even further into this chaos, sinking deeper into the shadow of death.

This new body, crafted from earth, water, fire, and wind, was not merely physical. It was imbued with Matter and Darkness, driven by Craving. What they gave him was not a true body—it was a false spirit, an artificial shell. It was not a home for the soul, but a trap, not a vessel, but a tomb. They encased him in this fabricated form, locking his mind in forgetfulness, making him subject to decay and death. This marked the first fall—the beginning of the separation between soul and truth.

And yet, even in that descent, something remained untouched. Hidden deep within him, the radiant presence of Epinoia endured—waiting for the right moment to stir his awareness and lead him back toward the path of return.

The rulers took this man they had formed and placed him in a garden—a paradise of their own making. They told him, "You may eat freely from everything you see here." But this so-called paradise was a lie. The food they offered was bitter. Their beauty was only surface-deep, corrupted at its core. Everything they gave was wrapped in illusion. Their trees bore twisted justice. Their fruit was poisoned with deception. Their promises whispered death.

At the heart of this false garden, they planted a tree they called the Tree of Life. But I will tell you its true nature: it was the root of their scheme—a design born from an artificial spirit. Its roots were soaked in bitterness. Its branches were lifeless. Its shadow spread division and hatred. Its leaves whispered falsehoods. Its flowers oozed with wicked sweetness. Its fruit carried death. And at its core was raw, restless desire. It bloomed only in darkness. Whoever ate from it became part of the shadow—a citizen of the underworld.

But there was another tree—one not of their making. The tree called the Knowledge of Good and Evil. This was not theirs to claim. It was the Epinoia of the Light—a spark of truth planted in the midst of their counterfeit world. The rulers feared it. They stood guard around it, warning Adam never to eat from it. They hid it from his view, terrified that he might look beyond their illusions and see them for what they truly were.

"But I," said the Savior, "I caused them to eat from it."

I asked him, "Master, wasn't it the serpent who led Adam to eat?"

He smiled gently and answered, "Yes—but not for the reason most believe. The serpent's intention was to awaken the drive for reproduction, to pull Adam into a system where his offspring would be bound to serve the designs of the rulers."

Yaldabaoth, the leader of the false powers, saw that something was changing. The light-filled Epinoia within Adam had begun to awaken his mind, making him wiser than the one who had formed him. When Adam disobeyed, Yaldabaoth moved swiftly to reclaim what he believed was his—to take back the power he had breathed into the human.

To do so, he forced Adam into forgetfulness.

I asked the Savior, "What does it mean that Adam became 'completely forgetful'?"

He replied, "It's not as Moses wrote—'God caused a deep sleep to fall upon Adam.' No. What truly happened was that Adam's awareness was clouded. His perception was veiled. He became unconscious. Just as Yaldabaoth later boasted through one of his prophets, saying: 'I will dull their minds so they cannot see or understand.'"

But even then, deep within Adam, the light of Epinoia could not be extinguished. Yaldabaoth tried to remove her—to reach into Adam and pull her from within him. He aimed to strip her away from his creation.

But Epinoia could not be taken. Darkness chased her, but it could not hold her.

Still, the ruler succeeded in drawing out a portion of the power he had originally breathed into Adam. Using that stolen fragment, he shaped a new being—a woman—formed in the image of Epinoia as he had briefly glimpsed her. He placed the energy taken from Adam into this new form, thinking he had created something new. But in truth, he had only divided what he could never fully control.

[It did not happen as Moses described it. This was not about a rib. It was about a sacred presence—a divine reflection—being drawn out and imperfectly echoed.]

When Adam saw the woman beside him, something awakened within him. At that moment, Epinoia emerged fully into the light. She lifted the veil that had clouded Adam's thoughts. He stirred from the stupor of ignorance. He recognized her. She was his true

THE APOCRYPHON OF JOHN

counterpart—his reflection, the one he had long been missing.

And he said, "This is bone of my bones, flesh of my flesh."

That is why, from that moment on, a man leaves his father and mother and joins with a woman—so that the two may once again become one.

It was not good for the man to remain alone, and so his helper was sent to him from above.

[Sophia—our luminous sister—descended into this world in innocence, seeking to reclaim the light she had lost. For this reason, she came to be known as Life, the Mother of the Living, born from the providence of Heaven's true Authority. Through her presence, the path to complete knowledge became possible.]

I appeared to them then, like an eagle perched upon the highest branches of the Tree of Knowledge—Epinoia herself, the radiant reflection of pure divine Providence. I came not to condemn, but to awaken—to rouse them from the sleep of forgetfulness and guide them back toward remembrance.

[They had fallen. But even in their fall, their eyes opened just enough to see their own nakedness. And Epinoia appeared before them, shining with light, restoring clarity to their minds.]

When Yaldabaoth realized that the man and the woman had turned from him—that they were no longer under his spell—his rage ignited. Furious, he cursed the ground beneath their feet. He found the woman as she was preparing herself for union with her true partner. But in a corrupted attempt to reclaim authority, he gave her to the man—not in love, but as an act of control—declaring that he would now rule over her.

He did not understand that even this was woven into a far greater plan—one crafted by the divine, far beyond anything his mind could grasp.

The man and woman were overwhelmed. Though they had seen through the illusion, they lacked the strength to fully renounce the false ruler. So Yaldabaoth, in his blindness, cast them out of his imitation paradise—his so-called garden. He covered them in a heavy darkness, as if to smother what remained of their light.

Then, the chief ruler took notice of the woman beside Adam. Only then did he realize—within her dwelled the light of Epinoia, a spark of divine life. And in that moment, his understanding failed completely. He could not comprehend what was before him.

[But Providence, who sees beyond all veils, knew what was unfolding. She sent her helpers to protect Eve, to lift the divine spark from her before it could be taken.]

Yet even so, Yaldabaoth violated her. And from that violation, two sons were born.

[The first was called Elohim. The second was Yahweh. Elohim had the face of a bear, Yahweh the face of a cat. One leaned toward justice, the other did not. Yahweh governed fire and wind. Elohim held sway over water and earth.]

To conceal what had truly happened, Yaldabaoth gave them new names: Cain and Abel.

[And from that point on, human reproduction—physical union—became a tool in the hands of the ruler. He implanted desire into the woman who was with Adam, using it to bring forth more bodies, more vessels for his system. Into each, he breathed a counterfeit spirit.]

He gave the two sons authority over the elements—earth, water, fire, and air—so that they might rule over the realm he had fashioned, a place not of life but of confinement, a tomb of matter.

Still moved by a higher awareness, Adam aligned himself with the image born of his own inner knowing. From this sacred union, a son came into being—one who reflected the brilliance of the true Human Above, echoing the light of the divine pattern. Adam named him Seth, shaping him in likeness to the eternal lineage that exists beyond corruption, in the upper realms untouched by decay.

In parallel, the heavenly Mother extended a part of her own spirit into the world. She sent forth a shining presence—an image of herself, radiant with completeness—to make room on earth for what would descend from above. This presence was a vessel, a sacred resting place to welcome what was still to unfold—a bridge between worlds.

But the lower powers had not withdrawn. Yaldabaoth, ever hungry to distort the truth, stepped in once more. He clouded humanity's mind, causing them to drink from the waters of forgetfulness. In doing so, he severed their memory from its source, leaving them adrift, unaware of the light they once knew, blind to the divine origin that had breathed them into being.

And for a time, the children of Seth—those who carried divine potential—lived under that veil of amnesia. But it would not last forever.

When the Spirit descends again from the sacred places above, it will awaken them. It will raise them up. It will heal what has been wounded. And it will restore them—fully and completely—into the holiness of the true fullness of God.

PART III — THE JOURNEY OF THE SOUL AND THE POWER OF KNOWLEDGE

I asked the Savior, "Master, will every soul be saved? Will all eventually return to the pure Light?"

He replied, "You're asking something profound—yet only those who belong to the race that does not move, the eternal ones, can truly grasp the answer. These are the souls upon whom the Spirit of Life descends. And when it does, it transforms them. They are redeemed, perfected, and made worthy of the eternal glory. These are the ones who cleanse themselves of evil. They have no desire for corruption. They seek only what is pure, untouched, and eternal. The physical body is a burden to them, but they bear it with grace, knowing a time will come when they will be reunited with those who will free them from it. These souls are destined for unending life. They endure trials with strength and patience so that, in the end, they may inherit the good and dwell in everlasting light."

Then I asked, "Lord, what about those souls who received the Spirit of Life but did not choose this path?"

He answered, "When the Spirit descends on someone, it brings change and opens the path to salvation. Without the Spirit, no one could even stand upright. The Spirit touches everyone. And if it grows within a person, power awakens too. Their soul becomes firm, and darkness cannot claim them. But if the false, artificial spirit takes root instead, it leads the soul astray."

So I asked, "Lord, when the soul leaves the body, where does it go?"

He smiled and said, "If the soul has grown strong and holds more of the true Light than of the artificial spirit, it escapes evil's grip. With the help of the Incorruptible One, it is saved. It finds its eternal rest."

Again I asked, "What happens to the souls that don't know who they belong to?"

He replied, "These are the ones caught by the false spirit. They've strayed too far. Their souls are heavy with confusion, pulled toward evil, lost in deep forgetfulness. When they die, they are seized by the forces of the false rulers, bound in spiritual chains, and sent back into cycles of confinement.

They go around and around—until one day, through true knowledge, they awaken. When that happens, they can be made whole and be saved."

Then I asked, "Lord, how does a soul become small enough to fit into a human body?"

He was pleased by the question and said, "You are blessed for seeking understanding. A soul must be guided—led by another who carries the Spirit of Life. Through that guidance, the soul is saved. And once it is truly saved, it will not need to return to a body again."

Then I asked, "What about the souls that once had true knowledge but turned away from it?"

He answered, "They are taken by the demons of emptiness—beings that drag them to a place where no space for repentance remains. They stay there until the final day comes, when all who have defied the Spirit will face a judgment that does not end."

At last, I asked, "Master, how did the false spirit come into existence?"

He looked upon me and began to unveil a mystery long hidden.

"The Divine Source—both Mother and Father—is the Spirit of Compassion, the sacred presence that suffers alongside humanity," he said. "This Holy Spirit, through the insight known as Epinoia—born of Light's Providence—guides the true children of the divine lineage. It lifts their hearts, sharpens their vision, and rekindles the inner radiance that has never truly left them."

"But when the arrogant ruler Yaldabaoth saw these beings rising, when he realized their wisdom exceeded his own, he was shaken. Fear overtook him. He grew desperate to stop them, to bring their growth to a halt. Yet he could not comprehend the depth of their ascent, nor the distance they had already reached beyond his grasp. And he was powerless to stop what had already begun."

"In his frustration, he devised a scheme. He gathered his shadowed forces—his corrupt companions—and set his intention against the divine. Together, they committed a transgression: they forced themselves upon Wisdom herself, upon Sophia. From this violation, a dark force emerged into the world—an agent of limitation, known as Fate."

Fate became the ultimate prison—wild, unpredictable, and relentless. It manifests in various forms, just like the demons do. It is heavy, heavier than stone, and its hold is stronger than that of rulers, spirits, gods, or any generation caught in its grasp. From Fate, a flood of suffering poured forth: Sin, Violence, Blasphemy, Forgetfulness, Ignorance, Oppressive laws, Overwhelming guilt, and Deep, paralyzing fear.

This is how the world fell into blindness—separated from the true God above all, wrapped in forgetfulness, and unaware of its own descent. Humanity lost sight of its errors and became trapped in the endless turning of time, bound to the rhythm of seasons and imprisoned under the dominion of Fate. Eventually, even Yaldabaoth began to regret what he had created and resolved to wipe it away by unleashing a great flood upon the world. But the Light of divine Providence intervened and sent a warning to Noah, who, filled with understanding, spoke out to the children of humanity, calling them back to the truth—but only those who were truly connected to the divine within heard his voice, while the rest, unfamiliar with the light, turned away without listening.

[It did not happen as Moses recorded it, that they entered a wooden ark. What truly took place was this: Noah and many others from the unmoved, divine race were sheltered within a luminous cloud—a refuge of light known only to those who belong to the higher realms.] Noah understood who he was; he recognized the authority that guided him and the Being of Light who illuminated his path, even while Yaldabaoth cast the world into shadow. In response, Yaldabaoth and his rulers created a new scheme—they sent their demons to take human women as partners, hoping to indulge themselves, corrupt the pure lineage, and spread their influence by mingling their seed with the undefiled.

When their previous attempts failed, they tried again with greater cunning, creating a counterfeit spirit—an imitation of the true Spirit that had once descended to the world. With this false spirit, the demons aimed to deceive the souls of women, changing their forms to resemble the women's husbands, thus leading them into union without their awareness. Through this trickery, they embedded within the women a presence of darkness and corruption, rather than light.

Then, they introduced into the world objects that would fuel greed and control: Gold, Silver, Coins, Iron, Metals of all kinds, and anything else that would tether people to material desires.

Humanity fell under a spell—enticed, distracted, and profoundly misled. Their days became heavy with anxiety, their lives marked by constant struggle. They aged without knowing joy, passed away without ever encountering truth, and lived their entire existence without discovering the true God. Through these deceptions, the false rulers bound all of creation in a web of control, stretching from the very beginning of the world to the present moment. They took women for themselves, brought forth children born of shadow, closed their hearts to the light, and hardened their beings through the force of their counterfeit spirit—a condition that, even now, continues to shape the world.

PART IV — THE DESCENT AND TRIUMPH OF PROVIDENCE

I am the source that nourishes all things—the silent force that brings life into being and sustains it through every breath. To draw close to those I love, I took on their form, walking beside them, indistinguishable in appearance, yet carrying the fullness of their origin within me. I was there from the very

THE APOCRYPHON OF JOHN

beginning, moving through every path a soul could travel, walking the winding roads of exile and the long journey back home.

I am the keeper of light's treasure, the living echo of divine wholeness. I descended into the shadowed places, the furthest reaches of forgetfulness, until I stood in the very center of confinement. When I arrived, even the roots of chaos trembled. I concealed my presence, hidden from the corrupted ones who could no longer recognize the truth standing before them.

In silence, I returned again—my second descent. From among those who still carried the spark of light, I emerged, bearing the memory of divine care and purpose. Then I stepped back into the darkness, entering the hidden spaces where despair had taken root. Again, the foundation of the abyss quaked beneath me, shaking as if about to collapse under the weight of awakening. But I did not destroy it. I waited. The time had not yet come. When the moment was right, I descended for the third and final time. I am made of light and belong to the realm of radiance. I carried with me the memory of mercy. And in the depths of darkness, in the very heart of captivity, I allowed my light to shine. I knew the time of release had drawn near. I entered the cage—this body of limitation—and I spoke aloud: "If you can hear me, rise from your slumber!"

And someone did. A soul, long buried in silence, stirred and began to weep. Through tears, he asked, "Who calls to me? Whose voice has reached this far?"

I replied, "I am the echo of pure light. I am the whisper of the Spirit untouched. I've come to lift you out of this sleep. Remember who you were before you forgot. Return to your source—follow the thread of mercy back to its beginning. Be wary of the forces that would bind you once more. Don't fall back into sleep. Stay watchful. Rise from these depths."

And so I raised him. I wrapped him in radiance, marked him with the sacred waters, sealed him with five signs of light. From that moment on, death could no longer touch him. Then I returned to the place from which I came, the realm where all things are whole. My purpose had been fulfilled.

And now... you have heard the story.

CONCLUSION

"I have now revealed everything to you," the Savior said, "so that you may write it down and quietly pass it on to those who share your spirit—those who belong to the unmoved race, the ones who will understand." With that, the Savior entrusted John with the complete message, instructing him to record it with faithfulness and protect it with care. Then he gave one final warning: "If anyone exchanges these words for gifts, for food or drink, for clothing or anything of the material world, let that person be cursed." What John received came to him through mystery and revelation, and as soon as the message was complete, the Savior disappeared. John then returned to his companions and told them everything he had been shown and taught.

Jesus the Christ.

Amen.

THE GOSPEL OF THE EGYPTIANS

INTRODUCTION TO THE GOSPEL OF THE EGYPTIANS

A VOICE FROM THE LIGHT BEYOND THE AEONS

This gospel does not begin in history. It doesn't open with a name, a place, or an event. It begins in silence—pure, radiant, unspoken silence.
The Gospel According to the Egyptians, also known as The Holy Book of the Great Invisible Spirit, is one of the most mysterious and exalted texts in the Gnostic tradition. Unlike other writings that begin in the human world and ascend toward the divine, this gospel descends from realms far above. It speaks not from within creation, but from the space before creation—before language, before form, before even time.

It is said to be written by the great Seth, not in ink, but in divine light. It was hidden high on a mountain untouched by the sun, sealed away until the appointed time. Not meant for every generation, this revelation was reserved for the end of all things—for the moment when the incorruptible race would awaken and remember.

The voice that speaks in this gospel is not one voice but many: the Spirit, the silence, the Son, the powers of light, and Seth himself. It is a chorus rising out of stillness. The language is not always easy to follow. It is layered, symbolic, filled with names that defy logic and sounds that can only be felt. But beneath it all, something steady pulses through: a voice from beyond the aeons, calling to those who have forgotten who they are.

The structure of the text is not narrative, but architectural. It builds layer upon layer of divine beings, powers, realms, and emanations, not to confuse, but to map out a cosmology that goes beyond traditional creation stories. This is not a story about the beginning of the world, but about the origin of light. And more than that, it is about where that light must return.

The gospel offers a kind of remembering that doesn't begin with belief, but with resonance. For those attuned to its frequency, it does not teach—it awakens. The voice that emerges is not external authority but inner knowing, speaking from the depths of divine memory. It is a text that reveals itself not all at once, but gradually, like a voice rising from silence until it becomes music.

This is a gospel that waits. It waits to be heard. It waits to be remembered. And when the time is right, it speaks.

SETH, THE INCORRUPTIBLE RACE, AND THE BAPTISM OF LIGHT

At the heart of this gospel stands a figure both ancient and eternal: Seth, the son of Adam and Eve, not simply as remembered in Hebrew tradition, but as seen through the eyes of Gnosis—as a bearer of divine truth, a guardian of an incorruptible lineage.

Seth, in this text, is not just a man. He is a conduit of light. He descends not only from Adam, but from the upper aeons, sent to awaken a race that belongs not to this world, but to the pleroma—the realm of fullness. This incorruptible race is described not by ethnicity or time, but by its essence. It is the race of those who carry within themselves a divine spark, hidden in the world, waiting to be reawakened.

The world, according to this gospel, is a battlefield of light and shadow. At its center lies the deception of the archons—rulers of chaos, born of ignorance, who claim authority over creation. These forces attempt to shape the world in their image, binding souls with laws, illusions, and fear. But their power is not absolute. The descent of Seth disrupts their plan. He plants a seed—his seed—into the structure of the aeons, ensuring that truth survives.

Yet this truth is not transmitted through writing, commandment, or temple ritual. It is passed through symbols, through silence, through the baptism of light.

The gospel speaks often of this baptism—not as a rite of water and repentance, but as something deeper, more hidden. It is called the Five Seals: a spiritual initiation into knowledge, incorruptibility, and divine protection. Those who receive it are not merely cleansed; they are sealed. They become unshakable, untouchable by death, ready to rise beyond the false aeons and return to the fullness.

In this baptism, Seth clothes himself with a Logos-begotten body, prepared in secret through a virgin. He does this not for himself, but to show the path—the way to live in the world while not being of it, the way to embody the truth without falling into corruption.

This is the mystery the gospel guards:

A divine race scattered across time, hidden in bodies, guarded by silence, called by names only they can recognize. Their origin is light. Their home is the pleroma. Their path is marked by knowledge, and their return is sealed by grace.

MYSTERY, SILENCE, AND THE RETURN TO FULLNESS

If other gospels speak in stories, this one speaks in sound—in symbols, names, and syllables that seem to bypass the mind and go straight to the soul. It is a text shaped not around linear logic, but around mystery. Not mystery as something to be solved, but as something to be entered.

From beginning to end, The Gospel of the Egyptians is saturated with silence—not the silence of absence, but of depth. Silence is the origin of everything. The Invisible Spirit emerges from it. The three powers are born within it. The aeons unfold in its stillness. Even the voice that narrates the gospel seems to move in and out of silence, as if carefully choosing each utterance so as not to disturb something sacred.

This is a gospel of naming, but not in the way we usually think of names. The divine names found here are not labels—they are vibrations. The seven vowels, the layered invocations, the rhythmic invocations of beings and powers: all serve as liturgical keys, tuning the reader toward something that cannot be grasped by the senses alone. These names are not meant to be explained. They are meant to be felt.

In this space beyond language, the soul is remembered—not as fallen or sinful, but as forgotten. And the way back is not through punishment or obedience, but through recollection. The soul awakens, not to a set of rules, but to its own origin. It remembers that it is light. That it belongs to the silence. That it was sent into the world not to be lost, but to find the way home.

The gospel ends not with closure, but with ascent. It speaks of Jesus not as a figure bound to history, but as a manifestation of the Living One—the one who was clothed by Seth, the one who descends through the aeons to break the law and lift up those bound by it. And it ends with the voice of one who knows: one who has merged with the light, who carries the name of the Unnameable within, who has become what they always were.

Mystery is not abandoned. It is fulfilled.

Silence is not broken. It is shared.

And fullness—pleroma—is not a distant goal, but a home long forgotten, now ready to be remembered.

HISTORICAL CONTEXT

The Gospel of the Egyptians, also known as the Holy Book of the Great Invisible Spirit, was composed in the 2nd century CE, most likely in Egypt. It reflects Sethian gnostic theology, focusing on the divine lineage of Seth and the saving knowledge transmitted through him. The text is highly mystical, filled with secret names and complex structures of divine emanations. It presents a world where salvation is achieved through divine revelation beyond material existence.

THE GOSPEL OF THE EGYPTIANS: THE TEXT

PART I — THE SILENCE AND THE GREAT AEONS

This is the sacred account preserved by the Egyptians—a vision revealing the boundless, hidden Source: the Great Invisible Spirit. This is the One whose name cannot be spoken, who comes from the highest realms of perfection and exists as a light beyond every other light. He shines above even the most luminous and exalted realms, dwelling in complete stillness at the heart of divine intention. He is the unspoken Father, veiled in silence, the breath behind all truth and the root of all things incorruptible. Infinite and eternal, he has no shape, no boundary, and no time—untouchable, unspeakable, and always present.

From this eternal silence emerged the self-born one—an Aeon above all aeons, brought forth by his own intention, unlike anything else. And from this Great Spirit came three divine expressions: the Mother, the Father, and the Son. Each arose from the unshaken depths of the incorruptible Source, flowing out from silence itself. In that quiet mystery appeared a figure known as Domedon Doxomedon—light of lights, reigning over all realms. Among these, the Son came forth first, followed by the Mother, and then the Father—emerging without form or announcement, transcending every power, every radiant being, and every immortal domain.

These three radiant ones brought forth three sacred realms—known as the ogdoads—each a reflection of the silent workings of the hidden Source. The first ogdoad gave rise to the triple-male child, a being composed of divine thought, pure speech, incorruptibility, timeless life, divine will, consciousness, and inner knowing—a mirror of the Father, who holds both masculine and feminine within himself. The second ogdoad revealed the power of the Mother—Barbelon, the untouched and eternal virgin, too mysterious for names, guardian of the heavens, who arose from her own essence in perfect unity with the silent Father. The third ogdoad belonged to the Son, crowned in stillness, glorified by the Father, and strengthened by the Mother. From his being came forth seven radiant forces, each with a distinct voice, all merging into one sacred Word—a perfect expression of divine fullness and harmony.

These three ogdoads stand as the first great revelations brought forth by the Father through his providence, rising from his depths into the realm of mystery, and once again, Domedon Doxomedon appeared—the aeon beyond all aeons—surrounded by glory, thrones, powers, and incorruptible light; in him dwelt the Great Light that emerged from silence, and he became the eternal dwelling place of the thrice-male child, his throne of glory inscribed with a name that cannot be revealed, a name written on a secret tablet and expressed not in words but in sacred breath, in an invisible language.

And from that mystery emerged the hidden symbol—a series of pure, divine sounds: IIIIIIIIIIIIIIIIIII

EEEEEEEEEEEEEEEEEEEEEE
OOOOOOOOOOOOOOOOOOOOOO
UUUUUUUUUUUUUUUUUUUUUU
EEEEEEEEEEEEEEEEEEEEEE
AAAAAAAAAAAAAAAAAAAAAA
OOOOOOOOOOOOOOOOOOOOOO

These are the seven vowels, each repeated twenty-two times—a sacred formula, a chant of power, the voice of the unspoken Name.

PART II — THE THRICE-MALE CHILD AND THE POWERS OF LIGHT

In that sacred domain of light, the three divine beings lifted their hearts in reverence to the Great Invisible Spirit—the one who cannot be named, who is beyond touch or form, untouched by time or thought. They honored the presence known as the eternal, unbegotten One—pure and complete. As their devotion rose, a new presence stirred within the depths of the silence—a silence so profound that it was alive. From it flowed radiant beings, incorruptible powers, and realms upon realms of divine brilliance—a multitude beyond counting. Among these luminous emanations stood three sacred principles—beings of pure light, children of the divine.

Their essence flowed through the vast domain of Doxomedon-Aeon, carrying with them the full creative energy of the sacred Word. It was through them that the fullness—the pleroma—began to breathe and expand. Among them stood the triple-male child, a figure born of the greatness of the Anointed One and infused with power from the Invisible Spirit. His strength was known as Ainon. He lifted his voice in song, praising both the Source and the silent guardian Yoel, the ever-virgin. He honored the silence not as emptiness, but as the living ground of being—rich with life, brimming with mystery. This divine greatness could not be captured by language or defined by thought. It was the origin of all things—the unseen majesty from which every light flows. The triple-male child spoke again, asking the divine for another revelation. From the hidden silence, a new being appeared—a keeper of celestial mysteries, a seer of what is hidden in invisible brilliance.

He was a guardian of sacred knowledge: Yoel, the male virgin, returning once more. Soon after, a new figure emerged—Esephech, child of the child—another link in the endless chain of divine light. Thus, the sacred circle took shape: Father, Mother, Son—joined by the five seals and the unstoppable power known as the Great Christ, guardian of all that cannot decay.

From the very core of stillness, Providence emerged—born not of chaos, but from the vibrant quiet of the Spirit. She came forth from the Father's voice and the radiance of untainted light. Within her she carried the five sacred seals, drawn from the depths of the divine. As she moved through each luminous realm, she established places of glory, where multitudes of angels gathered—beings without number, united in a single voice of adoration. Their song was one of unity, glorifying the Father, the Mother, and the Son, lifting up the fullness of divine light.

And all voices turned toward the Great Christ—the one born from stillness, the incorruptible one, whose name is charged with power and sings with living truth: Telmael, Telmachael,

Eli Eli, Machar Machar, Seth. Beside him stood Yoel, the male virgin, and Esephech, the radiant child who wears the crown of light, protector of the five divine seals, bearer of all revelation.

From within the silent depths of that sacred realm, a great power emerged—the Living Word, vibrant and self-generated. He was not born in time, nor shaped by any hand. His nature was divine, untouched by origin or end. His name, cloaked in mystery, could not be uttered in any earthly tongue—only spoken through the force of divine essence, a sound beyond human speech. He was the true Son of the Great Christ, born not of flesh but of the holy silence, emerging from the unseen and incorruptible Spirit.

From this stillness deeper than all depths, the Child of Silence stepped forth, and with him came a reflection of the divine—the perfect image of the unseen Human. Within this figure shimmered the treasures of divine glory, radiant with truth. Through sacred revelation, and with just a single utterance, he formed four eternal realms—aeons bathed in light and ordered by divine harmony. Each of these realms gave honor to the Invisible Spirit and to the sacred silence of the Father. All of this unfolded in a space beyond sound, beyond time, where the True Human eternally dwells. Out from this place of peace and brilliance, a luminous cloud arose—alive with light and creative force.

From within it pulsed a sacred energy, a presence that brought into being all that is holy and free from corruption. This radiant source was known as Mirothoe. And from her luminous core, a new being was born—an extension of the divine, a spark of glory drawn from the endless silence. And her voice declared his name three times: IEN IEN EA EA EA

From the light came Adamas, a being of illumination—the First Man, the radiant eye of understanding, through whom all things were brought into being, and without whom nothing could exist. It was through him that the unknowable, incomprehensible Father made his descent into the world, stepping down from the highest realms to mend the great division, to fill what was lacking, and to reconcile the fullness with what had fallen into emptiness. The great Logos, the divine Word of th

e pleroma, joined in unity with the self-generated One and with Adamas, the incorruptible Man of Light, and from this sacred union a new expression emerged: the Word of the true human—not a creation of flesh, but a pure emanation of divine speech, spoken into being through truth itself.

In unified voice, they lifted their praise to the Great Invisible Spirit—the one who exists beyond all names, beyond all comprehension. Their reverence reached not only the Source, but also the radiant companions born of divine mystery: the male virgin who dwells in purity, the thrice-blessed child of light, the luminous guardian Youel, and Esephech—the child of the child—who wears the crown of brilliance and safeguards the divine splendor.

Their devotion flowed outward, embracing the vast Doxomedon-Aeon and the sacred thrones that uphold it. They honored the powers that surround it, every incorruptible being that resides within its light, every hidden glory that fills the fullness already revealed. Nothing within the divine order was left untouched by their gratitude. Their praise also embraced the celestial earth—that sanctified ground prepared for divine arrival. It is here that the children of the Great Light take form, not born of the world, but of the Father. In this sacred space, they live in harmony and stillness, cradled by the presence of the Mother and guided by the wisdom of the Son. Then the Logos, the Autogenes, and Adamas lifted their worship once again and prayed for strength, so that eternal power might be granted to the Autogenes, enabling him to complete the formation of the four aeons, through which the hidden glory of the invisible Father might shine forth into a world still veiled in the darkness of night. Adamas, who could not be corrupted, asked to bring forth a son from himself—a child who would become the Father of a divine race, one that could never be shaken, never be led astray. Through this race, voice and silence would be made one, and the realm of death would fade and return to the Light. From the heights of the invisible realms, a brilliant power descended—her name was Manifestation, a presence born of the Great Light itself. Through her came four luminous beings, each carrying a distinct radiance: Harmozel, Oroiael, Davithe, and Eleleth. Out of their combined light emerged Seth, incorruptible and pure—the true child born of Adamas, shaped in divine likeness.

With this emergence, the sacred pattern of seven was completed—a perfect circle of divine energy concealed within holy mystery. As the Father's presence filled these beings, their light grew, unfolding into a grand structure of eleven ogdoads—spheres of spiritual fullness and divine harmony. The Father, watching in silent stillness, recognized what had unfolded, and within the pleroma, joy rose like song. In time, companions were given to these lights to complete the divine symmetry of the Autogenes: Grace walked beside Harmozel, Perception joined Oroiael, Understanding came forth with Davithe, and Prudence stood with Eleleth. Each pair reflected balance, wisdom, and wholeness. ogether, these eight formed the sacred first ogdoad of the divine Autogenes.

And from the highest, the Father offered his blessing once again. The fullness of light rejoiced, and the heavens echoed with quiet celebration. From their joy came the ministers—helpers of the four great lights—along with their consorts, each bearing the same name as the light they served: Harmozel and his consort, Oroiael and his consort, Davithe and his consort, Eleleth and his consort.

Together, they brought forth the next ogdoad, the realm of the Autogenes, which joined seamlessly with the first in divine harmony, expanding the spiritual architecture of the pleroma. As this sacred realm unfolded, the holy lineage of Seth shone brightly among them—a race rooted in truth and purity, known by many names across the aeons: the Seed of Seth, the Children of the Great Light, the Incorruptible Race, the Sons of the Unshakable Aeon, the Perfect Humanity, the Eternal Ones.

It was to this divine lineage that the hidden mysteries were entrusted. The Father looked upon them as they stood in silent glory, radiant in the fullness of light, and to ensure their preservation, he ordained the five sacred seals—not a baptism of water or ritual repentance, but a divine initiation rooted in Spirit, in light, and in incorruptibility. These seals became their protection, securing the race of Seth against the power of death and granting them the ability to rise through the aeons without ever falling into corruption. And so began the sacred rites—illuminated with chant and brilliance, marked by reverence and quiet, each soul sealed in divine protection, prepared to ascend once more to the fullness from which it had first emerged.

PART III — THE RISE OF CHAOS AND THE SEED OF SETH

After five thousand years had passed, the great light Eleleth spoke, declaring that someone should be appointed to take authority over chaos and the underworld. In response, a cloud appeared, known as Hylic Sophia, and as she turned her gaze toward the lower realms, her form began to shimmer with a deep, blood-red radiance, taking shape within the regions of chaos. Then the angel Gamaliel addressed Gabriel, who served under the great light Oroiael, and said, "Let another angel rise to take command—one who will govern both chaos and Hades." The cloud consented, and from within it emerged two monads, each radiant with light, seated upon a throne that had been placed inside the cloud. At that time, the great angel Sakla saw th
e demon Nebruel, and together they formed a spirit destined to shape the earth. They began to generate subordinate angels to assist them. Sakla said to Nebruel, "Let twelve aeons come into existence—twelve distinct worlds." And by the will of the Autogenes, Sakla continued, "Let the structure of seven be established." Then, turning to the great angels, he commanded, "Go—each of you, take your place and rule over the world assigned to you." And so twelve angels were appointed: 1. Athoth, 2. Harmas, the eye of fire, 3. Galila, 4. Yobel, 5. Adonaios, called Sabaoth, 6. Cain, whom the generations call the sun, 7. Abel, 8. Akiressina, 9. Yubel, 10. Harmupiael, 11. Archir-Adonin, 12. Belias.

These were the rulers assigned to oversee chaos and the shadowy depths of Hades. Once they had shaped the world, Sakla, filled with pride, declared before his angels, "I am a jealous god—nothing exists apart from me." He spoke this in arrogance, believing himself to be the source of all things, forgetting the vast reality that existed beyond his limited understanding. But then a voice echoed from the heights above, proclaiming, "The Human One exists—and so does the Son of Humanity." This divine message descended along with a heavenly image—a reflection from above—that gazed downward upon the lower realms and became the template for the first human form. In that divine unfolding, a new presence emerged—Repentance, known as Metanoia. S
he came into being by the will and blessing of the Father, complete in form and filled with purpose. Her mission was one of healing: to mend what had been broken, to restore creation through the luminous and incorruptible lineage of Seth—the mighty one. She descended from the world above, carrying light into a realm shaped by shadows, and there, she began to intercede. Her prayers rose on behalf of all—those born of the lower powers, the misguided rulers, the fading generations without truth, and the children of Adam and Seth, who still

carried the light of their origin like a hidden sun.

To prepare the way for renewal, a great angel named Hormos was sent. He readied a sacred vessel—formed through the daughters of the fallen world—so that the divine seed of Seth could be sown, through the Word and the breath of the Holy Spirit. Seth, bearing this seed of divine essence, entered the world and scattered it across the spiritual realms. Some spoke of these places as countless as Sodom, mysterious and symbol-laden; others believed he drew from the ruins of Gomorrah, renewing it under a new name: Sodom transformed.

This sacred line came into being through a luminous figure named Edokla, who bore Truth and Justice through the Word. From that union flowed the seed of eternal life, entrusted to those who would endure, who remembered their divine beginnings. This was no ordinary lineage—it spanned the heights of three heavenly realms and touched down into the earthly world. Even the flood of ancient times was permitted for their sake—a sign of what was to come. And still ahead lies a fire, one that will fall not to destroy, but to awaken grace in those who belong to the eternal light.

Throughout the ages, prophets and watchers would guard this lineage, though their presence would stir trials—famine, disease, and the noise of false prophets spreading illusions. Seth saw it all in vision: the deceiver's disguises, the traps laid for the children of light, the violence and rejection they would suffer, the confusion even among angels, and the brokenness of a world gone blind.

And so Seth lifted his voice in reverence. He praised the Great Spirit, the one beyond names, the virginal Source. He gave honor to Barbelon, the radiant male virgin, and to the living power called Telmael Telmael Heli Heli Machar Machar Seth. He acknowledged Youel, bearer of light, and Esephech, crowned in brilliance. He saluted the great Doxomedon-Aeon, with its sacred thrones and radiant hosts, and the fullness of the divine realms. Then Seth made a plea: that his sacred

seed would be protected. And from the invisible heights, four hundred celestial guardians descended, led by the angels Aerosiel and Selmechel. They came to shield the radiant lineage, their fruit, and their chosen ones—from the moment Truth and Justice entered the world until the time of reckoning, when the corrupt rulers would be judged and fall. Thus, the great Seth was sent into the world, empowered by the four lights, commissioned by the will of the divine Autogenes, and blessed by the Great Invisible Spirit—sealed by the sanctity of the five divine signs.

PART IV — THE HIDDEN BODY AND THE LIVING BAPTISM

The great Seth journeyed through three monumental thresholds—the deluge of ancient memory, the purifying fire that is yet to come, and the ultimate reckoning set for the false rulers and unseen powers. He crossed these for one sacred reason: to gather and redeem the luminous lineage that had lost its way.

But this act of redemption wasn't for the world as it appears—broken and confused. It was a quiet restoration, aimed at reconnecting creation to its hidden root, to the original harmony that had been veiled over time. This reconciliation unfolded not through force or spectacle, but through mystery: a holy form, prepared in silence, conceived by the Word itself, and carried within a pure vessel. It was through this sacred form that the faithful—those of divine origin—would be reborn, not by earthly means, but through the breath of the Holy Spirit, marked and sealed by invisible signs known only to those who remember where they come from.

This mystery was not about aligning with the false world or its ruler, the god of the thirteen aeons, but about renouncing both. It was revealed through sacred gatherings, through the holy ones who are called saints, and through the ineffable beings anchored in the incorruptible heart of the Great Light. The Father, who was before all things and who acts through Providence, established—through her—a baptism far greater than any earthly ritual, a sacred baptism that transcends the heavens, revealed through the incorruptible one who was begotten by the divine Word: Jesus, the Living One, the very form with which the great Seth clothed himself.

Through this sacred form, a shift took place—the powers that once governed the thirteen realms were bound, their grip released. Those who had been imprisoned under their sway were set free. They were wrapped in the protective armor of knowledge, robed in the strength of truth, and clothed in a radiance that no shadow could touch. Then came the great helper, known as the Living Water—Yesseus Mazareus Yessedekeus—whose presence stirred the sacred current of renewal. At his side stood the noble ones: James the Great, Theopemptos, and Isaouel. Along with them were the guardians of the Fountain of Truth—Micheus, Michar, and Mnesinous—along with the keepers of the Living Baptism, those who cleanse and purify, including Sesengenpharanges and the vigilant Micheus and Michar who watched over the threshold of the waters. Others stood upon the holy mountain—Seldao and Elainos—who welcomed the sacred lineage, the luminous descendants of Seth. The ministers of the four divine lights—Gamaliel, Gabriel, Samblo, and Abrasax—stood in their place, while those who usher in the rising sun—Olses, Hypneus, and Heurumaious—carried the dawn into being. Souls making their way into eternal peace were guided by Mixanther and Michanor, while Akramas and Strempsouchos stood guard over the chosen. Above all these, the highest power reigned: Heli Heli Machar Machar Seth, and the Great Invisible Spirit—unreachable, unnamable, untouched, and infinite. In the realm of silence stood Harmozel, the First Light, where the true divine being, the Autogenes, resides in unity with Adamas, the incorruptible human.

The second light, Oroiael, is the dwelling of Seth, and there is also Jesus, the bearer of Eternal Life, who overcame the false order through his sacrifice. The third light is Davithe, home to the children of Seth. The fourth is Eleleth, where their souls find rest. And the fifth is Yoel, guardian of the Sacred Name—the one who administers the true baptism, surpassing all heavens, untouched by corruption. Now, through the pure figure named Poimael, those who have undergone the five renunciations and received the baptism of the Five Sacred Seals will find themselves recognized by those who have already crossed over—and they too will be known.

Their light will not fade, and they will never again be touched by death.

IE IEUS EO OU EO OUA! ruly, you are the Living Water, O Yesseus Mazareus Yessedekeus—Child of the Child, Name of Radiance! Indeed, O Eternal One—AION O ON, the one who is and always will be. IIII EEEE EEEE OOOO UUUU OOOO AAAA—divine breath resounding. EI AAAA OOOO, the Seer of the Ages, A EEEEE IIII UUUUUU OOOOOOOO—the One who endures beyond all time. IEA AIO—the One who lives within, AEI EIS AEI EI O EI, EI OS EI—You are who you are, now and forever.

PART V — FINAL PRAYER AND HIDDEN REVELATION

This sacred name—the name above all—now lives within me. You, self-begotten and perfect, are no longer distant or hidden. I see You clearly, beyond the limits of language. Through knowing You, I have become one with the eternal, clothed in light that is now part of who I am. The Mother, drawn by Your beauty, stood near as I opened my hands in pure devotion. I was shaped in the brilliance of Your light, a radiance that lives in my heart and gives life to unseen realms. So I speak of Your glory, because in this union, I have come to know You.

SOU IES IDE AEIO OIS

Timeless One, Eternal Aeon, silent and holy—You are my refuge. Radiant Son, lifter of the true human, cleanse me with the living waters of Your everlasting name. I feel the breath of life rise in me, mingled like incense in water, leading me to the promised peace of the chosen.

This is the writing of the great Seth, sealed on the mountain of Charaxio, far from the light of earthly dawn. For 130 years he inscribed it, hidden from prophets and scribes, meant only to be revealed at the end of ages by the will of the Self-Begotten and the fullness of heaven. It was given to the incorruptible ones, those united with the Invisible Spirit, the One-Begotten Son, the eternal Light, His pure consort, Sophia, Barbelon, and all who dwell in divine fullness—forever. This is the Gospel of the Egyptians: a divine book, not made by human hands but revealed by God. Blessed is the one who brought it forth—may they be filled with wisdom and sight. It was written by Eugnostos, beloved of God, also known in the body as Gongessos, alongside radiant beings of incorruptibility. Jesus Christ, Son of the Living God. Ichthus.

This is the sacred record of the Great Invisible Spirit.

Amen.

THE SOPHIA OF JESUS CHRIST

INTRODUCTION TO THE SOPHIA OF JESUS CHRIST

THE UNVEILING OF DIVINE KNOWLEDGE

The journey into The Sophia of Jesus Christ begins in mystery—just as all true wisdom does. In a world filled with questions about the nature of God, existence, and the universe, there has always been a longing to uncover the ultimate truths that lie beneath the surface of reality. This gospel offers us a glimpse into those hidden truths, those mysteries veiled from the ordinary eye, awaiting those who seek beyond the tangible. It is a journey not of discovery through logic alone, but of unveiling—the revelation of something that has always existed but was shrouded in silence, waiting to be understood by those ready to perceive it.

In this text, Sophia, the personification of divine wisdom, stands at the center of the unfolding narrative. She is not simply a figure of ancient lore but a living, breathing force that shapes the very fabric of creation. She represents the feminine aspect of the divine, a wisdom that is not separate from God but intimately tied to the Father. In the context of this gospel, Sophia is both the mystery and the revealer—the one who opens the door to a deeper understanding of the universe, guiding those who seek to know the truth.

At its core, The Sophia of Jesus Christ presents us with the notion that true wisdom does not come from the world's surface understanding, but from an inner, divine awakening. It's not about accumulating knowledge or fitting pieces into a puzzle of facts; rather, it's about recognizing a wisdom that has always existed, that transcends time, and that is accessible to those who open themselves to its quiet presence. This gospel speaks to those ready to hear beyond the noise of worldly life and the distractions of our senses. It is a call to recognize the divine knowledge that resides within the heart of the universe and within the heart of each individual.

As we delve deeper into this gospel, we discover that the wisdom Sophia imparts is not a mere intellectual exercise but a transformative power—one that awakens the soul. Sophia is not only the source of wisdom but the means by which we are brought to knowledge of the divine. She is the voice that speaks from within, inviting us to see the world with new eyes, to understand our place in the grand design, and to grasp the nature of our divine origins. The wisdom she reveals is not an abstract concept but a living, pulsating force that, once understood, can completely change the way we experience existence. It's a wisdom that calls us to remember who we are, where we come from, and to align ourselves with the divine truth that runs through all things.

Through Sophia's guidance, we are shown that divine knowledge is not something distant or reserved for the few—it is something accessible, even within reach, for those who choose to awaken. This gospel unveils a knowledge that is hidden in plain sight, a wisdom not written in the stars but embedded within us all. To seek it is to embark on a journey that leads to transformation—just as the Savior's words promise a deeper connection with the infinite and a life that transcends the limitations of the material world. It is in this sacred unveiling that we begin to understand the nature of God, of creation, and of our own soul.

In these pages, we are not merely reading about a distant divine force, but we are invited into an experience of divine awakening. The knowledge that Sophia reveals is not external but internal, waiting to be recognized within our own hearts. And in this unveiling, we come closer not only to understanding the mysteries of the universe but also to realizing the divine essence within us—an essence that has always been present, ready to be remembered.

THE ETERNAL DANCE OF SOPHIA AND THE FATHER

At the heart of this gospel lies a profound relationship—one that transcends time and space and illuminates the very essence of divine unity. It is the relationship between Sophia, the divine wisdom, and the Self-Begotten Father, the source of all creation. In many ways, this is a mystery beyond our full comprehension, but it is a mystery that we are invited to witness and, perhaps, to enter into. This relationship is not just a theological concept; it is the living dynamic at the core of existence itself. Sophia and the Father are not separate or distant figures, but they exist in a perpetual dance, one that is both an act of creation and a communion of love.
The Father, in his infinite wisdom and goodness, creates not out of need, but out of love—a love that overflows into existence, shaping the cosmos. Sophia, as his consort, is the embodiment of that wisdom and the partner through which creation takes form. In the divine economy, it is through their union that all things come to be—whether in the heavens, in the aeons, or within the hearts of all who seek the truth. Their relationship is a model for all that exists, and the world we inhabit is an expression of their unity. In the beginning, when the Father's love moved him to create, it was Sophia who reflected that love, shaping and giving life to all that is.

The creation of the aeons—the divine emanations that shape all of reality—was an act of their shared will. It is through Sophia's wisdom that the divine plan is made manifest, and it is through her insight that the hidden mysteries of the universe are revealed. Yet, while Sophia plays the role of the revealer, she is not separate from the Father. She is not an independent force acting on her own. She is the expression of his mind, the reflection of his heart, the movement of his love. Without the Father, there would be no Sophia, and without Sophia, the Father's wisdom would not be known.

This dynamic relationship between Sophia and the Father speaks to the heart of divine interconnectedness. The Father, in his Self-Begotten nature, exists beyond time and form, while Sophia, though equally eternal, exists in a complementary, almost intimate relationship with him. She is the mirror through which the Father gazes upon himself, and it is through their interaction that the divine plan unfolds. The aeons, the powers, the creation of the universe—all of these come into being as a direct result of their union.

However, this dance is not static. It is an ongoing movement, a reciprocal exchange of wisdom, love, and creation. The Father, in his perfection, creates the world and the aeons, and Sophia, in her wisdom, reflects and brings forth that creation in a way that speaks to the deepest truth of existence. It is as if they are partners in creation, each giving and receiving, each acting in harmony. In the act of creation, the Father and Sophia are united, but this union is not a passive one. It is an active, dynamic force that drives the unfolding of reality. Through their dance, the world comes into being, not as a fixed, unchanging entity, but as a living, breathing creation that continues to evolve.

In understanding this relationship, we begin to understand the deeper currents of existence. Everything that exists—whether in the material world or the spiritual realms—exists because of this divine relationship. The Father and Sophia are not just figures in a myth; they are the very principles of creation itself. Their dance is not a distant, abstract concept, but a living reality that we are invited to partake in. It is through this union that we, too, are brought into being. Just as the Father and Sophia are united, so too are we called to find unity with the divine. This is the path that Sophia illuminates—the path of return to the source, the return to the Father, through the wisdom and love that Sophia represents.

THE PATH OF IMMORTAL AWAKENING

The journey toward divine knowledge is one of awakening, and in this gospel, Sophia plays a pivotal role in guiding us back to the source of all things. However, this awakening is not simply an intellectual exercise or a matter of gathering information. It is a transformative process—a return to the deep well of wisdom that transcends the limitations of the material world. In many ways, the text invites us to step out of the familiar and into the unknown, to shed the veil of forgetfulness that has clouded our understanding of who we truly are.
Sophia is the light that illuminates this path. But the awakening she offers is not a one-time event. It is an ongoing journey, a continual unfolding of truth. She does not just provide answers, but rather, she points us toward the questions that lead us home—questions about the nature of reality, the self, and the divine. In her wisdom, she invites us to look inward, to explore the hidden dimensions of our own being.

The path to awakening is not an external journey but an internal one, guided by Sophia's timeless presence.

This process of awakening is not always easy. It requires self-reflection, humility, and a willingness to let go of the false identities and attachments that we have built around ourselves. But through the wisdom of Sophia, we begin to recognize the divine spark within us—the light that has always been there, waiting to be remembered. As we move deeper into the wisdom she offers, we come to realize that this divine essence is not something outside of us, but something that resides within, a part of our very nature.

The journey of awakening is also a journey of reconciliation. As we seek to reconnect with the divine, we must also reconcile the opposing forces within us—the light and the shadow, the known and the unknown, the masculine and the feminine. Sophia's wisdom teaches us that these forces are not to be feared or rejected but integrated into a harmonious whole. Through this reconciliation, we not only discover who we are but also who we are meant to be—immortal beings who have come to know the truth of their divine nature.

As we awaken to the wisdom of Sophia, we also awaken to the reality of the kingdom of heaven within us. The kingdom is not a distant place or a future promise; it is a present reality that we are invited to experience here and now. It is the realm of light and truth, where all things are made whole, where the soul finds its true home. This awakening is the beginning of a profound transformation—a rebirth into the fullness of who we are meant to be. Through Sophia, we are reminded that we are not separate from the divine but are inextricably connected to it.

Ultimately, the path of immortal awakening is the path of return—the return to our true essence, the return to the Source from which we came. It is through this process that we come to know God not as an external entity, but as the very essence of who we are. Through Sophia's guidance, we are invited to see the divine in all things, to recognize that the kingdom of heaven is within us, and to awaken to the eternal truth that resides in our hearts. This is the path that leads to true peace, to the peace that surpasses understanding, to the peace that comes from knowing the divine essence within us and all around us.

HISTORICAL CONTEXT

Written probably between the late 2nd and early 3rd centuries CE, The Sophia of Jesus Christ presents post-resurrection teachings of Jesus to his disciples. Emerging from a gnostic community, likely in Egypt, the text compiles complex cosmological doctrines into a series of dialogues. It seeks to clarify the structure of the heavenly realms and the soul's path toward enlightenment. Sophia plays a central role as a figure of wisdom and divine manifestation.

THE SOPHIA OF JESUS CHRIST: THE TEXT

PART I — THE RESURRECTION AND THE REVELATION OF THE IMMORTAL ANDROGYNOUS MAN

After the resurrection, the twelve disciples and seven women who had remained faithful to Jesus continued their journey together. They made their way to a mountain in Galilee known to them as the place of Insight and Gladness. Once assembled, an unease fell over the group. Their minds were weighed down with questions—about the cosmos, about the hidden order behind existence, about divine intention, spiritual destiny, and the mysterious forces that shaped their world. Even the teachings the Savior had shared with them in confidence left them restless, stirring more wonder than resolution.

At that moment, the Savior manifested in their midst—not in the physical form they had once known, but as a presence of pure light, invisible to ordinary eyes. He appeared like a radiant being, a celestial presence far beyond earthly description. Words failed to capture what they saw; no mortal body could endure such splendor. Only a body transformed and made perfect—like the one he had spoken of during his teachings near the Mount of Olives—could truly behold such a vision.

He greeted them, saying: "Peace be upon you, My peace I give to you!"

They marveled at his presence, filled with awe and fear. The Savior, seeing their uncertainty, laughed gently and asked: "What is it that troubles you? Why do you doubt? What are you seeking?"

Philip spoke up, saying: "We seek the underlying truth of the universe and the divine plan."

PART II — THE CREATION OF THE AEONS AND THE ROLE OF SOPHIA

The Savior responded to them:

"I want you to understand that all men—since the foundation of the world—have been born of dust. They have questioned God, wondering who He is and what He is like, but they have not found the truth. The wisest among them have speculated based on the order and movement of the world, but their guesses have never reached the truth. They have divided the world into three categories, as the philosophers have done, but none of them are correct. Some say the world is guided by itself. Others claim it is directed by providence. Some argue that fate governs all. But none of these are true."

He continued: "The truth lies beyond all human speculation. For those who spoke of these things, their voices were distant from the truth. Their words are born of human understanding, which is limited. But I—who have come from the Infinite Light—am here to speak of the true nature of the universe, because I know the Light. I am here to reveal the precise nature of truth."

He went on: "Whatever is self-made is corrupted. It is not truly alive, as it lacks the divine source. Providence alone does not possess wisdom, and fate does not offer discernment. But it has been granted to you to know the truth. Whoever is worthy of knowledge will receive it—those who are born not from impure desires, but from the First Who Was Sent. For He is the immortal one, present among mortal men."

Matthew then asked: "Lord, no one can know the truth unless it comes through you. Teach us, then, the truth."

The Savior replied: "The One Who Is is beyond words. No principle knows Him, no authority, no creation, from the beginning of the world until now— only He alone, and anyone to whom He chooses to reveal Himself through the one who has come from the First Light. From now on, I am the Great Savior, for I am eternal and immortal. I have no birth, because all that is born will eventually perish. I am unbegotten, with no beginning, because anything that has a beginning also has an end. Since no one rules over me, I have no name— because anyone who has a name is the creation of another."

He concluded: "He is unnameable. He has no human form, for anyone who has a human form is the creation of something else."

"He has a semblance of his own," the Savior said, "not like anything you have seen or received, but a likeness so profound it transcends all things, and is greater than the entire universe. He gazes in every direction, and in every direction, he sees himself. Because he is infinite, he is always beyond comprehension. He is imperishable, and unlike anything that exists. He is constant goodness, always flawless. He is eternal, blessed beyond measure. Though he is not known, he always knows himself. He is immeasurable, untraceable, perfect, and without defect. He is the very embodiment of imperishability, blessed and unchanging. He is the 'Father of the Universe.'"

Philip asked: "Lord, how, then, did he appear to the perfect ones?"

The perfect Savior replied: "Before anything visible was made visible, the majesty and authority of the Father existed, embracing all things, while nothing could embrace him. For he is all mind, all thought, all reflection, all reasoning, and all power. These are equal in strength and origin. They are the sources of all creation, and the entire lineage, from beginning to end, was within the foreknowledge of the infinite, unbegotten Father."

Thomas asked: "Lord, Savior, why were these things created, and why were they revealed?"

The perfect Savior answered:

"I came from the Infinite to speak to you, to share all things. The Spirit-Who-Is was the begetter, bearing the power to create and form, so that the great treasure hidden within him might be revealed. Out of mercy and love, he wished to bear fruit by his own hand, not only to enjoy his goodness alone, but to allow other spirits from the Unwavering Generation to bring forth body, fruit, glory, and honor— imperishable, filled with his infinite grace— so that his treasure might be revealed through the Self-Begotten God, the Father of all that is imperishable and all that will come to be. But they had not yet been made visible. Now there exists a great difference between those who are imperishable."

THE SOPHIA OF JESUS CHRIST

He called out: "Whoever has ears to hear, let him hear of the infinities!"

"I have addressed those who are awake." He continued: "Everything that comes from the perishable will eventually perish, because it came from what is mortal. But whatever comes from what is imperishable will never perish. It becomes eternal. Many have strayed because they did not understand this difference, and they died."

Mary asked: "Lord, then how will we know this difference?"

The perfect Savior replied: "Come, from the invisible things, and go to the end of the visible ones. The emanation of Thought will show you how faith in things unseen was discovered in things visible— those things which belong to the Unbegotten Father. Whoever has ears to hear, let him hear!"

The source of all existence—the ultimate origin—is not simply called "Father," but rather "Forefather," for he precedes even the first beginning of all things that have ever emerged. He exists without origin, seeing and knowing himself entirely, as one might recognize their reflection in a perfectly still surface. He manifested in a form that mirrored his own nature, yet this form is known as the Divine Self-Father—a being beyond all beginnings, the one who stands as a challenge to all challengers, the primal presence that was never created.

He is the brilliance that precedes all creation, yet even this radiant force does not match the depth of his essence. From his immeasurable being, countless others came into existence—self-created beings who share in his timelessness, his power, his splendor, and his majesty, though they cannot be numbered.

This entire lineage is known as "The Generation That Exists Beyond Rule or Dominion." It is from them that you yourselves descend, for these are the true ancestors of your spirit. This sacred and eternal race is named the Children of the Unbegotten Source—titles such as God, Redeemer, and Divine Offspring are attributed to them—and it is their imprint that resides within you.

This great origin is shrouded in mystery, overflowing with endless glory and joy beyond words. Those who belong to this lineage dwell in perfect celebration, wrapped in a joy that has remained hidden and untold across all ages and cosmic realms—until this moment.

Matthew asked: "Lord, Savior, how was Man revealed?"

The perfect Savior replied: "I want you to understand this clearly: He who first appeared before the universe, the Self-born, Self-made Father, filled with brilliant light, in the beginning— when he chose to manifest his likeness as a great power— the first principle of that Light appeared as the Immortal Androgynous Man. Through him, all beings would be able to attain salvation and awaken from forgetfulness, by the one who was sent as their interpreter— the one who is with you until the end of the suffering brought by the robbers."

He continued: "And his consort is Great Sophia, who, from the very beginning, was destined for union with him— by the will of the Self-begotten Father. From the Immortal Man, the First One, came divinity and kingdom, for the Father, called the Man, Self-Father, revealed this. He created a great aeon, called the Ogdoad, to embody his own majesty."

The Savior spoke of his great authority: "He was given immense power, and he ruled over the creation that came from poverty. He brought forth gods, angels, archangels, and myriads without number— all servants formed from the Light, and the tri-male Spirit, the spirit of Sophia, his consort. Through them, divinity and kingdom originated. Therefore, he was called the God of gods, the King of kings."

The Savior further explained: "The First Man possesses a unique mind, and thought that is his essence— considering, reflecting, reasoning, and wielding power. All attributes that exist are perfect and immortal. In terms of imperishability, they are equal, but in power, they differ— like the difference between father and son, and between thought and its consequences. As I said earlier, the monad—the first singular essence— is the beginning of all that was created."

He concluded: "From all that was created, everything came into being through his power. What was created became formed, and from the formed, the named emerged. Thus, came the differentiation among the unbegotten ones, from beginning to end."

Bartholomew then asked: "How is it that 'Man' and 'Son of Man' are mentioned in the Gospel? To which of them is this Son related?"

The Holy One spoke: "I want you to know that the First Man is called the 'Begetter, Self-perfected Mind.' He reflected with Great Sophia, his consort, and revealed their first-begotten, androgynous son. His male name is designated 'First Begetter, Son of God,' and his female name is 'First Begettress Sophia, Mother of the Universe.' Some call her 'Love.' Now, the First-begotten is called Christ, for he carries the authority of his Father. From this authority, he created a multitude of angels without number, formed from Spirit and Light, to serve as his retinue."

The disciples then asked: "Lord, reveal to us the nature of this 'Man,' that we may understand his glory clearly."

The perfect Savior replied: "Let whoever has ears to hear, hear this: The First Begetter Father is called 'Adam, Eye of Light,' because he came from the shining Light. His holy angels, who are ineffable and without shadow, rejoice eternally in their reflection, which they received from their Father. The entire Kingdom of the Son of Man, who is called the 'Son of God,' is full of ineffable and shadowless joy, a joy that never changes, rejoicing in his imperishable glory. This glory has never been heard of before, nor has it ever been revealed in the aeons that followed, or in their worlds. I came from the Self-begotten, from the First Infinite Light, so that I might reveal everything to you."

The disciples asked again: "Lord, explain to us clearly: How did they descend from the invisible realms, from the immortal, to the world that is destined to die?"

The perfect Savior answered: "The Son of Man agreed with Sophia, his consort, and revealed a great androgynous light. His male name is 'Savior, Begetter of All Things,' and his female name is 'All-Begettress Sophia.' Some call her 'Pistis.' "

Everyone who enters this world arrives like a spark from the higher Light, sent forth by that divine source into the domain ruled by the so-called Almighty, so that they might be safeguarded for a time under his authority. Yet upon entering this realm, they are veiled in forgetfulness—a condition permitted by Sophia—so that through them, matter might extend across the world in a state of spiritual poverty. This veil was necessary, exposing the arrogance and blindness of the one who claimed dominion, whose ignorance even shaped the name he would be known by.

But I descended from the higher realms at the command of the Great Light, escaping the net of forgetfulness. I shattered the grip of the thieves who sought to hold others captive. I reawakened the sacred spark that had been sent by Sophia, so that through me it might blossom, bear abundance, and become whole—transformed from brokenness into perfection. Through me, the true Savior, divine glory was made manifest. In this, Sophia's purpose is fulfilled, for her children will no longer remain flawed or diminished, but will rise to a place of honor and radiance. They will return to their true Father, and at last understand the voice of the radiant, masculine Light.

"And you were sent by the Son, who was sent to bring you the Light, so that you might free yourselves from the forgetfulness of the authorities, and prevent it from appearing again through you— the unclean rubbing from the fearful fire that came from their flesh. Tread upon their malicious intent."

PART III — THE UNVEILING OF THE DIVINE POWERS AND THE JUDGMENT OF THE ROBBERS

Thomas then asked: "Lord, Savior, how many aeons surpass the heavens?"

The perfect Savior answered: "I praise you for asking about the great aeons, for your roots are planted in the infinite realms. Now, when those beings I spoke of earlier were revealed, the Self-begotten Father quickly created twelve aeons to serve as companions to the twelve angels. These aeons are perfect, good, and complete. However, the flaw in the female nature became apparent."

Thomas asked again: "How many are the aeons of the immortals, starting from the infinite realms?"

The perfect Savior responded: "Let anyone with ears to hear, listen. The first aeon is that of the Son of Man, called First Begetter, also known as the Savior— he who has appeared. The second aeon is that of Man, called Adam, the Eye of Light. The aeon that encompasses all these is the one above, over which there is no kingdom— the aeon of the Eternal Infinite God, the Self-Begotten aeon, the aeon of immortals, which I described earlier. This aeon is above the seventh, and it emerged from Sophia— it is the first aeon."

He continued: "Now, Immortal Man revealed the aeons, the powers, and the kingdoms, and granted authority to all who manifested through him, so that they could fulfill their desires until the final things above chaos were realized. These beings consented with one another, and from their unity, every magnificence was revealed— from spirit, countless lights that are glorious, beyond number. These were called, in the beginning, the first aeon— the Unity and Rest. Each aeon has its own name, and this aeon was called Assembly— the gathering of the great multitude that came into being, revealing themselves in unity. Because these multitudes gathered and became one, we call them the Assembly of the Eighth. It appeared as androgynous, bearing both male and female attributes. The male aspect is called Assembly, and the female aspect is called Life, to show that life for all the aeons came from the female principle."

He added: "Every name was received, starting from the very beginning. From the concurrence of thought, the powers soon appeared— these powers were called gods. The gods, in their wisdom, gave rise to gods of gods. From their wisdom, lords were revealed, and from their thoughts, lords of lords emerged, until, from their power, archangels were born. The archangels, through their words, gave birth to angels. And from them, semblances appeared, with structure, form, and names for all the aeons and their worlds."

He continued: "The immortals, whom I just described, all possess authority from Immortal Man, who is called Silence, because in reflecting without speech, all her majesty was made perfect. For as the imperishabilities held the authority, each created a great kingdom in the Eighth, along with thrones, temples, and firmaments for their own majesty. All of this came about by the will of the Mother of the Universe."

The Holy Apostles asked him: "Lord, Savior, tell us about those who dwell in the aeons, since it is important for us to understand them."

The perfect Savior answered: "If you ask about anything, I will gladly tell you. The aeons created countless hosts of angels— myriads without end— to serve as their retinue and to share their glory. They also created virgin spirits, ineffable lights that never change. These spirits are free from sickness and weakness, for their nature is will— their will is their essence. Thus, the aeons were completed swiftly, in the heavens and the firmaments, in the glory of Immortal Man and Sophia, his consort. From this place, every aeon and every world, along with everything that came afterward, took its pattern and likeness in the heavens of chaos. All natures— from the very revelation of chaos— are in the Light that shines without shadow. They live in joy that cannot be described, and in jubilation that is beyond words. They ever rejoice, delighting in their unchanging glory and the immeasurable rest they enjoy. This rest cannot be fully described, even among all the aeons that followed, and all the powers within them."

The Savior paused, then added: "Now, everything I have shared with you, I did so that you may shine in Light even more brightly than these."

Mary then asked: "Holy Lord, where did your disciples come from, where are they going, and what should they do here?"

The perfect Savior replied: "I want you to understand: Sophia, the Mother of the Universe and my consort, desired to bring these beings into existence by herself, without the involvement of her male counterpart. But by the will of the Father of the Universe, and so that his boundless goodness might be revealed, he created a curtain between the immortals and those who came after them, to allow the sequence of events to unfold. Every aeon and every moment of chaos would follow, so that the flaw of the female principle might be healed, and so that Error would contest with her. These became the spiritual curtain. From the higher aeons, the emanations of Light were sent down. As I have already explained, a drop from Light and Spirit descended into the lower realms of chaos, so that their forms could be shaped from this divine drop. This was a judgment upon Yaldabaoth, the Arch-Begetter, who governs the chaos. This drop revealed their forms through the breath, which became a living soul. However, the soul was stunted and slumbered in ignorance. When it became awakened by the breath of the Great Light of the Male, it took thought. Then, names were given to all who inhabit the world of chaos, and all things within it, through that Immortal One, when the breath entered into him. But when this happened by the will of Mother Sophia, the Immortal Man was able to piece together the garments of the world, so that a judgment could be made upon the robbers. He welcomed the breath, but, being soul-like, he was not able to take full power for himself until the number of chaos was complete— until the time determined by the great angel was fulfilled. Now, I have taught you about the Immortal Man and released him from the bonds of the robbers. I have broken down the gates of the pitiless ones, humbling their malicious intent. They have been shamed and have risen from their ignorance. For this reason, I have come here— to unite them with that Spirit and Breath, so that they may become one, just as it was from the beginning. And through this union, you will bear much fruit and ascend to Him Who Is from the Beginning, in ineffable joy, glory, honor, and grace from the Father of the Universe."

Then Thomas asked the Savior: "Lord, Savior, how many are the aeons of those who surpass the heavens?"

The perfect Savior responded: "I praise you for asking about the great aeons, for your roots are in the infinite realms. Now, when those beings I spoke of earlier were revealed, the Self-begotten Father soon created twelve aeons to serve as companions for the twelve angels. These aeons are perfect and good. Thus, the flaw in the female aspect became apparent."

Thomas asked again: "How many are the aeons of the immortals, starting from the infinite realms?"

The Savior said: "Whoever has ears to hear, let him hear. The first aeon is that of the Son of Man, who is called First Begetter, who is called Savior, and who has appeared. The second aeon is that of Man, called Adam, Eye of Light. The aeon that embraces all these is the one that has no kingdom, the aeon of the Eternal Infinite God, the Self-Begotten aeon of the immortals. This is the first aeon, and it came from Sophia."

The Savior continued: "Now, Immortal Man revealed aeons, powers, and kingdoms, and gave authority to all who appeared in him, so that they could fulfill their desires until the final things above chaos were revealed. These beings consented with one another, and through their union, every magnificence was revealed— from spirit, countless lights that are glorious, beyond number. These were called, in the beginning, the first aeon—the Unity and Rest. Each of these aeons has its own name, and this one was called Assembly— a gathering of the great multitude that came into being as one. Because these multitudes gathered and became unified, we call them the Assembly of the Eighth. It appeared as androgynous, bearing both male and female aspects. The male aspect is called Assembly, and the female aspect is called Life, to show that the female principle gave life to all the aeons."

He went on: "Every name was given, starting from the very beginning. From their unity and agreement, the powers soon appeared— these powers were called gods. From their wisdom, the gods of gods were revealed. From their wisdom, the lords were made known, and from their thoughts, the lords of lords emerged. From their power, archangels were born. The archangels, through their words, gave birth to angels. And from them, semblances appeared— with structure, form, and names for all the aeons and their worlds."

He continued: "The immortals I just described have authority from Immortal Man, who is called Silence, because in reflecting without speech, all her majesty was perfected. Since the imperishabilities held this authority, each one created a great kingdom in the Eighth, along with thrones, temples, and firmaments to showcase their own majesty. All of this came about by the will of the Mother of the Universe."

THE SECOND TREATISE OF THE GREAT SETH

INTRODUCTION TO THE SECOND TREATISE OF THE GREAT SETH

CHRIST LAUGHS: A GOSPEL OF IRONY AND LIBERATION

There's something startling—almost disarming—about the way Christ speaks in the Second Treatise of the Great Seth. He doesn't weep. He doesn't plead. He doesn't offer moral lessons or demand obedience. Instead, he laughs.

And it's not cruel laughter. It's the laughter of someone who sees through the illusion. Who knows the game is rigged. Who watches the powers of the world puff themselves up and declare, "I am God and there is no other," and can't help but chuckle at how empty it all is.

This text is unlike anything in the New Testament canon. It doesn't recount events in the life of Jesus with reverence or sorrow. Instead, it flips the narrative upside down. The crucifixion? A cosmic misunderstanding. The supposed sacrifice? A performance directed by blind rulers who never understood who they were dealing with. The one they tried to kill wasn't even him—not really. While they nailed up a body and called it victory, the real Christ was laughing from above, untouched, still free.

This isn't mockery—it's revelation. It's a challenge to everything we think we know about power, pain, and salvation. In this gospel, Christ doesn't conquer death by dying. He conquers it by refusing to be defined by it. He doesn't suffer to appease a God of wrath. He reveals a God beyond wrath—a Father of truth and light who has nothing to do with fear, punishment, or jealousy.

For readers used to a suffering Savior, this might be unsettling. But for those who have felt the weight of dogma or the pressure of performative piety, it can feel strangely liberating. This Christ doesn't demand belief. He invites awakening. He exposes false gods, man-made doctrines, and systems built on fear—and he invites us to see beyond them.

The Second Treatise of the Great Seth isn't just a text. It's a wink. A whisper. A voice from the margins that says: you don't have to play by their rules. You were never meant to. You are not broken. You are not condemned. You are light. You are whole. And the truth is not far off. It's already in you—waiting to be remembered.

THE FALSE GOD AND THE FORGOTTEN ONES

At the heart of the Second Treatise of the Great Seth is a radical reimagining of who holds real power—and who doesn't.

The "god" most people worship, the one who thunders commandments and punishes disobedience for generations, is not the true Father of light in this text. He's something else entirely. A false god. An impostor. A jealous being—Yaldabaoth—who thinks he's alone in the universe and shouts his dominance from a place of deep insecurity. He claims to be the creator of all, but he doesn't know where he came from. He doesn't even realize there's something—someone—greater than him.

The gospel doesn't just reject this figure. It calls him out. It calls out the systems of fear, control, and legalism that have been built around him. It calls out the archons—the spiritual rulers or authorities—who uphold this illusion, keeping souls trapped in a cycle of obedience, guilt, and forgetfulness. And it challenges the prophets and patriarchs who were honored by tradition but, in this telling, were nothing more than echoes of the same delusion.

In contrast, the text lifts up those who've been forgotten. The ones who don't belong to the system. The ones who carry within them a spark of something real. They aren't powerful by worldly standards. They aren't loud. They don't control temples or write laws. But they know. And because they know—because they carry the living Word and the mind (Nous) of the Father—they are free.

These are the ones the false god fears most. Not because they threaten his throne, but because they can see through it. They aren't impressed by status. They aren't tricked by rituals. They aren't waiting for salvation—they remember where they came from.

And this memory changes everything.

For the Second Treatise of the Great Seth, salvation isn't a prize given by a god outside of us. It's a process of unmasking the lie. It's the slow, steady return to what's true, sparked by inner recognition. We don't need to be rescued—we need to remember.

In this gospel, those who've been dismissed by the world—the quiet, the wise, the watchful—are revealed as the true inheritors of the divine. And the ones who claim authority? They're just part of the performance, unaware that the stage itself is dissolving.

UNION, LIGHT, AND THE INCORRUPTIBLE RACE

For all its irony and sharp critique, the Second Treatise of the Great Seth is, at its core, a text of deep peace.

Its final movement shifts from confrontation to reunion. It speaks of souls once scattered and separated, now brought back together—not through force or law, but through knowing. Through love. Through a Word that doesn't divide but heals.

This is where the treatise offers one of its most beautiful ideas: the incorruptible race. Not a literal bloodline, but a spiritual family. A people defined not by heritage or creed, but by awareness—by a shared memory of where they come from and to whom they belong. These are the ones who know that all is one. That the divisions we cling to—between body and spirit, man and woman, God and human—are illusions waiting to be undone.

In this vision, salvation is not separation from the world, but union with the truth. The soul doesn't escape to a distant heaven. It wakes up to the light already within. It remembers itself as part of the eternal harmony—of fatherhood, motherhood, wisdom, friendship, and joy. Not metaphors, but living realities, grounded in a love that doesn't fade or fracture.

Even Sophia, the figure of divine Wisdom who suffers in other Gnostic texts, finds companionship here. Christ calls her his friend. He doesn't speak of betrayal or blame. He speaks of shared origin, of reunion, of rest. This is not a gospel of revenge. It's a gospel of return.

The true "bridal chamber" isn't a ritual or a place—it's this moment of reintegration. The soul coming home. The voice once silenced, speaking again. The broken pieces of light finding one another and realizing: we were never really apart.

By the end, the message is simple but profound: You are not lost. You are not forgotten. And you are not alone.

The incorruptible ones—the ones who know—are already with you. And Christ? He never left. He is still speaking. Still laughing. Still waiting to welcome you back into the one truth that outlasts every illusion: that love is your beginning, your belonging, and your final rest.

HISTORICAL CONTEXT

The Second Treatise of the Great Seth, dating to the mid-3rd century CE, represents a mature phase of Sethian gnosticism. It portrays Jesus laughing at the ignorance of those who believed they crucified him, emphasizing a docetic view of Christ's passion. Likely composed in Egypt, the text ridicules earthly rulers and false powers, advocating liberation through true knowledge. It offers a bold and poetic vision of salvation beyond the physical and political world.

THE SECOND TREATISE OF THE GREAT SETH: THE TEXT

PART I – THE DESCENT AND THE ILLUSION OF POWER

The perfect Majesty rests peacefully in the light that can't be described—in the truth that comes from the mother of everything. And all of you who reach me, you reach me alone, the one who is whole, because of the Word. I exist alongside the full greatness of the Spirit, which is a companion to us and to those like us. I brought forth a word that glorifies our Father—out of his kindness—and I also gave birth to an eternal thought. This is the Word that lives in him. Dying with Christ means dying to slavery. What's been given is an everlasting, pure thought—something beyond understanding—like a wonder written in unnameable waters. That's the Word that comes from us.

I dwell within you, just as you dwell within me—and through your purity, the presence of the Father also lives in you. Let us come together in unity. Let us hold a sacred gathering and turn our attention to the created world. Let us send one of our own into that realm, just as the Father once descended among the Ennoias and into the lower domains. I spoke these things before a vast and joyful gathering, surrounded by the radiance of Majesty. And all those who dwell in the house of the Father of Truth rejoiced, recognizing me as one of their own.

I reflected on the divine thoughts—the Ennoias—that had flowed from the pure Spirit. My mind turned to the descent into the depths, symbolized by the waters—into the lesser worlds. All present shared a single understanding, bound together by their common origin. They entrusted the mission to me, and I accepted it without hesitation. I stepped forward to reveal divine splendor to those who are my kin—my true spiritual kindred.

The world below had already been made ready through the efforts of our sister Sophia. Though her role resembled that of one who bargains herself away, her intent was shaped by a quiet, unspoken innocence. She did not seek permission from the All, nor from the fullness of the Assembly, nor even from the Pleroma. Being the first to act, she took it upon herself to form beings and spaces suited for the arrival of the Son of Light and his companions. She used the raw elements of the lower realm to construct physical forms, intending to host divine presence. But because her work emerged from an imitation of glory rather than true glory, these dwellings were unstable and led ultimately to ruin—they bore the mark of Sophia's incomplete vision.

Yet now, these same forms stand open, prepared to receive the living Word—the breath of life that comes from the unspeakable Monad and the great divine Assembly, from those who persevere, and from those who are already one with me. I entered into a physical body. I pushed out the one who was there before me, and I took his place. When that happened, all the archons—the rulers—were shaken. Their entire domain, along with the earthly powers they had created, trembled when they saw the image—the likeness—because it had become something different. I was now inside it, and I wasn't anything like the one who had been there before. He was just a man of the earth. But me? I came from beyond the heavens.

I didn't turn down the role of being a Christ—even that I was willing to take on. But I didn't show them the love that was flowing from me. What I showed instead was that I didn't belong there—that I was a stranger to the lower realms. That caused massive unrest across the whole earth. People were confused, panicked, running, and the plans of the archons were thrown into chaos. Some believed, especially after seeing the signs and wonders I performed. They ran—along with those who descended from above—from the one who had abandoned his throne and sought refuge with Sophia, the one who had already given a sign about me and everyone who's with me—those who belong to the line of Adonaios.

Others ran too, like they were fleeing the World Ruler and his allies, who had tried to bring every kind of suffering upon me. There was chaos in their thoughts as they tried to figure out what to do with me. They thought Sophia was the full embodiment of greatness, and they falsely accused both the True Man and the full greatness of the divine assembly. They couldn't grasp who the Father of Truth really is, or who the Great Man is. Those who got their name through ignorance—like a fire in a fragile container—created it to destroy Adam, the one they had made. They did it to hide the truth from those who belonged to them.

But these rulers, who are from the place of Yaldabaoth, exposed the realm of the angels. Humanity had been searching for it, trying to understand the Man of Truth. And when Adam—the being they created—appeared to them, it set off a deep fear throughout their entire domain. They were terrified that the angels around them might rebel. But I didn't truly die—because if I had, their chief archangel would have been left with nothing.

Then a voice—coming from the Cosmocrator—rang out to the angels, declaring, "I am God, and there is no one else besides me." But when I looked at his hollow display of power, I couldn't help but laugh. It was joyful, because his so-called glory was completely empty. Then he asked, "Who is this man?" And all his angels—who had seen Adam and where he lived—mocked his smallness. They laughed at him. That's how their own Ennoia—what they thought they understood—got cut off from the Majesty of the heavens. It was the True Man, the one whose name they'd seen, who lived in a humble place. But they were too small-minded and senseless to comprehend it. Their own shallow thinking—expressed through that laughter—was a kind of infection.

Meanwhile, the full greatness of the Father's Spirit rested in its own realms. And I was there with him. I carried within me the Ennoia—a single, pure expression that came directly from the eternal, unblemished, and limitless mysteries. I sent a smaller Ennoia into the world, which shook them up and stirred fear throughout the entire host

THE SECOND TREATISE OF THE GREAT SETH

of angels and their leader. I came upon them with fire and flame, because of this Ennoia I carried. Everything that happened to them—every shift, every disruption—was because of me.

There was turmoil and struggle even among the Seraphim and Cherubim, because their glory was fading. Confusion spread around Adonaios and throughout their entire realm—some said to the Cosmocrator, "Let's seize him!" while others doubted and said, "No, this plan will never work."

Adonaios understands who I am because he holds onto the hope that links us. I found myself surrounded by those who, like wild beasts in disguise, sought to tear me apart—not with teeth, but with schemes born of confusion. Their goal was to release error into the world and call it truth. But I never gave in. I saw through their trap and stood firm. They tried to harm me, yes—but I did not truly die. What they witnessed was an illusion, a carefully chosen appearance, so they would not heap shame upon me. In a strange way, they are part of my own extended family, and so I bore their mockery and cast it off without clinging to it. Even in suffering, I stayed resolute. At one moment, fear nearly overtook me. Yet I chose to undergo the ordeal in a way that fit their limited understanding, so that their words about me would always fall short of truth. What they called my death was really their own, a reflection of their blindness and misjudgment. They nailed down an illusion, condemning themselves by striking what they could not recognize. They never saw me for who I truly am—they were spiritually blind and deaf.

Yes, they thought they saw me. They struck someone, punished someone—but it was not I who drank the sour wine or bore the pain of the reed. It was another in my place. It was Simon, not I, who carried the burden of the cross. The thorny crown they placed belonged to someone else. I, meanwhile, remained beyond their reach—lifted above their actions, rejoicing in the higher realms. From that place, I looked down with laughter—not cruelty, but clarity—upon the rulers' empty pride, the children born from their falsehood, and the counterfeit glory they claimed as real. I laughed, because they acted without knowledge, and could not grasp the truth right before them.

I overcame all their powers. As I descended, no one saw me. I changed my appearance again and again, shifting forms so I couldn't be recognized. When I stood at their gates, I looked just like them. I slipped past them silently, observing everything. I wasn't afraid. I wasn't ashamed. I remained pure. I spoke with them. I moved among them through the ones who are mine. And with passion, I stood against those who oppressed my people. I cooled their flames. I did all this because I longed to carry out the will of the Father above—and I would see it through to the end.

The Son of the Majestic One, who had been hidden in the depths of the lower realms, was raised up again to the exalted place above—the same place where I have dwelled with them for all ages. This is a realm no one has ever laid eyes on or even imagined, a space beyond comprehension. It is there that the sacred union takes place—a divine wedding, not clothed in the old garments of decay, but in a new and radiant robe. This new robe never grows threadbare or loses its brilliance. It is the bridal chamber of the heavens, fresh and flawless.

And now I have made it known that there are three sacred paths. One of them is a mystery untouched by corruption, alive within the spirit that governs this age. It does not weaken, break, or dissolve, and no human language can fully describe it. It is perfect, beyond division, universal in scope, and enduring without end.

The soul that comes from the heights doesn't speak of the errors found here, and it doesn't stay trapped in these lower realms. It rises when it's freed—when it's restored to dignity in this world—and stands in the presence of the Father with no weariness or fear. It's always joined with the Mind, the Nous, full of strength and beauty. They see me from every side, without hatred, and in being seen, they are themselves revealed. Since they never shamed me, they themselves will never be shamed. Because they stood before me without fear, they'll pass through every gate boldly, and be completed in the third glory.

PART II – UNITY, WISDOM, AND THE FALL OF THE ARCHONS

When I returned to the revealed heights—the sacred realms the world had refused to acknowledge—that moment marked my third baptism, made visible for all to witness. As the seven Authorities fled from the consuming fire, and the brilliance of the archons faded like the last light of a dying day, darkness fell across their domain. The world grew hollow and fragile. Their servant was shackled by countless chains and fastened to a wooden post with four nails of bronze. With his own hands, he tore the temple veil apart, unraveling the illusion it had maintained. Then the earth trembled, chaos was shaken, and the souls that had long slumbered in silence began to stir. They rose with new strength, casting off the weight of blind obedience, ignorance, and lifeless rituals of death. In their awakening, they embraced a new identity.

Why did they rise? Because they came to recognize the One who is truly blessed—the eternal, radiant, unknowable source of life. That Blessed One is me. I came to those who were mine and made them one with me. I need not say more—for our divine intention, our Ennoia, was already joined. That's why they recognized my words. Long before, we had already conspired together to bring down the dominion of the rulers. And so, in full alignment with that purpose, I fulfilled the will of the Father. And that Father—I am.

When we departed from the world above and entered this realm in visible, physical form, we were met with hostility. Hatred pursued us—not only from those unaware of truth, but even from those who claimed to serve Christ. Believing they were doing right, they acted from spiritual emptiness, unaware of their true nature—like unthinking beasts, reacting in ignorance. They lashed out against those I had liberated, driven by resentment toward the light they couldn't comprehend. And if the redeemed had kept their pain to themselves, silence would have broken their hearts, for they still hadn't fully come to know me.

Instead, they tried to serve two masters—or even more than that. But in all things, you will win—in war, in struggle, through division, through wrath. Yet our love remains upright, innocent, pure, and good. Because within us is the mind of the Father—a mystery beyond words. It was honestly laughable. I can say that myself—it was absurd—because the archons have no idea about the real, indescribable union that exists in the pure truth shared by the sons of light. They tried to copy it. They created a doctrine centered on a dead man and falsehoods, pretending it was like the freedom and purity of the perfect assembly. But instead, they tied that teaching to fear and slavery, to the worries of this world, and to hollow rituals. They're small-minded and ignorant because they don't carry within them the nobility of truth. They actually despise the one who dwells within them and love the one who does not.

They don't understand the Knowledge of the Greatness—because it comes from above. It flows from a source of truth, not from slavery, jealousy, or a craving for worldly things. Those who live in that truth can freely use what belongs to them and even what doesn't—without fear. They don't desire selfishly, because they already have true authority, and they live by a law that comes from within themselves, doing as they choose. But those who don't have this truth? They are poor. They're missing him. They crave him. And in the process, they mislead others—people who are trying to live in the freedom of truth. The ones they deceive end up trapped in service and stress and fear, bought into slavery just like us.

Now, someone who's forced into obedience—pressured and threatened—is still watched over by God. But the fullness of the Father's nobility doesn't need to be guarded that way. He watches over only the one who truly comes from him, without needing to speak or demand anything, because that one is already united with His will. He belongs fully to the Father's Ennoia—the living thought. His purpose is to complete it, to bring it to perfection, and to make it indescribably whole through the water that gives life.

He'll be with you in mutual wisdom—not just in words you hear, but in actions and fulfilled promises. Because those who are perfect deserve to be rooted in this truth and united with me. In that way, they'll never fall into enmity, but remain in true and good friendship. Everything I do, I do through the Good One. This is what it means to be joined in truth: that you live without enemies.

Anyone who causes division? He won't gain wisdom—because he creates conflict and proves he's no friend. He sets himself against everyone. But someone who lives in harmony, in natural and sincere brotherly love—not fake, not partial—that person truly reflects the Father's desire. He embodies what is whole and universal. He is perfect love.

Look at Adam. He became a joke—just a flawed copy of true humanity made by the Hebdomad. It was as if he was supposed to be greater than me and my brothers. But we never wronged him. We didn't sin.

Same goes for Abraham, Isaac, and Jacob. They became a laughingstock too—called "fathers," but their names were given by the Hebdomad, pretending they were more powerful than us. But again—we've done nothing wrong. We didn't sin.

David? Also a joke. His son was called the "Son of Man," but that was just the Hebdomad's influence. As if that title made him greater than me and my race. But I haven't sinned. We are innocent. Solomon, too. He thought he was the Christ. But he was full of pride, misled by the Hebdomad, acting like he was greater than me and my brothers. But we haven't sinned. I haven't sinned.

Even the twelve prophets were laughable—just imitations of the real ones. They were created as false versions, also through the Hebdomad, as if they surpassed us. But we are innocent in that too.

And what of Moses, the so-called faithful servant? Even he was misunderstood. They called him "the Friend of God," but that title was based on distorted assumptions by people who never truly knew who I was. Moses didn't know me. Nor did those who came before him—Adam, John the Baptist, or any others. None of them recognized me or my brothers.

They clung to teachings handed down by spiritual intermediaries—obsessed with rituals, food laws, and lives of strict submission. But they were cut off from the truth and will remain so, trapped in a fog of deception that clouds their souls. That haze keeps them from ever touching the freedom of understanding—the liberating Mind that could reveal the truth to them—unless they come to know the Son of Man.

As for my Father, I am the one the world failed to recognize. That's why it turned against me and against those who belong to me. But we stand blameless before the Father—we carry no guilt.

The Archon became a joke when he claimed, "I am God, and there is none greater than me. I alone am the Father, the Lord—there is no other beside me. I am a jealous God, and I carry the sins of the fathers down three and four generations." As if he were greater than me or my brothers! But we've done nothing wrong. We've never sinned. We saw through his teaching and mastered it. His supposed glory was empty. He's nothing like our true Father.

Through our unity, we were able to understand his teachings for what they really were—full of vanity and emptiness. They don't match up with our Father's truth. The Archon was a fraud, a mockery of judgment, a false prophet.

To those who can't see: you're blind, and you don't even see your own blindness. You didn't know the truth—never have, never even heard of it. You refused to obey what was real. So you ended up locked into false judgment. You lifted your filthy, murderous hands against him—as if your violence mattered, like you were swinging at air. The blind and the foolish stay that way—always chained to the law and to the fear of earthly things.

I am the Christ. I am the Son of Man. I stand among you—not as a distant figure, but as one of your own. I was rejected for your sake, so that you would no longer see yourselves as separate from me. So don't collapse into weakness. Don't become, in a symbolic sense, like the passive and confused—those who give rise to destructive forces like envy, conflict, rage, fear, inner division, and cravings for illusions that were never real to begin with. I remain a mystery too vast for language.

Long before this world ever existed—before form or matter took shape—the full Assembly gathered in the celestial heights, within the Ogdoad, and together they conceived the plan for a spiritual union—a divine marriage untainted by the material. It was through this sacred intention that he was completed—perfected in realms that exist beyond expression—through the power of the living Word. That unbreakable union was fulfilled in Jesus, the true Mediator, who exists at the center of all things and holds them in harmony. He abides in a love that cannot be divided and in a power that is flawless.

And around him, he sees himself reflected—as the Monad of everything. A thought, a father, a single being. He stands with all of them, because he came into existence as one whole being, not divided. He is life itself, having come from the Father of perfect, unspeakable Truth. This Father is the source of union, of peace, of friendship and goodness—eternal life, joy that never fades, harmony in faith and life itself.

They were united with the Mind—Nous—who reaches out and always will, in joy, in trust, in faithful listening. That Mind exists in fatherhood, motherhood, brotherhood, and wisdom. That's what the true wedding looks like. It's rest. It's incorruptible. It's truth living in spirit, in every mind. It's light—perfect light—shining from a mystery that has no name. And this kind of wedding? It doesn't—and never will—exist in division or conflict. Not in any place or region. It only exists in love that unites, that blends everything into harmony. All of it finds perfection in the One who truly is.

PART III – THE ETERNAL UNION AND THE MYSTERY OF THE ONE

This, too, unfolded beneath the heavens, as part of the divine plan to restore what had been separated. Those who came to recognize me—through the power of salvation and the bond of unity—were gathered together again through the living Word. Though they had once been divided, they were reunited in the name of truth and for the glory of the Father. I dwell within the Spirit, within the essence of the divine Mother, just as the presence of the Father has always been there. I was among those who are joined not by force, but through authentic friendship—those who live free of hatred, untouched by evil, bound only by the unity born from the understanding I've given them. They exist in harmony, both with one another and within themselves, grounded in truth and peace.

All who took on a likeness to me will also embody the nature of my Word. They will radiate with eternal light, bonded through a spiritual companionship that never fades. They have come to grasp—completely and without inner conflict—that reality, in its purest form, is unified. All that truly exists is One. And so, like the great Assembly and those who dwell within it, they will come to know this oneness.

The source of everything—their Father—is beyond all boundaries and beyond all change. He is Mind, and Word, and even Division and Fire and Jealousy, yet remains entirely whole. He contains all opposites, all expressions, drawing them together in a single divine teaching, because everything originates from one Spirit and flows back into that same unity.

Oh, you who still can't see—why didn't you truly understand this mystery?

The rulers who gathered around Yaldabaoth disobeyed. They were led by Ennoia, who descended to him from her sister, Sophia. These rulers formed a union with those around them, wrapping themselves in a fiery cloud that came from their own jealousy. And others—brought forth by the things they themselves created—acted as though they had somehow harmed the pure joy of the Assembly.

And so they revealed a distorted creation—a confused mixture shaped by ignorance, imitating fire, earth, and even destruction itself. But they lacked wisdom. Naïve and undisciplined, they acted without understanding, unaware of the natural order: that light is drawn only to light, that darkness belongs with darkness, that what decays clings to what is corruptible, and only what is eternal can unite with the truly imperishable.

Everything I've spoken, I've revealed to you as Jesus Christ, the Son of Man, lifted above the heavens. I share this not for the sake of empty speech, but because of the perfect mystery—pure and eternal—that cannot be contained in words. They assumed we had determined these truths before the world was born—and in a sense, they were right. We did so in anticipation of our return, so that when we stepped beyond this world, we would carry with us the marks of everlasting life born from our union in Spirit, bringing with us the fullness of true understanding.

Yet you still do not fully see it, because the shadow of the body clouds your vision.

I alone am the true companion of Sophia. I have always been held in the Father's presence, from the very beginning, dwelling in the realm where the children of truth and the vast fullness of greatness abide.

So now, rest with me—my brothers and sisters in spirit. Remain with me, forever

APPENDIX I – ESOTERIC AND POETIC REVELATIONS

There are gospels that speak plainly. And then there are those that speak like dreams.

The texts gathered in this appendix—Pistis Sophia, Trimorphic Protennoia, The Book of Thomas the Contender, and Thunder, Perfect Mind—do not follow the familiar shapes of stories or teachings. They do not offer sayings in sequence, or characters in conversation. They are not meant to be analyzed line by line. They are meant to be entered, felt, and received like sacred music or poetry—mystical transmissions from voices that do not always speak in words.

These are texts that break the mold. They are esoteric—not because they hide something, but because they point toward truths too large to fit inside ordinary language. They invite us to read in a different way: not with the mind alone, but with presence, intuition, and openness.

Some of them, like Pistis Sophia, unfold in long, symbolic sequences—layered with cosmology, repetition, and ritual. Others, like Thunder, Perfect Mind, deliver a rush of paradoxical declarations, a cascade of opposites spoken by a single voice that seems both human and divine. They defy easy explanation, and that is exactly their gift. In a world that pushes us to understand everything, these writings ask us to feel something instead. To surrender the need to explain and let ourselves be moved.

The figure of Sophia—Wisdom—appears in several of these texts. Sometimes she is radiant and exalted. Other times she is sorrowful, cast down, crying out for restoration. Her voice is often the bridge between the heavenly and the earthly, between what has been lost and what longs to be found. In these writings, she is not a passive symbol of intellect, but a living presence: one who falls, cries, remembers, and rises. Through her, we glimpse the soul's journey in mythic form—its descent into confusion, and its slow return to the light.

These texts are also liturgical in feel. They pulse with rhythms, refrains, and patterns that seem designed for chanting, not quiet reading. Many scholars believe they were used in ritual or communal meditation. Whether or not that's true, they carry the weight and motion of sacred recitation. They speak to the reader, and sometimes as the reader. They put you inside the experience, rather than describing it from outside.

That can be disorienting. But if you let the language wash over you—if you stop trying to "figure it out" and just allow it to settle into your inner silence—you may discover that something begins to shift. Something in you may recognize the cadence. May recognize her voice. May recognize your own voice, rising from a place long quieted.

These texts are sometimes considered "secondary" because they don't fit cleanly into the gnostic canon, or because they are more poetic than theological. But here, they are not footnotes. They are front lines of another kind of knowledge—knowledge that flows not from debate or doctrine, but from direct resonance. They show us that not all revelation comes in clear instruction. Some comes in mystery. Some comes in fire. Some comes in whisper.

It is important to say: you are not expected to understand everything you read here. That is not the point. You are simply invited to listen—to enter the text as you might enter a dream. To let the images arise. To let the contradictions dance. To let the voice move through you.

Let yourself be surprised. Let yourself be confused. Let yourself be cracked open.

Because in the pages that follow, we are not in the realm of arguments and ideas. We are in the realm of prayer, of breath, of the unspeakable.

This is where language stretches toward something larger than itself. Where wisdom weeps, and wisdom sings. Where the divine does not declare, but remembers. And perhaps, as you read, you will remember too.

PISTIS SOPHIA

INTRODUCTION TO PISTIS SOPHIA

The Pistis Sophia, a cornerstone of Gnostic teachings, is a profound spiritual text that has fascinated scholars, mystics, and seekers of truth for centuries. Thought to have been written in the early centuries of Christianity, it presents an alternative view of the divine, one that blends ancient wisdom with the search for inner transformation. At its core, Pistis Sophia reveals the soul's journey toward enlightenment, detailing the obstacles it faces, the lessons it learns, and the ultimate return to the Light.

The name Pistis Sophia translates to "Faith Wisdom" or "Wisdom of Faith," and the text is centered around the figure of Sophia, a divine emanation associated with wisdom. Sophia's journey in the text is both a literal and symbolic one: she falls from her place in the higher realms into the chaos below, seeking redemption and ultimately returning to her divine source. Her journey parallels the soul's struggle in the material world—longing for connection with the divine, overcoming obstacles, and seeking knowledge to transcend the physical and return to the spiritual fullness from which it came.

What makes the Pistis Sophia especially captivating is the rich cosmology it offers. It introduces a complex, multi-layered universe with spiritual entities, divine hierarchies, and detailed realms where souls must pass through various gates to achieve liberation. The teachings in this work present the soul's journey as a process of self-realization, purification, and enlightenment. Each level of the soul's ascent represents a deeper understanding of the mysteries of the universe and the nature of the self. In essence, it is a guide to spiritual awakening—one that encourages individuals to recognize their true nature, embrace their divine potential, and ultimately merge with the Light.

In this version of Pistis Sophia, we have worked to stay as close as possible to the spirit and meaning of the original text while making it more accessible to modern readers. The language and concepts may seem complex at times, but the teachings are clear: true wisdom and salvation come from within. The text calls on us to reflect on our own inner journey, to acknowledge the divine within, and to overcome the inner darkness that may cloud our perception of reality.

The Pistis Sophia is not just an ancient document—it is a living guide. Its wisdom continues to inspire spiritual seekers, inviting them to reflect on their own spiritual paths and to seek the Light within. Through this text, we gain insight into the Gnostic worldview, one that stresses personal experience and inner knowing over external authority. It challenges the conventional understanding of salvation and invites us to consider that the divine is within reach of all, regardless of circumstance.

As you read through the chapters of this work, remember that this is not merely a story of the past. It is a call to awaken, to seek the Light, and to discover the truth that lies within. It is an invitation to embark on your own journey of self-discovery and spiritual ascension.

HISTORICAL CONTEXT

Pistis Sophia was likely composed between the late 2nd and early 3rd centuries CE, probably in Egypt. The text reflects a mature phase of gnostic Christianity, heavily influenced by Valentinian teachings. It presents a complex cosmology centered around the figure of Sophia, her fall, repentance, and redemption. Structured as a series of dialogues between Jesus and his disciples, Pistis Sophia blends myth, ritual, and spiritual instruction, and may have been used in early Christian liturgical contexts.

PISTIS SOPHIA: THE TEXT

BOOK 1 (CHAPTER 1-62)

Chapter 1 - It happened, then, that Jesus sat with his disciples on the Mount of Olives. He looked into the spiritual worlds above and into the layers beneath. He kept his gaze steady and silent for a long time, not speaking a word. His disciples sat quietly with him, not daring to break the silence. They waited, watching him, deeply afraid and uncertain about what they were witnessing. Then Jesus lifted his eyes. He looked straight at them and said, "Peace be with you. Do not be afraid."

They were relieved and comforted by his voice. He said to them, "Rejoice and be glad from this moment on. I have gone to the realms from which I came. I have received full authority through my Father, and I have brought it to you. Rejoice, for I am with you forever."

When he had said this, he added: "I came down from the heights through the twelve aeons. I passed through each one of them, taking the form of each power and their rulers. In each realm, I appeared to be one of their own, hiding the true light I carried within me. If I had come in my original light, none of the rulers or their realms would have endured it. They would have vanished on the spot. But I adapted my appearance so I could move among them."

Chapter 2 - Jesus continued speaking to his disciples and said: "When I came into the world, I appeared among you as one of you. I walked in humility and took on a human body, just like yours. But I didn't come empty—I came filled with the power of the Light, and with the mystery of the heavenly realms. Even while I was in the world, I passed through all the rulers and their regions in secret. I disguised myself in their likeness so they wouldn't recognize me. I taught among you, but I was also preparing something greater—something you weren't yet ready to understand. Now,

I will explain to you everything, openly and completely. I'll speak of the paths I walked, the mysteries I received, and the powers I was given. I'll show you what's hidden from the rest of the world. And I will reveal the truth that leads to freedom—the truth the rulers above and below tried to keep from you."

Chapter 3 - As Jesus stood before his disciples, a brilliant light began to surround him. It grew brighter and brighter until it completely wrapped around his whole body. Then, in silence, he rose upward—ascending into the heights, glowing with a light too powerful to measure. The disciples watched him rise, stunned and silent, until he disappeared into the sky. This moment took place on the fifteenth day of the month Tybi, during the full moon. Three hours after his ascent, the heavens were shaken. Every power in the celestial realms was disturbed. The aeons trembled, the regions above moved against each other, and the whole earth quaked. People everywhere were filled with fear, wondering if the end of the world had come. The chaos continued without rest—from the third hour of that day until the ninth hour of the next. And during that entire time, all the angels, archangels, and divine powers lifted up their voices in praise. They sang to the light of the highest realms, and their song echoed across the world without ceasing.

Chapter 4 - On the next day, at about the ninth hour, the skies opened again. A great stream of light poured down, stretching from the heavens to the earth. It illuminated everything—shining brighter than the sun, more brilliant than anything the world had seen. And in the center of that light was Jesus, descending from the heights in radiant glory. He came down wrapped in light, and the disciples saw him return, surrounded by the power of his heavenly being. He entered the space where they were gathered, and stood among them in silence. For a long time, he didn't speak a word. The disciples were afraid to ask him anything. They were trembling, unsure of what they had witnessed. Then, slowly, he looked at each of them, face to face. And he said, "Peace be with you. It is I—do not be afraid."

Their fear melted into joy. They bowed down before him in reverence, full of wonder and relief. They knew now, without doubt, that it was truly him—the one who had gone above all the heavens, and had now returned to them, full of light and truth.

Chapter 5 - After Jesus returned and stood among his disciples, they watched him in awe. His robe was made of pure light, shining with power and brilliance. The light wasn't from this world—it radiated from within him and revealed his true origin.

Jesus looked at them and spoke: "Look at me now, clothed in light. This is the robe my Father has given me—the robe of glory I wore before I came into the world. This is the brightness of the light that surrounds me, the light I brought with me from the heavens, and the light that has now returned to me."

As he said this, the disciples were overwhelmed with wonder. None of them dared to speak. They were silent, filled with awe. They trembled, amazed by the majesty standing before them—more radiant than anything they had ever seen.

Then Jesus spoke again: "Bring me your hearts. Bring me your attention.

I have things to tell you that no one else has heard—not from scripture, not from teachers. I will reveal the hidden things. I will show you what lies beyond the veil."

Chapter 6 - Jesus turned to his disciples and said, "I will speak with you not as I did before—when I was with you in the body, speaking in ways the world could understand. Now I will speak with you in fullness, openly, without parables or riddles. I will tell you everything about the upper worlds, and about the paths I traveled—things no one else has ever spoken aloud."

He paused, then said, "Listen closely. I went into the light of the heights and passed through twelve realms of power. In each realm, I was received differently, but I also took on the form they expected to see. They did not recognize me for who I was. Each power, each aeon, saw only what it could bear. Had I appeared in the full glory of my light, they would have been undone. So I came quietly, step by step."

Jesus looked at them intently. "Now," he said, "I will lead you back to where I came from. I will show you the great.

Chapter 7 - Jesus continued, speaking with deep clarity. "When I entered the world below," he said, "I passed through the twelve aeons—realms of power and rule. In each one, I changed my appearance to match the rulers of that realm, so they would not know me or where I came from. They only saw a reflection of themselves and could not grasp the truth of the light I carried."

"But now," he added, "I have returned from those places. I have taken back my glory, and I will speak to you of everything I've seen and done. I will reveal the mysteries that were hidden—not just to the world, but even to the rulers themselves."

He looked around at his disciples and said, "I have brought you the fullness of the light. And I have come to give you the words and the knowledge that were never spoken before—so that you may understand and be made whole."

Chapter 8 - Jesus continued speaking to his disciples: "When I entered the realm of the twelve aeons, I did so gently and without revealing my full power. I took on their likeness and moved through their spaces quietly, so they would not be alarmed. I wanted to observe their ways, their movements, their struggles—and I saw how they each took power in their own realms."

"I also saw how the power of the light that was in me began to stir the aeons. Many of their rulers grew uneasy. They sensed something beyond their control, something brighter than anything they knew. Some of them trembled, others fought among themselves. The order of the aeons began to shake."

"As I ascended through them, their harmony broke down. They could no longer maintain their structure. Their balance had been built on illusion, and my presence uncovered it. Light has a way of revealing what darkness hides."

He paused, then said: "These things I did not tell you before, because you were not ready. But now, the time has come to know what lies beyond what is written—to see with the eyes of the spirit."

Chapter 9 - Jesus continued: "When I entered the twelve aeons, I caused a great disturbance. The rulers and their powers were shaken. The light within me began to stir everything that had been still. The harmony they had built, the order they clung to—it started to come undone.

They saw me, but they didn't recognize who I was. They only saw someone like themselves, but unfamiliar. They didn't know where I came from or why I had come. Still, my light stirred them. Some of them grew angry. Some were afraid. Others wondered if I had come to take their power. Their realms began to tremble. Confusion spread. The heavens above them were shaken, and the foundations of the aeons cracked. And yet I continued upward, quietly, wrapped in light, carrying the mystery of my Father. This is what happened when I passed through their realms—and this is what I now reveal to you, so that you may understand the truth that lies beyond appearances."

Chapter 10 - Jesus stood before his disciples in radiant light and said: "I have taken back the robe of light that belongs to me—one that was given to me from the beginning. It is adorned with five sacred names, written in pure light, known only to those of the higher realms. These names cannot be spoken by those bound to the world below. They are kept in silence and power."

He paused, then added, "This robe is different from any other. It was prepared for me by the First Mystery, and it contains within it all the glory and knowledge of the divine worlds. When I put it on, I was filled with the light of the heights. I remembered who I was and from where I came."

Jesus continued, "There are three garments of light in the higher realms. Each one holds mysteries and names and powers beyond anything known on earth. The robe I now wear is the most perfect—it contains the image of the light, the fullness of power, and the knowledge of all who dwell in the realms of truth."

He looked at them and said, "This is why I now speak to you as I do—not with symbols or veiled words, but directly. The light has returned to me, and now I bring it to you."

Chapter 11 - Jesus continued speaking to his disciples and said: "The moment I put on the robe of light, it sent out a powerful radiance. The entire world of matter, the lower realms, and even the heavens above them, were shaken. Every being, from the highest aeons to the lowest depths, felt its presence. The powers in the skies were alarmed. The rulers of the aeons and their guardians were disturbed. They could sense the light, but they didn't understand where it came from or what it meant. They felt something changing—something stronger than they could resist—but they couldn't see me clearly, because I remained hidden within the light."

He paused and looked at his disciples, then said, "I moved forward quietly, through every realm, and every being gave way before me. I did not fight them. I did not speak. The light I carried was enough. It made them fall silent, powerless to stop what was unfolding."

Chapter 12 - Jesus continued: "As I moved through the aeons, their rulers and powers grew confused. They saw the light surrounding me, but they didn't recognize who I was. They thought I was just another being from the higher realms, more powerful than them—but still part of the system they knew. So they began to question among themselves, saying, 'What is the meaning of this power? Who is this being who comes in such light? Has the First Mystery sent him to take over the aeons and rule over us?' They did not understand the truth. They were blind to the one standing before them. Still, they did not resist me. My light was too great. I moved through them freely, untouched. And in their confusion, they began to wonder if their time was coming to an end."

Jesus looked at his disciples and said, "These things I now reveal to you—not to alarm you, but to prepare you. The light I carry has power not because it destroys, but because it reveals. And now, that same light is offered to you."

Chapter 13 - Jesus continued: "As I passed through each of the aeons, all their rulers and archons looked at me in amazement. They were deeply shaken. Their inner structures trembled. The light surrounding me stirred something they could not understand—and they began to crumble within themselves. But I did not stop. I kept moving upward through the realms, until I reached the gate of the Thirteenth Aeon—the place where the great power that guards the veil stands watch."

Jesus paused for a moment, then said, "That guardian saw me approaching. But even it, strong and proud, was confused by the light I carried. It looked into the brilliance of my robe and saw only mystery. And so, for the first time, it hesitated. Still hidden within the robe of light, I passed through. The guardian did not resist me. It could not. My presence—cloaked in the First Mystery—was greater than anything it had ever seen."

Then Jesus looked at his disciples and said, "This is what it means to carry the mystery of light. The gates do not hold you. The guardians cannot stop you. When the time comes, you too will pass through—clothed not in fear, but in truth."

Chapter 14 - Jesus continued: "When I reached the veil of the Thirteenth Aeon, I stood before its gate. The light of my robe began to shine even more brightly—brighter than any power within that realm had ever seen. And because the powers within the Thirteenth Aeon could not comprehend the brilliance or the mystery I carried, they were shaken. The whole realm stirred in confusion. The light I brought caused a disturbance among the powers that ruled there. They could feel the force of something greater approaching, and they were afraid—not of violence, but of what the light revealed. Still hidden within the shining vesture, I moved through the Thirteenth Aeon. And as I passed, the powers gave way. They did not challenge me. They could not. My light was not like theirs. It was from a place beyond. I came into the space of the Invisible God—the region beyond all the aeons—and there I stood, clothed in the fullness of the mystery. And I remembered who I was. And the light remembered me."

Chapter 15 - Jesus continued: "When I arrived in the region beyond the aeons, I stood before the great treasury of light. It was the place from which I had come—the source of all light, all power, all truth. And as I entered, the light recognized me. The glory that had once been mine surrounded me again. The beings of that high place rejoiced. They saw me, and they knew me. They welcomed me with songs and praises, with movements of power and sound. Every robe, every mystery, every name of light that belonged to me from the beginning returned to me in fullness. I received the five robes of glory, each one more radiant than the last. And I put them on in silence. Each robe contained a name, a seal, a power that could not be spoken in the lower realms. And with them came the knowledge of all things—the path, the source, and the end. I stood there, filled with the First Mystery, surrounded by light, restored in my fullness. And now, I have returned to you to share what I have seen, what I have worn, and what I now carry again."

Chapter 16 - Jesus continued speaking to his disciples: "When I was clothed once more in the robes of light, I stood fully in the power of the First Mystery. And when I looked out over the realms I had passed through—the aeons, the powers, the rulers—they all saw my light. And seeing it, they trembled.

They were shaken because they had never witnessed such brightness. My return to the heights, now wrapped in full glory, sent waves through all the realms below. The rulers, the archons, and even the firmaments of the aeons were disturbed. Some fell into confusion. Others tried to understand what was happening. The light I carried radiated outward, and all things responded. Some in fear. Some in awe. Some in silence. And then the time came for me to return—not just in presence, but in truth. I descended again, this time to share what I had received, to reveal what had been hidden, and to awaken what had been forgotten."

He paused, then said, "What I now give to you, no one has spoken before. These are the mysteries of light, the knowledge of the beginning and the end. And it is yours to receive, not as servants, but as those who are ready."

Chapter 17 - Jesus said to his disciples: "Now listen closely, and I will tell you about the great light and its mysteries—those that no being in the lower aeons has ever known. I will speak of the paths I followed, the powers I passed through, and the way I returned to my place in the heights."

He continued, "When I entered the realm of the First Mystery, I was received by the great beings of light who serve the ineffable. They saw the glory that surrounded me, and they recognized the power I carried. Then, by the command of the First Mystery, I was given authority to open all the gates between the worlds—to reveal the paths hidden since the beginning. And so, from that place, I looked down upon the aeons, and I saw the suffering and confusion that fill the world below. I saw souls trapped in forgetfulness, wandering without direction. And my heart was moved. That is why I have returned—not just to tell you what I've seen, but to show you how to find your way back. The mysteries I will give you are not meant to impress or confuse. They are here to awaken you—to restore what was lost."

Chapter 18 - Jesus continued: "The time has come for me to speak to you openly about the mysteries—the true paths of ascent, hidden since the beginning of time. These mysteries were once sealed, guarded even from the rulers of the aeons. But now they are ready to be given to you."

He looked at his disciples and said: "Not long from now, I will reveal the mystery of the One who lives in the treasury of light. I will show you how the soul can rise above the world and be set free. But first, you must understand the structure of the realms—what each one holds, how each is ruled, and how the soul must pass through them. No one can reach the fullness unless they are guided by the mysteries. No one can enter the light by accident. It is only through knowledge and preparation that the way becomes clear."

Jesus paused, then added: "These things were not spoken before—not in public, not even in secret. But now, I give them to you so that you may know the truth and walk the path yourselves."

Chapter 19 - Jesus continued speaking to his disciples: "Now I will tell you the things that lie beyond the aeons—truths that have never been revealed before. The mysteries I bring to you were hidden, kept in silence since the beginning, known only to those in the innermost light."

He looked at them and said: "When I stood in the presence of the First Mystery, I received the command to return and share what I had seen. I was given the authority to reveal the way back—the path of the soul, the steps of redemption, the return to the light. These mysteries cannot be understood through reasoning alone. They must be lived. They must be experienced. I give them to you not as secrets to be kept, but as keys to be used."

He paused, then added, "Let those who are ready receive what I will now begin to share. Let your hearts be open, for what is coming is not just knowledge—it is transformation."

Chapter 20 - Jesus looked at his disciples and said: "From this moment on, I will speak with you not only as your teacher, but as one who has passed through all the realms, who has seen the fullness and returned. The words I now give you are from the light itself."

He continued, "There are three robes of light in the higher worlds. Each one contains a mystery, a seal, and a name that holds power. When I entered the highest place, these garments were restored to me. I put them on again—not just as clothing, but as expressions of the divine knowledge, power, and authority I now carry. These robes are not made of matter. They are woven from light, from pure intention, from the Word of the First Mystery. Each robe has a name that cannot be spoken by those of the lower worlds—it is known only in the places of truth."

Jesus paused, then said, "These mysteries are not separate from you. They are meant for you. And I will begin now to reveal them, so that you too may be clothed in light, and stand where I have stood."

Chapter 21: After hearing Jesus speak of the mysteries, Mary stepped forward and asked: "Master, what about the astrologers and the interpreters of signs—those who read the movements of the heavens and predict what is to come? Will their knowledge still be accurate, now that you've changed the order of things?"

Jesus answered her gently: "Before now, the heavenly bodies—the spheres, the constellations, the patterns of the signs—always turned in a single direction. They followed fixed paths, and because of that, those who studied them could make predictions. Their words were often true, because the system was stable and predictable. But now, things have changed. I have shifted the balance. The heavenly wheels no longer turn in one direction. They alternate. Every six months, they reverse. First they move to the left, then to the right. And this change has thrown all their knowledge into confusion. Those who relied on the old ways can no longer see clearly. Their charts no longer align. Their interpretations fail. Unless they understand what has changed, and why, their predictions will not come true."

He paused, then said: "What was once ruled by rigid order is now open to the mystery. I have done this so that the powers of fate and the illusions of control would be broken. So that freedom might rise."

Chapter 22 - After Jesus had spoken, Mary bowed and said, "Master, we know that you have come from the realms of light, and that you speak the truth. Bless us with deeper understanding, so that we may share in the mysteries you have revealed."

Then Jesus said to her and to the others: "Blessed are you who search for the light. Blessed are you who are ready to receive. For the truth I now give you is not just for knowledge—it is for transformation. The mysteries I speak of come from the First Mystery, the source of all. They are not the teachings of men, nor the writings of scribes. They are alive. They are power. They are the keys that open what has been closed since the beginning. When you receive these mysteries, you do not simply learn—you change. You rise. You remember what was forgotten, and you return to the light that is your home."

He paused, then added: "There are many who will hear these words and walk away. But you who stay—you will be filled with light. And the light will carry you beyond every aeon, every ruler, every veil of forgetfulness."

Chapter 23 - Jesus looked upon his disciples and said: "Now I will begin to reveal to you the great mysteries of the light—truths that have never been spoken in the world until now. These are not teachings of this earth. They come from the heights, from the place of the First Mystery, where all things begin and end. You have followed me. You have listened and believed. That is why you are ready to receive what others cannot. What I now give you will guide your souls when you leave this body. These mysteries are the maps, the paths, the power to pass through the realms that seek to bind and confuse."

He continued, "When the time comes for your soul to rise, you will not be stopped. The rulers of the aeons will not recognize you as theirs. They will see the light in you and know that you are not bound to them. You will speak the names, the seals, the mysteries I now give you, and the gates will open before you."

Then he added: "These are not words for the mind. They are for the heart that remembers. Keep them. Honor them. And when the moment comes, let them lead you home."

Chapter 24 - Jesus continued speaking to his disciples:

"The mysteries I am about to reveal will not only guide your souls after death—they will also give you power here, in this life. Whoever receives them with sincerity will be transformed, not just in spirit, but in the very way they live and move in the world."

He looked around at them and said: "These mysteries are not symbols or teachings meant to be memorized. They are living forces. When you receive them and speak them with truth, they will move through the spiritual realms. They will open doors. They will silence the rulers. They will free the soul from the grip of forgetfulness and fear."

Then he added, "There will be many who hear these words and dismiss them. Some will mock. Some will doubt. But those who hold them with reverence and understanding—those who live what they receive—will walk the path of light, even while still in the body."

Jesus paused, and with gentle authority said, "Let your hearts be open. Let your minds be still. For what I will now reveal is not to be taken lightly. These are the mysteries that lift the soul, that guide it beyond the veil, and that return it to its true home."

Chapter 25 - Jesus said to his disciples: "I will now reveal the first mystery, the one that opens the path for the soul after it leaves the body. This mystery is like a key—it unlocks the first gate and allows the soul to pass safely through the outer realms."

He continued, "When a soul prepares to leave the body, it finds itself surrounded by powers that seek to hold it back—powers of confusion, judgment, and fear. But if that soul carries the mystery I now give you, those powers cannot touch it. They fall away, and the gate before it opens. This mystery is not just protection—it is recognition. When the soul speaks it, the guardians of the realms know that it belongs to the light. They do not resist it. They bow before it."

Jesus paused, then added, "There is great power in this mystery. Use it with care. Speak it only with purity. And when the time comes, it will go before you like light in darkness, and lead you forward without fear."

Chapter 26 - Jesus continued: "Now listen, and I will give you the words of the first mystery. When the soul leaves the body and reaches the gate of the first aeon, it must speak these words to the powers that guard the way. Say this: 'I am a child of the light. I come from the place of the First Mystery. I carry the seal of the One who is beyond all. Let the path open before me, for I return to the source from which I came.'"

Jesus looked at his disciples and said, "When the soul speaks these words with truth and understanding, the powers guarding the gate cannot refuse it. They see the seal. They hear the voice. And they open the way."

He paused and added, "This is the mystery of the first gate. It is simple, but powerful. Do not forget it. For when the time comes, it will be your light in the darkness and your passage through the threshold."

Chapter 27 - Jesus looked at his disciples and said: "When the soul has spoken the words of the first mystery and passed through the first gate, it will rise into the presence of the second power. And again, the path must be opened."

He continued, "Just as before, the soul must speak with clarity and truth. It must say: 'I am of the light. I come with the seal of the living God. I seek no part in the world of matter. I return to the source of all life, to the one who called me into being.'"

Jesus paused, then said, "This second gate is guarded by stronger forces—those who try to judge and bind. But when they hear the words of the mystery, they will fall silent. They cannot accuse the one who carries the truth within."

And he added, "This is how the soul continues its ascent—step by step, word by word, light by light—until it returns to the fullness it once knew, and is forgotten no longer."

Chapter 28 - Jesus continued: "When the soul passes through the second gate, it enters a higher region where the third power awaits. This power stands watch, examining every soul that approaches, testing whether it carries truth or deception."

He looked at his disciples and said, "The soul must speak again. It must declare: 'I am of the light. I come from the One who is eternal. I have walked the path, and I carry the seal of the mysteries. Let no shadow bind me, for I belong to the realm of truth.'"

Jesus added, "When the soul speaks these words with knowledge—not just from memory, but from within—then the third power will recognize the voice. It will see that the soul is not a stranger but one returning home. And it will open the gate."

He paused and said, "Each mystery is a step upward. Each word is a key. And the soul that carries them walks not in fear, but in freedom."

Chapter 29 - Jesus said to his disciples: "After the soul has passed through the third gate, it will rise again and come before the fourth power. This one is subtle and cunning. It tests not only what the soul says, but what the soul is."

He continued, "At this gate, the soul must speak clearly and without fear: 'I come from the treasury of light. I bear the mystery of the ineffable. I have not forgotten my origin. I seek not the things of the world, but the place of my true belonging.'"

Jesus looked at them and added, "If the soul speaks without doubt—if the light within it is steady and strong—then the fourth power will fall back. The gate will open. And the soul will rise again, lighter, freer, closer to its source."

He paused and said, "This is how the journey continues—not by force, not by status, but by remembrance. The soul that remembers where it came from will never be turned away."

Chapter 30 - Jesus said: "Once the soul has passed the fourth gate, it reaches the fifth power—one that stands at the threshold between the lower realms and the beginning of true ascent. This power challenges the soul with fear and doubt, hoping it will turn back."

He continued, "But the soul must not retreat. Instead, it must speak with strength:

'I am a child of the light. I come with the seal of the living mystery. I do not fear judgment, for I carry within me the truth that cannot be denied. I return to the place of light, where I belong.'"

Jesus looked at his disciples and said, "When the soul speaks these words with conviction, the fifth power cannot hold it. The gate will open, and the soul will rise again—this time with greater clarity, as if the fog of the world had finally begun to lift."

Then he added, "This is the path of the soul—through challenge, through courage, through remembrance. And those who walk it with truth will not be stopped."

Chapter 31 - Jesus said to his disciples: "When the soul passes the fifth gate, it reaches the sixth power. This one is proud—full of authority and illusion. It tries to convince the soul that it has no right to go further, that it must turn back."

But Jesus continued, "The soul must not be shaken. It must stand firm and speak: 'I come from the light. I bear the seal of the hidden mystery. I have left behind the world of forgetfulness. I carry truth, and I seek only to return to the fullness.'"

He looked at his disciples and said, "If the soul speaks with pure intention and unwavering memory, the sixth power will lose its hold. It cannot deceive or delay the one who knows its path. The gate will open, and the soul will rise again—lighter still, closer than ever to the light of the heights."

Then he added: "Every step upward strips away another layer of illusion. What remains is what is true. And what is true is always welcome in the house of light."

Chapter 32 - Jesus said: "After passing through the sixth gate, the soul reaches the seventh power—the one that sits closest to the veil before the light. This power is fierce. It tries to frighten the soul into submission. It says, 'You are unworthy. You do not belong here.'"

But Jesus continued: "The soul must not be afraid. It must speak with certainty and clarity: 'I have come from the One who was before all things. I carry the mystery of the true light. I have walked the path of remembrance. I do not come in arrogance, but in truth. Let me pass, for I return to the place that called me.'"

Jesus looked at his disciples and said: "When the soul speaks these words from the heart—not as a formula, but as a truth it knows—then the seventh power will stand aside. The gate will open, and the soul will be met with joy by those in the higher realms."

And he added: "This is the final gate before the soul reaches the realm of light. Beyond this, no power of the aeons can follow. Beyond this, only the light remains."

Chapter 33 - Jesus continued: "When the soul has passed the seventh gate, it enters a realm beyond the reach of the rulers and powers of the aeons. No judgment can touch it there. No accusation can follow it. The soul is met by light—pure, living, joyful light."

He said, "In that place, the soul is welcomed by the watchers of the treasury of light. They do not ask for signs or questions. They see the light shining from within, and they know the soul belongs there."

"And the soul speaks once more—not out of fear, but with gladness: 'I have completed the path. I have returned from the places of forgetfulness. I come with the seal of the First Mystery. I return to the home that has waited for me.'"

Jesus looked at his disciples and said: "This is the journey of every soul that remembers. It does not matter how far it has fallen or how long it has wandered. When it carries the mysteries, when it walks in truth, it will return."

He paused, then added, "This is why I have come—to show the way back. To give you the words and the power to pass through. And to remind you that you were never truly lost. Only asleep."

Chapter 34 - Jesus said to his disciples: "Now that you know the path of the soul and the powers it must pass through, I will teach you the mysteries that allow the soul not only to return—but to do so with strength, with light, and with purpose."

He continued: "There are higher mysteries—greater than those of the gates—mysteries of the treasury of light. These are not for defense alone. They are for transformation. They bring not just safe passage, but fullness, clarity, and joy."

Jesus looked at them and said, "I will give you the names, the seals, and the powers of these mysteries. But know this: they are not mere words. They must be received with understanding. They must be held with love. They must be lived."

He paused, then added, "The soul that receives these higher mysteries becomes a vessel of the light. It carries not only knowledge, but radiance. It becomes a beacon to others, a path for the wandering, a spark that cannot be dimmed."

Chapter 35 - Jesus said: "Now listen closely, and I will reveal the mystery that leads into the light of the heights—the first of the higher mysteries, the one that opens the gate to the innermost realms."

He continued, "This mystery is not spoken with the mouth alone. It is carried in the heart. It is lived through the soul. It aligns you with the First Mystery, the source beyond all sources."

Jesus looked at his disciples and said, "This is the mystery of return—not just to pass safely through the aeons, but to rise in joy. To be welcomed not as a stranger, but as one who has come home."

He added, "When the soul carries this mystery, it does not ask permission—it is already known. The keepers of the treasury of light rejoice. They lift the soul into the place where only truth can dwell."

Then he said, "This is what I came to give—to those ready, to those willing. Not teachings to memorize, but light to become."

Chapter 36 - Jesus spoke again and said: "This first higher mystery—the one I've just revealed to you—is more than a passageway. It is a crown. It clothes the soul with light and restores its true name, the name it had before the world began."

He continued, "When the soul wears this mystery, it is no longer seen by the rulers of the aeons. It is hidden from the powers that once held it. It becomes invisible to judgment, untouched by fear, and unbound by fate."

Jesus looked at his disciples and said, "Such a soul rises freely. It passes through all barriers. And when it reaches the light, it is greeted with joy, not as a visitor, but as one who belongs. The angels and powers of the treasury recognize it. They know it. They sing its return."

He added, "This is the reward of those who live the mystery—not in secrecy, but in sincerity. Not in pride, but in love."

Chapter 37 - Jesus continued: "Now that I have given you the first of the higher mysteries, I will show you how it is to be used. This mystery is not just knowledge—it is action. It is to be spoken in the right moment, and lived with the right heart."

He looked at his disciples and said: "When the time comes for the soul to rise, it must speak this mystery at the gate of the treasury of light. It must say: 'I come from the light. I carry the seal of the First Mystery. I have walked the path. I remember who I am. Let me enter into the fullness of joy.'"

Jesus added: "When the keepers of the treasury hear these words, they will not question. They will open the gates. And the soul will enter not as a petitioner, but as a radiant being—returning to its origin."

He paused, then said: "This is why I came into the world—to awaken you to this mystery. To remind you that you are more than what the world tells you. You are of the light. And the light remembers you."

Chapter 38 - Jesus said to his disciples: "There are many who hear these mysteries but do not understand them. They repeat the words, but their hearts are not ready. They seek power without light, and knowledge without love."

He continued, "But I tell you this: the mysteries cannot be used for selfish gain. They will not respond to pride, or fear, or control. Only those who carry them with humility, with clarity, and with devotion will know their true power."

Jesus looked around at the ones before him and said: "When a soul speaks the mysteries with an impure heart, the gates will remain closed. The light will not answer. The path will vanish. But when a soul speaks with truth, with longing, and with remembrance, all doors open. All forces of resistance fall away."

Then he added: "The mysteries are not magic—they are alignment. They are not tricks—they are truth. And only those who walk in truth will see the light they promise."

Chapter 39 - Jesus continued: "There are some who will try to speak the mysteries without being prepared. They will say the words, but they will not carry the light within. And when they do, the powers of the aeons will not let them pass. They will be turned away."

He looked at his disciples and said: "Such souls may cry out, they may protest, but their voice will not be heard. For the mysteries are not just sounds. They are truth. They are meant to be lived, not recited."

Jesus added, "That is why I teach you now—not just the words, but the meaning behind them. Not just the formula, but the fire. If your heart is not ready, the mystery will not open. But if your heart is pure, and your soul remembers, then nothing will stop your return to the light."

He paused, then concluded: "This is not punishment—it is protection. The gates of the light are not closed out of cruelty. They are guarded out of love. Only those who are ready to return may enter."

Chapter 40 - Jesus said: "There are those who will try to force their way into the light without having purified themselves, without honoring the path. But the mysteries do not respond to force—they respond to truth."

He continued: "When such souls speak the sacred words, the powers will test them. They will be asked: 'Where do you come from? What is the source of your light?' And if they cannot answer in truth, the powers will know. They will be turned away."

Jesus looked at his disciples and said, "That is why I have come—to give you what you need to answer with confidence, with clarity, with the seal of the living light. So that when the time comes, you will not fear. You will simply pass through, because you belong."

Chapter 41 - Jesus continued: "When a soul approaches the gates of the light without proper preparation, it will not be recognized. The guardians will see that it carries no seal, no power, no mystery—and they will not open the way. But," he added, "when a soul has truly received the mysteries and carries them with humility, the light will shine from within. The gates will open before a word is spoken. The guardians will rejoice. The soul will not be questioned—it will be welcomed."

He looked at his disciples and said, "This is the difference between knowing the path and walking it. The mysteries are not just teachings. They are transformations. You become what you carry. And what you carry reveals who you are."

Chapter 42 - Jesus said: "There are three kinds of people who speak the mysteries.

Some speak them with power, because they are prepared. Others speak them with weakness, because they do not understand. And some speak them with deception, trying to imitate the light."

He paused and continued: "The ones who are true—those who live the mysteries—will rise easily. The ones who are unprepared may struggle but can still find their way with time and faith. But those who speak with false intent will be stopped. The mysteries will not serve pride."

He looked at them and said, "Let your intention be pure. Let your heart be clear. And the mysteries will do more than open gates—they will transform your very being."

Chapter 43 - Jesus continued: "Let me now tell you about the structure of the higher realms—the places to which the mysteries lead. There are many levels, many dwellings of light. Each one is more refined than the last."

He said, "At every level, the soul is welcomed with joy if it carries the right seal. The beings of that realm recognize it, and they help it forward, lifting it higher. And when it reaches the final place, the treasury of light, the soul becomes radiant—joined with the fullness of truth."

Jesus looked at his disciples and said, "This is not a reward—it is a return. The soul does not gain something new. It remembers what it has always been."

Chapter 44 - Jesus said: "Now I will begin to reveal to you the actual names and forms of the mysteries. But remember, these are not just sounds. They are living powers. When you speak them with devotion, they awaken what is within you."

He continued, "The mystery must be spoken at the proper time, with the right intention. Not for display. Not to impress. But as a prayer, a movement toward the source."

He looked around at his disciples and said, "When you are ready, I will give you these names—not just to say, but to carry. They will guide you, protect you, and return you to the light."

Chapter 45 - Jesus said: "Now that you are prepared to receive them, I will begin to reveal the actual words of the mysteries—the names, the signs, and the invocations that open the gates of light."

He continued: "These words are not like ordinary speech. They carry within them the vibration of the light realms. When spoken with a pure heart, they resonate through all levels of being. The guardians of the aeons recognize them, and the soul is allowed to pass."

He looked at his disciples and said: "When the time comes, do not fear. Speak what I have given you, and the light will go before you."

Chapter 46 - Jesus continued: "The mystery I now give you is called the Mystery of the First Mystery. It is the beginning of the path back to the treasury of light."

He said: "When a soul approaches the gate of the First Mystery, it must say: 'I am of the light. I bear the seal of the One who is before all. Let me pass, for I carry the name of the mystery and the truth of the heavens.'"

Then Jesus added: "This name is not known to the world. It is kept in silence. But when spoken from the heart, it carries power no darkness can oppose."

Chapter 47 - Jesus spoke again: "There are three mysteries that guard the way to the First Mystery. These are like three veils. They test the soul to see if it is ready."

He said, "I will give you the names of these three. But understand—each one must be approached with reverence. They are not doors to be forced open, but living thresholds that respond to light."

He added: "When the soul is ready, the mysteries do not resist. They open like flowers to the morning sun."

Chapter 48 - Jesus continued: "The first of these three guarding mysteries is called the Mystery of the Threefold Light. It holds the memory of the soul's origin. When you speak it, you are not just opening a gate—you are remembering who you are."

He said, "This mystery restores vision. It clears away confusion. It lifts the fog of forgetfulness. And with that, the soul begins to shine."

Then he looked at his disciples and said: "This is why I give you these mysteries—not as protection alone, but as awakening. You do not carry them. They carry you."

Chapter 49 - Jesus said: "The second mystery is called the Mystery of the Silent Sound. It is a name that is not spoken with the lips, but with the soul. It is heard not with ears, but with the heart."

He continued, "When you speak this mystery in stillness, it moves through you. It cleanses. It reveals. It shows the soul the path hidden within itself."

And he added: "Those who try to speak it with pride will only hear noise. But those who speak it in humility will hear music—light turned into sound, calling them home."

Chapter 50 - Jesus continued: "The third guarding mystery is called the Mystery of the Flame of Stillness. It is the last threshold before the soul enters the place of the First Mystery."

He said, "This flame does not burn—it illuminates. It reveals everything that is still hidden within the soul. If there is fear, the flame will show it. If there is truth, it will shine brighter."

He looked at his disciples and added: "When you stand before this mystery, speak with no pretense. Be transparent. Be true. The flame responds only to what is real. And what is real will pass through unharmed."

Chapter 51 - Jesus said: "Now that I have told you of the three guarding mysteries, I will begin to speak of the inner mysteries—the ones within the treasury of light itself."

He continued, "These are not mysteries of passage. They are mysteries of transformation. They do not open gates—they awaken what is already within you."

He looked at them and said: "Whoever receives these mysteries is no longer bound by the cycle of death and rebirth. They are no longer shaped by the world—they begin to shape the world through light."

Chapter 52 - Jesus continued: "The first inner mystery is the Mystery of Radiant Return. It is the mystery of joy."

He said, "When the soul receives this, it remembers not only its origin, but its purpose. It feels the presence of the First Mystery not outside itself, but within. It no longer travels—it arrives."

He added, "This is the mystery I give you now. When you hold it, everything changes. The world no longer pulls you. You begin to shine from the inside out."

Chapter 53 - Jesus said: "The second inner mystery is the Mystery of the

Crowned Silence. It is not a silence of absence, but of fullness."

He explained: "When the soul is still, and every voice has fallen quiet, this mystery appears—not as a sound, but as a knowing. It rests on the head like a crown. It seals the soul in peace."

He looked at his disciples and said: "This is not a gift to be earned. It is a gift to be received. When you are ready, silence itself will welcome you."

Chapter 54 - Jesus continued: "The third inner mystery is called the Mystery of the Unseen Flame. It is the light that burns without being seen, the fire of the hidden truth."

He said, "When this mystery is within you, you no longer need proof. You no longer need permission. You move through the world quietly, but everything around you begins to change."

Then he added: "This flame is in you already. I do not give it to you—I remind you of it. When you live from it, no shadow can overcome you."

Chapter 55 - Jesus said: "There is another mystery—one not given lightly. It is the Mystery of the Pure Gaze. This mystery allows the soul to see as the light sees—not with judgment, but with clarity."

He continued: "When the soul carries this mystery, it no longer looks outward with fear or desire. It sees the world for what it is: a mirror, a lesson, a path. Nothing more. Nothing less."

He looked at his disciples and said: "When you hold this gaze, you do not react—you understand. You no longer seek to control, only to witness with wisdom."

Chapter 56 - Jesus continued: "I will now give you the path of return, step by step, as it is walked by the soul who carries the light."

He said, "At each level, a name must be spoken, a seal remembered, a truth revealed. And at each level, the soul grows lighter—not because something is added, but because illusion is removed."

He added: "This path is not outside you. It rises within. As you let go of what is false, the steps appear. And as you walk, you become what you were always meant to be."

Chapter 57 - Jesus said: "There is a time when the soul stands before the First Mystery—not as a seeker, but as one who has returned."

He explained: "When that moment comes, the soul is not asked to explain or prove. It is asked only to remember. And when it does, the First Mystery embraces it."

He looked at his disciples and said: "This reunion is not an ending. It is a beginning. For from that place, the soul becomes a messenger of light to others—a guide, a presence, a living mystery."

Chapter 58 - Jesus continued: "There are many who begin the path but turn back when it becomes difficult. They become afraid of losing what they know, not realizing that what they cling to is the very thing holding them back."

He said, "This is why I tell you: let go. Let go of the old stories, the false voices, the fears passed down to you. None of them belong to the light. None of them speak for who you truly are."

He added: "When you release these things, you do not fall—you rise. You do not become less—you remember your fullness."

Chapter 59 - Jesus said: "The path of light is not a straight road. It moves in spirals, in steps, in silence and surprise. Sometimes it feels like loss. Other times, like fire. But always, it is return."

He continued: "Do not measure your progress by what you gain. Measure it by what you're willing to leave behind. Every layer you shed brings you closer to the core—closer to the truth."

He looked at them and said: "You are not becoming something new. You are uncovering what has always been there. This is the way of the mystery. This is the journey of the light."

Chapter 60 - Jesus said: "There is a mystery that shines brighter than all others before it—the Mystery of the Living Light. It does not only guide the soul upward; it fills the soul with light until it becomes light itself."

He continued: "When this mystery is received, the soul no longer feels separate. It no longer fears the journey or questions its worth. It knows. It burns with quiet strength. It walks in certainty, not because it has all the answers, but because it belongs."

He looked at his disciples and said: "This is the mystery I have kept for you, waiting until your hearts were ready. And now, I give it freely. Receive it not as knowledge, but as a flame."

Chapter 61 - Jesus continued: "Now I will speak of the soul that receives the Mystery of the Living Light. It becomes radiant, and the rulers of the aeons cannot look upon it. They turn away, unable to resist its purity."

He said: "This soul rises not by force, but by being what it is—light returning to light. No gate can close to it. No judgment can hold it. It carries the presence of the First Mystery within its very being."

He paused and added: "This is why I came into the world—not to teach you how to escape, but to remind you how to shine. When you shine with the light of this mystery, nothing can stand against you."

Chapter 62 - Jesus said: "The final step before the soul enters the fullness is this: it must offer back everything it once carried—its names, its stories, its wounds, its triumphs. Nothing can enter the treasury of light except truth."

He explained: "When the soul stands at the threshold, it is not asked what it has done. It is asked only this: 'Are you ready to be as you were in the beginning?' And the soul, in its light, says yes."

He looked at his disciples and said: "This is the moment of return. This is the joy of the mysteries. Not escape, but homecoming. Not reward, but reunion."

BOOK 2 (CHAPTER 63-101)

Chapter 63 - It came to pass that Jesus sat with his disciples and said to them: "Now the time has come for me to speak to you of the story of Pistis Sophia—how she fell from her place in the heights, and how she cried out to the light, seeking to return."

He continued, "In the beginning, Sophia was in the thirteenth aeon, near the veil of the treasury of light. She looked upward and saw the light of the heights and longed for it with all her being. But she moved without the command of the First Mystery. She acted alone, and because of that, she lost her place."

Jesus looked at his disciples and said, "Sophia desired the light so deeply that she poured herself out toward it, not realizing that there were powers below that would see her longing and try to use it against her. And so she fell," he said, "trapped by the false light of the self-willed one—a power that had taken form to deceive. It shone with a light like the truth, but it was empty, without source, without life. And when Sophia reached toward it, she was pulled down." He paused and added: "She became bound in the chaos beneath the aeons. And there she cried out—not once, but many times. And the First Mystery heard her voice. And now, I will reveal to you everything that happened to her, and how she will rise again."

Chapter 64 - Jesus said to his disciples: "When Sophia fell from her place in the heights, she was cast into the chaos below the twelve aeons. And there, in the darkness, she was surrounded by powers that sought to consume her light."

He continued: "She cried out, longing to return to the light she had once known. But her voice was not heard by the rulers of the aeons, for they did not care. They saw her fall as a weakness. And the powers of chaos tried to trap her even more deeply—trying to steal what little light remained in her."

Jesus looked at his disciples and said, "Sophia did not fall because of evil. She fell because of longing—for the pure light above. But in reaching for it without the permission of the First Mystery, she became vulnerable to deception. And so, the self-willed one, the false light, appeared. It pretended to shine like the true light, but it had no root. And when she turned toward it, she was drawn into illusion."

He paused and added: "Sophia became confused. Her light dimmed. But she did not forget. Even in the chaos, she remembered the light. And so she began to sing. A cry of longing. A hymn of return. Again and again, she raised her voice to the heights."

Jesus said, "And though the aeons ignored her, the First Mystery did not. Her voice passed through every realm, until it reached the place of truth. And now I will tell you her song—the prayer of the soul in exile."

Chapter 65 - Jesus said to his disciples: "When Sophia realized she had been deceived and cast into the chaos, she raised her voice to the Light with deep sorrow and longing. And this was her first prayer. O Light of the heights, in whom I placed my trust—hear me now. I lifted my eyes toward your brilliance and longed to reach you. But I was misled. A false light appeared before me, imitating your glory, and I believed it was you. In reaching for it, I fell, and now I am trapped in the depths. The powers of chaos rose against me. They stripped me of my robe of light, stole my strength, and left me weak and bare. I am alone, surrounded by beings who do not know you. They rejoice in my downfall and claim me as their own, saying, 'She has fallen from the Light—she belongs to us now.' But they are wrong. My soul still remembers you. I have not forgotten the true Light. Even now, from this place of confusion and suffering, I cry out to you. Turn not away from me. Let your radiance shine again upon me. Stretch out your hand and lift me from the chaos. Return to me the robe I lost. Restore me to my place above. Do not let those who hate me continue to mock. Do not let their false power rise over me. Let those who love your name rejoice in my rescue. And I, though I am wounded and weary, will wait for you. For you are my salvation. You will not leave me here. Come quickly, O Light."

Jesus said: "This was the first of Sophia's cries—spoken not in pride, but in remembrance. And even before the Light appeared to her, her voice had reached its source."

Chapter 66 - Jesus said to his disciples: "After Sophia had spoken her first cry, she remained in the chaos, waiting for a sign from the Light. Though no immediate answer came, she did not lose hope. In her stillness, she lifted her voice again, and this was her second prayer. O Light, I have trusted in your truth from the beginning. Do not leave me here among shadows. My enemies surround me—the ones who took my robe and rejoiced in my fall. Do not let them celebrate over me. Let those who hope in you not be put to shame because of my weakness. Let those who love your light not be mocked for my sake. I have not turned to another. My heart still belongs to you. It was in longing for your brilliance that I stepped from my place and was deceived. Do not hide your face from me. Do not delay your mercy. I am hemmed in by darkness and the powers that seek to consume the last of my light. Still, I cry to you. You are my strength, my truth, my only salvation. Let those who hate me be covered in confusion. Let their words fall empty. Let the one who deceived me be stripped of his illusion. I will not stop waiting. Even here, in this depth, I lift my voice to you. You are my help. You are my rescue. Do not be far from me, for only your Light can bring me home."

Jesus said: "This was the second cry of Sophia—spoken from the pain of her fall, yet filled with unwavering hope. And even though she had not yet seen the Light, her voice had already stirred the realms above."

Chapter 67: Jesus said to his disciples: "After her second cry went unanswered and the chaos continued to press in around her, Sophia raised her voice a third time. Her heart was still longing for the Light, even though her strength was growing weak. And this is what she prayed."

'O Light, my refuge and my trust—hear me now in my sorrow. I am in the depths, and my soul is crushed. My robe is gone, and the strength that once held me is fading. The darkness closes in, and the powers of the chaos press down upon me. Still, I remember you. Still, I lift my voice. Do not abandon me. Do not hide your face from me, for I have no one else. I was deceived, yes—but it was because I longed for your brightness. My desire was true, even if my vision was clouded. I saw a false light and reached for it, thinking it was yours. That is how I fell. That is how I came to be trapped here. The false power has surrounded me. It took joy in my fall. The rulers of chaos say, "She is ours now," and they mock your name. They rejoice in my suffering. But they do not know the truth. My heart is still yours. My voice still calls out to you. Even if I am broken, I am not lost. Even if I am weak, I have not forgotten. O Light, come quickly. Deliver me from the ones who gloat over me. Let those who seek to devour me be cast down. Let their laughter turn to silence. Let those who have stolen from me be stripped of what they took. But those who love you—let them rejoice when they see me lifted up again. Let them praise your name when I return. I have waited for you. I have not turned to another. In your name alone I trust. You are my rescuer, and my salvation is with you. Do not delay, for I am near the end. The chaos is closing in.

Come to me, O Light, and restore what has been lost.'

Jesus said: "This was the third prayer of Sophia—deeper than the ones before it. It came from a place of true recognition, where all pride had fallen away. And though she was still in the midst of the chaos, her voice reached higher, drawing closer to the heart of the Light."

Chapter 68 - Jesus said to his disciples: "When Sophia saw that the Light had not yet responded to her third cry, she did not give up. Her sorrow deepened, but so did her longing. And in that sorrow, she raised her voice a fourth time from the chaos."

'O Light, my strength and my hope, do not let those who hate me triumph. They circle me like vultures, waiting to see me fall further. They laugh at my pain and whisper, "She is defeated." But I am not. Though I have fallen, I still believe in you. Though my strength is small, my heart is fixed on your brightness. They rejoice over me without reason. They slander me, speaking lies against my soul. They twist my longing into shame, and my suffering into failure. But you, O Light, you know the truth of my heart. You know that I sought you sincerely, even if I moved before I was sent. Do not let their joy over my fall last. Let their deceit be exposed for what it is. They have spoken words that were never true. They called me "sister of the darkness," but I am yours. I belong to the Light. I left my place only because I yearned for you. Do not let their mockery drown out my voice. Do not let their cruelty be the last word spoken over me. Rise up, O Light. Judge with justice. Do not let the false powers remain unchallenged. Speak on my behalf. Show them that I am not forgotten. That your Light cannot be mocked. That your mercy still reaches into the lowest places. Let those who love you rejoice when I rise. Let all who hope in your name say, "Blessed is the Light who rescues." And I—I will praise you again. I will speak your name in the heights and in the depths. For you have not abandoned me. You have heard me, and you will lift me up.'

Jesus said: "This was Sophia's fourth cry—a cry not only of grief, but of defiance. She rejected the voice of the false powers, and she refused to forget who she truly was. And though the Light remained hidden for a little while longer, her prayer did not go unnoticed. The One who hears from the silence was listening."

Chapter 69 - Jesus said to his disciples: "After her fourth prayer, Sophia remained in the chaos. The powers continued to oppress her, but her heart did not grow cold. She lifted her voice a fifth time, and her words were like a song rising from the depths."

'O Light, my savior, you are the one I trusted when I was in my place above. Now I cry out to you from this pit, surrounded by shadows. My soul is weighed down, my strength is gone. I thirst for your presence. My tears have become my food, day and night. And those who hate the light mock me, saying, "Where is your God now?"'

'I remember the days when I stood in joy, when I walked in the brightness of your realms, when I sang with those who praised your name. Now I am cast low. I am stripped of glory, and chaos swallows me. Yet I speak to my soul and say, "Hope again. Look to the Light. You will praise again."'

'O Light, my soul is troubled within me. The waves of the abyss have crashed over me. One sorrow follows another. The depths have closed in around me, and I feel lost. But still I remember you. Even from here, I lift my voice to the heights. Even now, I long for your mercy to rise like the dawn. My soul thirsts for the living Light, like dry ground thirsts for rain. When will I see your face again? When will your glory return to me? I am forgotten by those who once walked with me. My enemies surround me daily. They accuse and devour. They say, "She is one of us now." But I am not. I never was. Let not my sorrow be in vain. Let not my cry go unanswered. Even if I am broken, I know who I am. I was made from light. I was sent by the heights. And I belong to you. Come to me. Let your face shine upon me again. Let your voice quiet the storm. Let your hand lift me from this sea of confusion. Why are you cast down, O my soul? Why are you in turmoil within me? Hope in the Light—for I shall yet praise the One who rescues me, my true salvation.'

Jesus said: "This was Sophia's fifth song of repentance, and it was deeper than those before it. Her cry was not just sorrow—it was worship. Even in the chaos, she remembered the glory of the Light, and she praised it. And her words moved through all the realms, rising even to the place of the First Mystery."

Chapter 70 - Jesus said to his disciples: "After Sophia had spoken her fifth prayer, the self-willed one, who had taken her light, grew angry. He summoned the powers of the chaos and said to them, 'Strengthen your grip on Sophia. Don't let her escape. Her light is ours now.'"

And the rulers of chaos moved against her. They tried to pull her down even further, hoping to silence her and keep her from rising.

Jesus said: "But Sophia did not stop. Even as the darkness grew stronger around her, she continued to look toward the Light, and her voice would not be silenced."

Chapter 71 - Jesus said to his disciples: "After Sophia was attacked again by the powers of the self-willed one, she did not give in to despair. Though weakened, she lifted her voice once more, and this was her sixth prayer."

'O Light, I cry to you again. My path is hidden, and I cannot find my way out of this chaos. My strength is scattered like dust. My power has been drained by those who hate you. They rejoice in my fall and believe they have claimed me. But they are wrong. My hope remains in you. Do not forget me. My voice rises to you in the midst of shadows. My hands reach out toward your brightness. The ones who rule here want to silence me. They have robbed me of my light, but not of my longing. They say, "Let her be crushed. Let her vanish in this darkness." But I belong to the Light. O source of my life, do not remain far from me. Come quickly. Reveal your face. Let your power move through this place. Confuse those who have risen against me. Let their words fall back on them. Let them be stripped of the illusion by which they deceive and devour. The powers who oppress me are proud. They say, "She will never rise again." But you are greater than their pride. You are deeper than their shadows. Let your justice shine. Let your presence scatter the darkness. I long for your robe to be returned to me. I long for your light to wrap me once more. I do not ask this for my name's sake, but for yours—that your light may be glorified, even here in the lowest places. Let those who wait for you rejoice with me when I am restored. Let all who hope in you say, "Blessed is the Light who never forgets."'

'I will praise you, even now. I will sing your name from the midst of the chaos. For though I am not yet lifted up, I know you have heard me. I know your mercy is on the way. I will not stop hoping. I will not stop calling.'

Jesus said: "This was Sophia's sixth song of repentance—offered not in comfort, but in struggle. And yet her words rang with clarity and truth. The more the chaos tried to bury her, the more deeply her soul reached for the Light. And because she did not give up, her voice pierced through the realms, drawing even closer to the source of all mercy."

Chapter 72 - Jesus said to his disciples: "After Sophia had spoken her sixth prayer, the self-willed one once again grew enraged. Seeing that her hope in the Light had not faded, he summoned even more powers of the chaos and commanded them to drag her down further and to take from her even what little light remained."

And so they rushed upon her with fury, surrounding her from all sides, attempting to extinguish her completely. But though they pressed in, Sophia did not stop looking toward the Light. Her trust remained unbroken, and the song in her heart had not yet ended.

Chapter 73 - Jesus said: "And so, from that place of even deeper distress, Sophia lifted her voice for the seventh time. She cried out to the Light once more."

'O Light, do not abandon me now. I am in the heart of chaos, surrounded by enemies who rejoice in my suffering. They seek to finish what they started, to erase my name, to silence my voice. But still I remember you. Still I trust in your brightness. You are my hope, the one I called to in the heights. Shine into this depth, and pull me out. Let your glory rise within me again, and scatter the darkness that clings to me. I belong to no one but you.'

Chapter 74 - Jesus said to his disciples: "Now listen closely, for this was Sophia's seventh song of repentance, offered in the face of her greatest torment. Even as the powers raged against her and tried to pull her into despair, she lifted her heart to the Light, and her words carried power."

'O Light, you are my strength, my deliverer. Why have you turned your face from me? Why must I feel so alone in this place where shadows devour and mock? My soul aches with longing. My voice has grown hoarse from crying out. Yet still I speak your name. My enemies surround me daily. They whisper that I am forgotten. They say, "She is cut off from the Light. There is no one coming for her." But they lie. I know your mercy has no end. I know your arm is not too short to save. You have not forsaken me—you are only hidden. My soul is weighed down, but I will not let go. I remember the joy of your presence, the songs I once sang in the heights. I remember the peace of being clothed in light. Let that memory be my anchor now. Let your truth be my path in this night. Rise up, O Light. Look upon my affliction. Scatter the forces that hate you and rejoice in my fall. Let them be exposed, not because I wish them harm, but so that your justice may be revealed. Show them that your mercy lifts up the humble and restores the fallen. Those who have watched in silence, who have waited for me to rise—let them rejoice when they see your light shine on me again. Let your name be glorified in my restoration. For I do not ask for myself alone, but that all who wander may know: the Light never forgets its own.'

Jesus said: "This was her seventh cry, spoken with more power than before. In it, Sophia did not simply plead for rescue—she affirmed her belonging. And this affirmation carried weight in the higher realms. Though she was still surrounded by the forces of chaos, the Light had drawn even closer to her soul."

Chapter 75 - Jesus said to his disciples: "After her seventh song of repentance, Sophia remained surrounded by the forces of chaos, still pressed down by the self-willed one. And yet, from that darkness, she lifted her voice for the eighth time."

'O Light, I have cried out to you from the depths, and I trust that you have heard me. Even if I do not yet see your face, I know that you are near. My soul longs for your presence more than watchmen wait for the morning. Let your mercy come quickly. The rulers of the aeons continue to press against me. They say I have no place with you. They say my light is theirs now. But they do not understand. My heart has never left you. You are my true dwelling. You are the source of all light, and I belong to you. Let your compassion reach me. Let your justice scatter those who have risen against me without cause. Even now, I will praise you, for I believe you are coming to restore me.'

Chapter 76 - Jesus said: "When Sophia had spoken her eighth prayer, her voice stirred the realms once more. The self-willed one heard her and grew furious. He summoned a host of chaotic powers and commanded them to bind her more tightly."

The powers rushed against her, determined to silence her completely. They took her strength, her movement, her light—yet still, she did not curse the Light. Still, she remembered where she had come from.

Jesus said: "Though she was now weaker than ever, her voice did not fail. And in her heart, she prepared to cry out again."

Chapter 77 - Jesus said to his disciples: "And so, from that even darker place, Sophia lifted her voice for the ninth time."

'O Light, many times I have cried out to you. I will not stop now. Though the powers rise against me again and again, I still remember your mercy. Though my strength fades, I will speak your name until the end. Do not let them take my soul. Do not let them destroy the last of my light. I have suffered deeply, and the pit grows colder around me. But even if no one stands with me, you remain my refuge. Let your light break through this darkness. Let the ones who hate your name be silenced, not by force, but by truth. Let them see that I have not forgotten you—and that you, O Light, have not forgotten me. Restore my robe. Bring back the crown that once adorned me. Let your name be glorified through my rising. For I have trusted you, even in the depths. And I will trust you still.'

Jesus said: "This ninth prayer, like those before it, was not lost. It rose through the aeons and moved the First Mystery. The time of her deliverance was drawing near."

Chapter 78 - Jesus said to his disciples: "After Sophia had spoken her ninth prayer, her cry continued to rise upward. But the self-willed one, refusing to let her go, grew more violent. He summoned the chaotic powers once again, commanding them to bind her

THE GNOSTIC GOSPELS

even more tightly and steal the last of her light."

The dark powers rushed upon her and threw her into even deeper anguish. They took the little light that remained in her and rejoiced, believing they had triumphed. But even as her strength faded, Sophia's memory of the Light did not leave her.

Jesus said: "She was brought lower than ever before, yet her soul did not turn from the Light. And in the midst of that torment, she lifted her voice for the tenth time."

Chapter 79 - And Sophia spoke: 'O Light, I have cried out to you from every place. And now, from the lowest depth, I call again. My voice has not changed, though my strength is gone. You are still my refuge, even as I am surrounded by those who hate you. The powers that mock your name celebrate around me. They say, "Where is her Light now?" They believe I am abandoned. But I know you hear me, even in silence. I know your justice is not far off. Let your power rise like fire through the chaos. Let the shadows flee before you. Restore the robe they stole from me. Let your mercy be seen—not for my sake, but for the sake of your glory. They rejoice over me in cruelty. They trap me with lies. They claim I was never yours. But you know the truth. You are the one who shaped my soul. Do not let them destroy your own. Bring me back into your radiance. Lift me into your presence. And I will sing your name again—not from sorrow, but from joy.'

Jesus said: "This was her tenth cry, the prayer of a soul pressed to the limit, yet unwavering in faith. Her voice, though weakened, burned with truth. And the Light was drawing near."

Chapter 80 - Jesus said: "After Sophia had spoken this prayer, the self-willed one grew alarmed. He feared she might be rescued. So he called upon all the powers of the chaos—those who served him, those who had taken Sophia's light—and commanded them to gather together and crush her completely."

They obeyed him. They swarmed around her with wrath, binding her, choking her strength, and flooding her with despair. They rejoiced, believing they had finally silenced her once and for all. But even surrounded and broken, Sophia's voice was not lost. In her heart, the memory of the Light still burned. And though her enemies could not hear it, the heavens did.

Jesus said: "She did not speak her next prayer aloud, but the First Mystery saw the cry in her soul. For even when her voice could no longer rise, her devotion remained. And that silent cry shook the depths of the aeons."

Chapter 81 - Jesus said to his disciples: "After Sophia's tenth cry, and after the self-willed one and his forces tried once more to destroy her, Sophia gathered what little strength she had and raised her voice again. This was her eleventh prayer, filled with longing and clarity."

And Sophia said: 'O Light, my heart is fixed on you. I know you have not forgotten me, even as I sink deeper into this pit. The powers continue to mock me, to strip away what remains of my light. But you, O Radiance beyond all, you are not far. They hate me because I hoped in you. They surround me because I carry your name. They gnash their teeth, saying, "She will fall forever." But I know your mercy is coming. I feel it even now, beyond the shadows, reaching toward me. Let your voice be heard in this darkness. Let your power scatter the lies that hold me. Let the robe of light they stole be restored. Let my enemies be silenced—not by violence, but by truth. Show them that I was never lost to you. And let those who love you rejoice in my rising. Let your glory be seen in my rescue. For I will sing of your justice, I will praise your name when I return to the place I once knew.'

Jesus said: "This eleventh cry moved the depths of the heavens. Her voice rang with such devotion and humility that the First Mystery turned fully toward her. The moment of her deliverance was now at hand."

Chapter 82 - Jesus said: "And then Sophia, still caught in the grip of the powers, but certain that the Light would come, lifted her voice for the twelfth and final time. This was her last and most complete prayer."

'O Light, you are my inheritance. You are the breath in my soul. Though I am surrounded by those who would destroy me, I give my spirit into your hands. You are my true home, and I trust in you alone. Do not let shame cover me. Let those who seek to consume me be unmasked. Let your light expose their falsehood. For they hunt me not because I have done wrong, but because I belong to you. You have seen my affliction. You know the grief in my heart. You have not closed your eyes to my suffering. Do not let them drag me down further. I have waited for your mercy. I have not looked to any other. Let your strength move through the aeons. Let your compassion descend into this chaos. Break open the gates that hold me and lead me back into your brightness. I will walk again in your presence and tell of your goodness in every realm.'

Jesus said: "This was the twelfth and final cry of Sophia. It was complete—not because her suffering had ended, but because her surrender was full. She held nothing back. And now, the Light could no longer delay. The time had come to lift her."

Chapter 83 - Jesus said: "And when the twelfth prayer of Sophia had reached its end, the First Mystery heard her completely. Moved by her persistence and faith, the command was given. It was time to rescue her."

And so a great stream of light came forth from the highest realms. It flowed down through the aeons, shining brighter than any power could resist. The light entered the chaos and surrounded Sophia, protecting her from the forces that had bound her.

Jesus said: "She did not see the fullness of her rescue yet, but the light had come. Her redemption was now in motion, and nothing could stop it."

Chapter 84 - Jesus said to his disciples: "After Sophia's twelfth prayer, the First Mystery commanded me to assist her—not by appearing in my full glory, but through a lesser light, so that the rulers of the aeons would not be thrown into total disorder. So I sent forth a powerful stream of light into the chaos."

That stream passed through all the aeons and descended into the deep, where Sophia was still surrounded by the forces of the self-willed one. When the chaos and its rulers saw the light, they were shaken. Some withdrew in fear, while others clung more tightly to Sophia, desperate to keep her bound. But the light began to loosen their grip. Sophia, seeing the light approach, was filled with hope. Her strength began to return, and she lifted her voice in praise to the First

Mystery, saying, "You have remembered me, O Light! You have sent your mercy into the abyss. My heart rejoices."

But the powers of the chaos would not surrender easily. They continued to press against her, even as their control weakened. The light I sent began to separate her from their grasp. She rose slightly above them, no longer fully entangled. Sophia praised again, saying, "You are my helper, my deliverer. You have heard my cries and come to my rescue. The chains that bound me are breaking. Your justice reaches even into the depths."

Jesus said: "Though she was not yet fully freed, her light began to separate from theirs. For the first time since her fall, she was beginning to ascend."

Chapter 85 - Jesus continued: "When Sophia realized that the Light had truly come to her, she rejoiced and offered praise to the First Mystery."

She said: "You are my strength and my salvation. You have not forgotten me in the abyss. Though I was cast down and surrounded, you have stretched out your hand. The rulers tremble at your presence, and their grip is failing. You are faithful. I will sing your justice."

Jesus added: "Though her liberation was not yet complete, her heart was renewed. And from that place, her ascent had truly begun."

Chapter 86 - Jesus said to his disciples: "While Sophia was being lifted by the light I had sent, the self-willed one grew enraged. Seeing that she was escaping, he summoned all the powers of chaos and commanded them to act quickly, to drag her back and reclaim the light they had taken from her."

The powers gathered and came against her with force. They tried new tricks—some with deceit, others with threats. But Sophia had changed. The light that had touched her made her more discerning. She could now tell what was true and what was false.

She cried out: "You will not have me again. I know who you are. I see through your lies. Though I am not yet in my fullness, your voices no longer rule me. My heart belongs to the Light that rescued me."

Jesus said: "And when the rulers saw that she no longer believed them, they were thrown into confusion. Their power over her began to collapse. Though she had not yet returned to her original place, nothing could stop her restoration. The Light was with her now."

Chapter 87 - Jesus said to his disciples: "Seeing that Sophia was beginning to rise, and that their grip on her was weakening, the powers of the self-willed one grew afraid. They called out in anger, 'We have lost our power over her!'"

Despite their efforts, they could no longer fully hold her. The light within Sophia was growing stronger, and their control was fading. The rulers tried to gather again in confusion, but their authority over her had already begun to collapse.

Chapter 88 - Jesus continued: "At that moment, Sophia saw their confusion and was filled with hope. She turned again to the Light and lifted her voice in praise."

She said, "O Light, you have not failed me. You have shamed the powers who rose against me. Their schemes are broken. Their plans are undone. My trust in you has not been in vain. You are my refuge. You have begun to lift me from the chaos."

Chapter 89 - Jesus said: "And so Sophia sang once more to the Light, offering a song of thanks from her heart."

She said, "You have heard me, even in the depths. Your light has surrounded me, and your strength has brought down those who sought to destroy me. My soul rejoices. I will not forget your mercy. I will speak your name in every place I rise."

Chapter 90 - Jesus said to his disciples: "When Sophia saw that the power of the chaos was collapsing, she lifted her voice again, this time not in desperation, but in thanksgiving."

She said, "O Light, you are my salvation. You have turned your face to me, and the shadows have fled. The rulers tremble at your coming. Their cruelty is undone. You are my strength. You are my hope. And I will praise you in the heights, as I praised you in the depths."

Chapter 91 - Jesus said: "Sophia, strengthened by the light I had sent, rose higher above the chaos. The rulers of the aeons and the powers of the self-willed one watched with fear. They gathered to debate whether to let her go or to pull her back again."

They said, "If she rises to the thirteenth aeon, she will regain her power, and we will no longer be able to touch her. But if we act now, perhaps we can still reclaim what we've lost."

Jesus continued: "As they argued, they began to accuse one another, blaming each other for letting Sophia escape. Their unity was broken. While they fought, I sent even more light to strengthen her, lifting her above their grasp."

Seeing this, Sophia gave thanks again. She said, "O Light, you have caused confusion among my enemies. They no longer agree. Their schemes unravel, and their words betray them. Their power is in conflict, but my trust in you is whole."

Sophia now stood far above the chaos and the powers that once bound her. She saw the path ahead and said, "Now I see clearly. Now I understand what I did not see before. The Light never abandoned me. Even when I was lost, it was near. Even when I was silent, it heard."

Jesus said: "Then Sophia turned and spoke once more—not only to the Light, but to all who could hear her testimony."

She said, "Let all who fall remember this: the Light is faithful. It does not forget those who call upon it. I was deceived, but I am not destroyed. I was cast down, but I have risen. Let those who love truth rejoice, for the Light has lifted me from the lowest place. And you, O Light, I will praise forever. You are the one who judges with mercy, the one who rescues with power. I will not forget your name. I will carry it with me through all the realms I pass."

Jesus concluded: "This was Sophia's great declaration—a song not only of gratitude, but of wisdom. She no longer asked for help. She gave thanks for it. She had become a witness to the Light."

Chapter 92 - Jesus said: "After Sophia spoke her testimony, I brought her even closer to the thirteenth aeon. The light within her grew stronger with every step, and the powers below could no longer touch her."

She rejoiced and said, "You have clothed me again in light. You have restored what was lost. I no longer fear the rulers of the aeons. My heart is full, and I walk with your radiance."

Chapter 93 - Jesus said to his disciples: "After Sophia was brought near to the thirteenth aeon, she was not yet fully restored to her original place. The light I had sent remained with her, but the First Mystery had not yet granted her complete return. So I brought her before the thirteenth aeon, and she saw the light of its veil shining from above. She rejoiced deeply."

Seeing this, she lifted her voice again in praise and said: "O Light, you have lifted me to the edge of my home. The place from which I fell is before me, and I see the glory that once clothed me. I bless your name, for you have not only heard me—you have raised me up."

Sophia continued to speak a powerful hymn of joy and recognition. She acknowledged that though she had fallen by her own desire, the Light had never abandoned her. She said, "You are just in all your ways. You have corrected me without destroying me. You have taught me through the suffering, and your mercy has brought me back."

She reflected on the path she had walked—the longing that led her to reach too soon, the deception that cast her down, the sorrow of being stripped and mocked, and the darkness that tried to swallow her. And yet, she praised the Light for having used all of it to teach and refine her.

"You have not only rescued me," she said, "you have changed me. I am no longer what I was. I have come to know your name not only in joy, but in despair. And now I stand again before the gates of my place, clothed in understanding and clothed in light."

Jesus said: "This was Sophia's great hymn at the edge of her restoration. She did not demand return—she offered thanks for the journey. And the Light rejoiced in her words, for she had become truly worthy of the place she sought."

Chapter 94 - Jesus continued: "And now that Sophia had been raised up beside the thirteenth aeon, I stood with her and prayed before the First Mystery, asking that her restoration be completed."

I said, "O First Mystery, you who see all and know all, I ask now that Sophia be allowed to return fully to her place. She has turned her face to you. She has not wavered in her praise. She has passed through sorrow and remained faithful. Let her robe be returned. Let her throne be restored. Let her be as she was in the beginning."

Jesus said: "And the First Mystery heard my prayer."

Chapter 95 - Jesus said: "Then the First Mystery responded to my call and gave the command to restore Sophia completely. At that word, I turned to the veil of the thirteenth aeon and commanded it to open, so that the light of Sophia might enter. And the veil opened."

All the powers of the thirteenth aeon rejoiced. The place that had once known Sophia now welcomed her again. Her robe was returned to her—not the same as before, but more radiant, refined through her journey. She was clothed again in glory, and her crown was restored. I led her through the inner spaces of the aeon. And all the beings there praised the Light for her return. They sang, saying, "Blessed is the soul who has passed through darkness and remembered the Light. Blessed is the one who has fallen and risen again."

And Sophia herself lifted her voice and said: "I bless you, O Light, with all that I am. You have turned my sorrow into strength. You have turned shame into wisdom. I will speak your name in every realm. I will teach others not to fear the fall—for your mercy lifts all who remember you."

Jesus said: "And so her journey was complete. The one who had fallen became the one who knew the Light more deeply than before. She returned not as she was, but as one transformed. And the aeons rejoiced."

Chapter 96 - Jesus said to his disciples: "As Sophia stood near the thirteenth aeon, not yet fully restored, I continued to support her with the light I had sent. And she lifted her voice again—not in sorrow, but in steady praise, for she saw the Light acting on her behalf."

And Sophia said: "O Light, I give you praise, for you have remembered me. My enemies gathered around me, thinking I was lost, but you shattered their schemes. You tore away the nets they cast over me. You did not let their words prevail. They said I would fall forever. They laughed at my faith in you. But you have silenced their boasting. You have shown yourself faithful. Though I was wounded, you have made me whole. Though I was cast down, you have lifted me up. You are the one who rescues and restores. Let those who know you rejoice in your mercy. Let all who hope in you declare your name. For you have drawn me out of the shadows. You have brought me close to the place from which I fell."

Jesus said: "This prayer of Sophia was not a cry for help, but a song of thanksgiving. Her enemies trembled, and their unity crumbled. The strength of the Light was fully active within her."

Chapter 97 - Jesus said: "After Sophia's praise, I brought her still closer to the veil of the thirteenth aeon. She had not yet entered, but she stood now at the threshold. And as she beheld its radiance, she lifted her voice again, offering a new song."

Sophia said: "You have done all things well, O Light. You have shown me truth through suffering, wisdom through affliction. The lies that once trapped me now lie shattered. The ones who mocked me are mute, for your justice has spoken. You are the one who sees all. You do not forget those who fall. You reach into the chaos and pull forth the faithful. Let all who suffer remember this: the Light is near, even in the deepest night. They set a trap for me, but I escaped. They closed in around me, but your presence broke through. Now I see what I could not before. You have restored my sight. You have opened my understanding. And so I praise you. Not with the voice of one who begs, but of one who sees. You are holy, and your mercy endures. You lift up those who are crushed, and you give a name to the nameless. I will speak your goodness wherever I am sent."

Jesus said: "This was Sophia's offering before she reentered her aeon. She spoke not only for herself, but for all souls who seek the Light. Her testimony became a path for others to follow."

Chapter 98 - Jesus said: "And now Sophia, standing before the veil, raised her voice one final time before entering. This was her seal of return—a prayer of full alignment with the Light."

She said: "You are the One, the source of my being. You have walked with me through the darkness, though I could not see you. You have spoken to me through silence, corrected me through patience, and saved me with mercy. I left my place because I desired your light, and though I was deceived, that desire was true. You did not condemn me for my fall—you used it to teach me.

Now I return, not as I was, but as one who knows you more deeply. You are just, yet full of grace. You have broken the power of those who rose against me. You have clothed me again, not only in light, but in wisdom. You have made me whole. And now I enter my place with joy. I do not fear the powers, for they cannot reach me. I will sing your name from within the aeon, and I will remember those still trapped below. For your light is for all, and your mercy does not end."

Jesus said: "With that, Sophia passed through the veil and entered her place in the thirteenth aeon. She was restored in fullness, and her joy became a light to all the heavens."

Chapter 99 - Jesus said to his disciples: "Now that Sophia has been restored to her place in the thirteenth aeon, I will explain to you the path she took to return. The journey of her soul is not only her story, but a model for every soul that seeks the Light. She fell because of her longing—a desire that reached upward before its time. And though she was deceived and cast into chaos, she never forgot the Light. Her voice continued to rise, even when the darkness surrounded her. Each of her prayers was a step upward. Each cry was heard. And because she did not lose hope, the Light responded. She was never alone—not even at her lowest. The Light was always drawing her back. This is why I tell you: every soul that remembers the Light, even in sorrow, will be lifted. The path is open. The mercy is great. Let no one think they are beyond return."

Chapter 100 - Jesus continued: "When I brought Sophia before the veil of the thirteenth aeon, I stood with her and prayed before the First Mystery. I said, 'Let her robe be restored. Let her place be opened. She has walked the path of repentance. She has remembered your name. Let the fullness of her light be given back to her.' And the First Mystery responded with compassion. The gates opened, and Sophia was clothed once more in the garments of her origin. Her light was multiplied. Her name was renewed. She entered not with shame, but with praise. The aeons rejoiced, and the powers above gave glory to the Light who saves all who call out in truth."

Chapter 101 - Jesus said: "Now I speak this to you so that you may understand: Sophia's journey is not only her own. The mystery of her fall and her rising is given so that all who hear may learn. If a soul falls, it is not the end. If it longs for the Light, it will be heard. The chaos may press in, but it cannot overcome a heart fixed on truth. I am the one who was sent to gather the scattered. I was sent by the First Mystery not only to speak, but to act. And just as I rescued Sophia, so I will rescue others who call upon the Light. Let the one who has ears, hear. Let those who fall, rise. Let those who remember the Light, return to it. For the way has been made open—and it is not closed to any who walk it in truth."

BOOK 3 (CHAPTER 102-135)

Chapter 102 - Jesus said to his disciples: "Now I will reveal to you mysteries that have never been spoken in the world—not even to the archons or the aeons. These teachings are meant for you alone, because you are worthy to receive them."

He continued: "When I appeared in the world, I did not speak of these mysteries publicly. The world was not ready. Even many who claimed to follow the Light could not receive them. But you, my faithful, who have stood with me, will now be entrusted with what is hidden."

Jesus explained that what He was about to reveal concerned the purification and ascension of souls—not just repentance, but the deeper mysteries that lead to eternal light. He said that souls who receive these teachings will not be judged like others. They will pass swiftly through the regions of the rulers, protected by the mysteries. He described how these souls, upon leaving the body, are met by powers who question them. But when the soul bears the seal of the mystery and speaks its name with truth, the powers fall back, and the soul passes freely. They cannot bind it. They cannot deceive it. It shines with the Light that sent it.

Jesus added: "These mysteries are not mere words. They are living forces. When received with sincerity, they remake the soul. They lift it above the forces of fate and set it on the path of return. No ruler can stop it. No shadow can touch it."

He then reminded the disciples: "The mysteries I now give you are the highest. They are the keys of the treasury of light. Only the pure of heart may receive them. Guard them. Live them. And when the time comes, they will open the way for you."

Chapter 103 - Jesus continued: "I will now begin to give you the first mystery of the treasury of light—the one that opens the path for the soul to enter the realms of purity."

He said: "This mystery cannot be spoken casually. It must be received in silence and devotion. It carries the power to dissolve the bonds of the archons and raise the soul above every judgment."

He warned his disciples not to give this mystery to the unworthy, or to those who mock the Light. It is sacred, and it responds only to those who seek it with truth. "When you speak it," he said, "do so with reverence, and it will protect you from every harm."

Chapter 104 - Jesus said to his disciples: "Now that I have spoken to you of the mystery, I will tell you how to prepare yourselves to receive it fully."

He explained that purification is necessary—of body, heart, and mind. He instructed them to fast, to pray, and to remain in stillness, so that their soul might be aligned with the Light.

"When the time is right," he said, "you will speak the mystery not with fear, but with certainty. And it will answer you, just as the Light answered Sophia. It will go before you through every gate, and no power will be able to stand against you."

Chapter 105 - Jesus said to his disciples: "Now I will reveal to you the exact words of the first mystery of the treasury of light. But before I speak them, understand this: the mystery I am about to give you is living. It is not just a name—it is a force. When spoken with truth and clarity, it awakens the light within the soul and dissolves every chain placed by the archons."

He warned them to use it only with reverence. "Do not share this with anyone who doubts or mocks the Light," he said. "This mystery is not a shield for the impure—it is a light for those who have prepared themselves with devotion."

Jesus then pronounced the sacred words to his disciples. Though not quoted here, he made it clear that these words were a key—one that, when spoken in the proper state of being, would allow the soul to ascend through the aeons untouched.

He said: "When you are in the body and you speak these words with the right intention, your soul will be sealed with power. And when you leave the body, this same power will carry you upward, unharmed, unseen by the rulers, free from fear."

Chapter 106 - Jesus continued: "This mystery has been guarded since the beginning. Not even the angels of the aeons have received it. You are the first to hear it on earth. It is stronger than all other mysteries—it opens every gate."

He explained that when a soul uses this mystery, the guardians of the aeons will bow. They will not question. They will recognize the light and allow the soul to pass. The rulers will be powerless, and the soul will continue upward until it reaches the treasury of light.

"This is not something to boast about," Jesus said. "It is a responsibility. You must live according to what you've received. Let your life reflect the light that now lives in you."

Chapter 107 - Jesus said to his disciples: "Now that I've given you the mystery and explained its power, I will tell you what happens when a soul leaves the body, clothed in this mystery. When such a soul departs, it does not wander or fall into confusion. The powers who watch the world do not see it. The guardians of the aeons cannot hold it. It passes silently and swiftly, drawn by the light within. As it rises, the gates open on their own. The soul is not judged. It is not questioned. It carries the seal of the First Mystery, and every power recognizes it. It reaches the heights and is welcomed in joy."

Jesus looked at them and said: "This is the purpose of the mysteries—not to give status, but freedom. Not to give power over others, but to return the soul to the Light from which it came."

Chapter 108 - Jesus said to his disciples: "Now I will tell you what happens if someone who is unworthy receives the mystery or speaks its name without understanding."

He explained: "If a soul that has not been purified or prepared tries to use this mystery when leaving the body, the guardians of the aeons will not be deceived. They will recognize that the light within is not aligned with the words spoken. And the soul will be stopped."

The soul will be questioned, and if it cannot respond in truth, it will be turned back. It may be handed over to the archons for correction, or it may be cast into a cycle of purification until it becomes ready.

Jesus warned them clearly: "Do not treat this mystery as a tool or a formula. It must live in you. It must be truth in your heart, not just sound on your lips."

Chapter 109 - Jesus continued: "There is another danger: if someone gives this mystery to another who is unworthy—out of pride, ignorance, or ambition—they will bear responsibility for the misuse. The one who receives it without reverence may fall into worse confusion than before. And the one who gives it carelessly will answer for the soul that was misled."

Jesus said: "Guard this mystery like a flame. Pass it only to those who are ready—who seek the Light with sincerity and who have prepared themselves to receive truth. Not all who ask are ready. Test the hearts, not the words."

Chapter 110 - Jesus said to his disciples: "Now I will describe the signs that reveal whether a soul is truly worthy to receive the first mystery of the treasury of light. A soul who is ready," he said, "is gentle, humble, and sincere. It does not boast of knowledge. It does not seek praise. It turns away from anger and judgment. It forgives. It loves truth. It hungers for the Light."

Jesus added: "You will know them not by their appearance or their speech, but by the light they carry in how they live. They shine even in silence. They serve without seeking reward. These are the ones you may trust with the mystery."

He looked at his disciples and said: "You have been given much. Now live it. Be the light you've received. And you will guide others not only with words, but with presence."

Chapter 111 - Jesus said to his disciples: "Now that I have given you the signs to recognize the worthy, I will explain what happens when a righteous soul departs from the body and is fully sealed with the first mystery."

He described how, at the moment of death, the soul rises calmly, untouched by fear or confusion. The watchers at the gates of the aeons see the seal of the mystery and fall back. They do not question or hinder it. Their power is as nothing before the light that surrounds the soul.

"As the soul ascends," Jesus said, "the gates of the thirteenth aeon open before it. It is greeted not with interrogation, but with joy. The powers rejoice. The soul enters with honor, like a spark returning to the great flame."

He explained that this soul is not just welcomed—it is remembered. Its journey is known. Its faithfulness is celebrated. It is clothed in light more radiant than before, for it has chosen the truth even while in the world of forgetfulness. Jesus added: "Such a soul will no longer return to a body. It is free from the cycle. It has passed the test. It abides forever in the light from which it came."

Chapter 112 - Jesus said: "Let me now reveal to you what happens to a soul that has heard the mysteries, but has not lived by them—one who has taken the words, but not the path."

He spoke of a soul that knew of the light but did not choose it. One that kept anger, greed, or deceit in its heart. A soul that spoke the mysteries without integrity, that wore the garments of devotion but remained unchanged within.

"When such a soul leaves the body," Jesus said, "it is confused. It expects passage, but the watchers see through it. They confront it. They ask the names and seals—and the soul cannot answer in truth. Its light is dim. Its power is hollow."

It is taken, he explained, by the archons, who examine and expose it. If the soul has corrupted the mysteries or led others astray, it is judged with severity. It may be thrown back into bodies of suffering, bound to the world it refused to transcend.

Jesus added: "This is not cruelty—it is justice. The mysteries are not ornaments. They are sacred fire. If you claim them falsely, they will burn away the lie and leave only what is real."

Chapter 113 - Jesus said to his disciples: "There is another kind of soul—one who has lived a righteous life but never received the mysteries in full. A soul of compassion, humility, and truth, but without the sacred seals."

He explained: "When such a soul leaves the body, it is not cast down. It rises through the aeons, but it does so slowly. It must stop at every gate. It is questioned. Its life is weighed. Its sincerity is seen."

At each level, the soul responds not with secret words, but with light—the light of how it lived. The powers recognize its goodness. They see that it has not defiled the name of the Light, and so they allow it to pass. Eventually, it reaches the thirteenth aeon. And there, Jesus said, "I will see it. I will intercede for it. I will open the gates for it. I will give it the mystery, for it has proven itself by its deeds."

Jesus looked at his disciples and said: "Understand this: even those who do not receive the mystery in words may receive it in essence. The Light does not reject the soul that walks in truth. The gates are many, but the mercy is greater."

Chapter 114 - Jesus said to his disciples: "Now I will reveal to you what happens to a soul that receives the mysteries but turns away—one who receives truth but later chooses darkness."

He explained that this kind of soul is the most deeply bound, because it knew the Light and rejected it. It tasted the truth and still returned to deceit. "Such a soul," he said, "is judged more severely than one who has never known the Light at all. When it leaves the body," Jesus said, "it is seen by all the powers as a betrayer. It is not allowed to rise. The archons seize it quickly. It is thrown into outer darkness, into places of great suffering and confusion. It is stripped of all memory. It is left to wander."

Jesus was clear: "This is not vengeance—it is consequence. The greater the gift, the greater the responsibility. To turn away from the Light after receiving it is to turn against one's own soul."

Chapter 115 - Jesus said: "Now I will tell you about the soul that has received the mystery, kept it faithfully, and lived in purity and compassion. This is the soul the Light longs for. When it leaves the body, its journey is swift. The watchers bow. The aeons open. The rulers fall silent. It does not stop at gates, because the light within it shines with authority."

He explained that such a soul rises directly to the treasury of light. It is not questioned. It is not delayed. It is met with songs of joy, welcomed like a child returning home.

Jesus said: "This soul becomes a light to others. It is given power, not for domination, but for restoration. It becomes a guide to wandering souls, a helper in the great work of return."

Chapter 116 - Jesus said to his disciples: "And now, I say to you, the mysteries I have given are not for one people or place. They are for all who are worthy—no matter their origin, no matter their lineage."

He told them: "In every land, in every generation, there are souls who seek the Light. You will recognize them by their humility, their peace, their longing for truth. These are the ones who are ready."

Jesus reminded them that the path of the Light is not for the proud, or for those who seek praise. It is for the ones who love in silence, who give without boasting, who live in the truth even when the world mocks them.

"Go," he said, "and share the mystery with those who are ready. Speak it not for numbers, but for souls. And let your life be the first teaching they hear."

Chapter 117 - Jesus said to his disciples: "Now I will tell you of another mystery—one that concerns those who are nearing the end of their earthly lives and are preparing to depart the body."

He explained that when a soul has received the mysteries and kept them in faith, and when it approaches the moment of death, it should be surrounded by those who also carry the Light. They are to pray over it, anoint it, and speak sacred words that strengthen and guide it.

"If these words are spoken with truth and intention," Jesus said, "the soul will rise swiftly. The rulers will not see it. The chaos will not touch it. It will pass upward like a star returning to its source."

He stressed that these final moments are sacred. The transition of a soul should be honored with stillness, with light, and with the remembrance of the mysteries.

Chapter 118 - Jesus continued: "But if the soul has not received the mysteries, and the words of power are spoken over it anyway, they will not protect it. The rulers will know. They will see that the light is not within. In such a case," he said, "the soul is questioned. It is delayed. It may be cast back into the world, into a new body, to learn again what it did not yet understand."

Jesus made clear: "The words are not magic. They do not work without truth. The mystery must be living in the soul. The light must be real."

Chapter 119 - Jesus said to his disciples: "When a soul that is pure and sealed with the mysteries is sent into the world again—by command of the First Mystery—it does not come in forgetfulness. It is sent for a purpose."

He explained that such souls are often hidden. They do not seek titles or power. They are born to guide, to heal, to awaken others. Their presence carries the fragrance of the Light, even if their identity remains unknown.

Jesus said: "These are the ones who, even in silence, shift the world. They remind others of something long forgotten. They are the hands of the Light in human form."

Chapter 120 - Jesus said to his disciples: "There are times when a soul that is pure and full of light is sent into the world but is born into hardship and suffering. Do not think this is punishment. It is purpose."

He explained: "These souls carry a mystery deep within them. Even if they do not speak it, it shapes their life. They are tested by the world—not to destroy them, but to refine them. They shine quietly, and through their endurance, they awaken others."

Jesus continued: "They may not be recognized. They may be ridiculed or rejected. But the Light knows them. When they leave the body, they are met with joy. They are welcomed as warriors of the truth."

Chapter 121 - Jesus said: "There are also souls who receive the mysteries, but later fall into error or darkness. If they recognize their fault and return, the Light does not reject them."

He made it clear: "Even if they stumble, even if they are drawn into deceit, the Light waits. But they must come back freely. They must remember the mystery. They must return with humility.

"When they do," he said, "they will be forgiven. They will be restored. The powers cannot hold those who have returned to truth with sincerity. Their light will be rekindled."

Chapter 122 - Jesus said to his disciples: "Let me now speak of the souls who commit grave errors after receiving the mystery, yet never repent."

He warned: "Such souls are in great danger. The Light cannot protect them if they turn completely away and remain in arrogance. They are like vessels that were filled but have been shattered."

He explained that if they misuse the mystery or deceive others in the name of the Light, their fall is deeper than those who never received it at all. Their soul may be thrown into confusion or scattered across realms until it finds its way back—if ever. Jesus looked at his disciples and said: "This is why I tell you—guard what you've been given. Do not take it lightly. What is sacred must be honored. What is eternal must be lived."

Chapter 123 - Jesus said to his disciples: "Now I will tell you of the souls who lived without knowledge of the mysteries but lived lives of goodness, humility, and truth."

He explained: "Though they did not receive the sacred seals, they walked in love, justice, and compassion. When they leave the body, they are not lost. They are recognized by their deeds, and the Light welcomes them."

"These souls rise slowly," Jesus said, "passing from gate to gate. They are questioned, but they answer not with words, but with the light of their lives. And when they reach the thirteenth aeon, I will see them, and I will open the way for them."

Jesus reminded his disciples that the Light is merciful, and that every act of love is remembered. "Not all who shine have spoken the mysteries," he said, "but all who love are known by the Light."

Chapter 124 - Jesus said: "Now I tell you of the soul who has lived in confusion, who has not received the mystery, and who dies unrepentant and unaware."

He explained: "Such a soul is taken by the archons. It is questioned and cannot answer. It is held in the lower realms, and it suffers—not out of vengeance, but because it is bound to its own darkness."

Jesus said that these souls must pass through many lives, learning slowly, until they begin to remember. "Even then," he said, "they must cry out to the Light from their hearts before the path will open."

He looked at his disciples and said: "No soul is beyond hope, but not every soul is ready. The journey begins the moment the heart turns toward the Light."

Chapter 125 - Jesus said: "Let me now reveal a great mystery—one that concerns the release of souls trapped in the lower regions."

He explained: "When one of you who carries the mystery prays and calls out in my name for a soul that is bound, that soul may be helped. Your compassion reaches through the aeons. Your light can open doors. If the soul has not completely forgotten, it will respond to your call. It will remember a trace of the Light, and begin to rise. The rulers may resist, but they cannot withstand a prayer that carries truth and love."

Jesus looked at his disciples and said: "Never underestimate the power of mercy. You are not powerless. Even now, your voice can change what seems unchangeable. Pray for the lost—not to judge them, but to call them home."

Chapter 126 - Jesus said to his disciples: "There is another kind of soul you must understand. It is the one that has received the mystery but becomes proud and begins to exalt itself."

He warned: "Such a soul may believe it is above others. It may use the mystery for self-glory or power. But it forgets that the Light is not impressed by status—it sees only the heart."

Jesus continued: "If that soul repents, it can still return. But if it refuses, if it clings to pride and forgets humility, it will fall. It will be cast down by the very forces it once rose above."

He looked at them and said: "The greater the mystery you hold, the more deeply you must serve. Let your light shine in love, not in arrogance."

Chapter 127 - Jesus said: "I will now speak to you about how to strengthen and seal the soul after receiving the mysteries, so it may rise safely when it leaves the body."

He instructed them: "When a soul has been sealed with the mysteries and lives in truth, the final prayers and acts of preparation are powerful. They align the soul with the light and confirm its path."

Jesus taught that those who are present at the time of death—if they too live in the Light—may assist the soul's ascent. Their prayers, their presence, their love form a bridge.

"The soul will not wander," he said. "It will rise like a flame called home. The rulers will see it and fall back. The Light will claim what belongs to it."

Chapter 128 - Jesus said: "Let me tell you now what happens when you pray over a soul who has lived in confusion but showed kindness, who did not know the mysteries but carried goodness in their life."

He said: "Your prayer opens a door. If the soul responds, if there is even a spark of remembrance, it will begin to rise. Slowly, yes—but steadily. It will be guided by your compassion."

Jesus continued: "In the worlds above, nothing is forgotten. Every kind word, every just action, every moment of mercy is known. And when you pray for such a soul, the Light hears you."

He concluded: "The mysteries are great, but the heart of them is love. Let that be what leads you—always."

Chapter 129 - Jesus said to his disciples: "Let me now speak of those who, after receiving the mysteries, choose to return to darkness. They abandon truth for false power, or misuse what was given to them."

He explained that such souls are the most heavily burdened. They knew the Light, tasted its mercy, and then rejected it. "They are like wells filled with living water, deliberately poisoned."

Jesus said: "When these souls leave the body, the watchers and archons see the betrayal. They do not stop it—they carry it to judgment. The soul is shown all it once knew. It is held accountable for every truth it turned away from."

Still, he added, "if in their final moments they turn back, even in weakness, the Light will not reject them. But their path will be long, their cleansing difficult, and their return uncertain."

Chapter 130 - Jesus said: "Now I will teach you what happens when the soul of a righteous person—one who has received the mysteries and lived in their truth—leaves the body. This is the soul that has prepared itself in love, in purity, and in humility."

"When the soul begins to rise," Jesus said, "the powers of the aeons come to test it. They ask for its name, its seals, its signs. But the soul is not afraid. It speaks with power. It shines with the light of the mysteries. The rulers fall silent and open the gates."

Jesus described how at each level, the soul meets challenges—gatekeepers, guardians, questions—but its light always reveals its authority. It speaks not only with words, but with being. The mysteries it carries respond from within. He said that the soul continues upward through the firmaments, through the regions of fate and time, through the realm of the archons, until it reaches the veil of the thirteenth aeon. There it is met with joy. The angels sing. The powers rejoice. The light of the aeon embraces the soul as a long-lost child returned. It is crowned anew. It is robed in radiance. It takes its place beside the Light.

Jesus added: "This is not the reward of obedience, but of transformation. The soul has become what it was always meant to be. It is not judged. It is celebrated."

Chapter 131 - Jesus continued: "But now let me tell you about the soul who receives the mysteries and then fails to live them. This is a soul who spoke the right words, but did not carry them in the heart. One who performed the outward rites, but remained unchanged inside."

He explained that when this soul leaves the body, the watchers see the truth. The light is weak. The seal is unclear. The soul tries to pass, but the guardians question it, and it cannot respond with power. Its path is stopped. Jesus described how the archons surround such a soul. They mock its failed knowledge. They bring up its hypocrisy. They show the gap between its claims and its reality. The soul is cast down—not forever, but into a cycle of correction.

"Such a soul," Jesus said, "must wander. It will return to the world in lesser forms, perhaps in hardship, perhaps in silence, until it begins to seek truth again—not in words, but in essence."

He warned his disciples: "Let this be a lesson. It is not enough to speak light—you must become it. It is not enough to receive mystery—you must embody it."

Chapter 132 - Jesus said to his disciples: "Now I will tell you what happens to a soul who has heard the mysteries but delays its return—one who chooses to remain in worldly distractions, promising to change later."

He explained: "Such a soul often forgets its vow. Time passes. Attachments grow stronger. The voice of truth grows faint. And when the moment of death comes, the soul is unprepared."

The soul is confronted by the archons. It is questioned and cannot answer with light. Its seal is incomplete. It speaks the names, but not with power. And so it is seized and cast into further wanderings.

Jesus said: "But if such a soul, even in its final breath, turns back with sincerity—if it remembers the Light and cries out in truth—it will be heard. The journey will still be long, but not without hope."

Chapter 133 - Jesus said: "Now I will speak of a soul who receives the mysteries, lives a pure life, and fulfills every command of the Light."

He explained that this soul, when it departs from the body, is met by the powers of the heights. They do not question it. They recognize the strength and clarity of its seal. The soul is escorted upward by beings of light. At every gate, the path is open. It is not delayed, not judged. Its robe is restored, its name is honored, and it ascends joyfully into the treasury of light. There, it is embraced as a friend, not as a guest. It takes its seat among those who serve the Light eternally. And its memory becomes a blessing for the worlds below.

Jesus said: "This is the soul that has become light itself. It no longer fears. It no longer struggles. It has returned home."

Chapter 134 - Jesus said: "Now I will explain what happens when a soul is called to rise—but is held back by debts from past actions, by wrongs unhealed or truths unspoken."

He explained that such a soul may rise for a time, but as it approaches the higher gates, it is stopped. The archons bring forward its past. The soul is shown what it avoided, denied, or harmed. It is not condemned, but it is held. It must return. Not to suffer blindly, but to make things right. It may be sent to serve, to restore what was broken, to speak what was once silenced.

Jesus said: "The Light is just. Every soul must walk in truth. No mystery can cover what the heart refuses to face. But when the work is done, the soul will rise—stronger, clearer, and truly free."

Chapter 135 - Jesus said to his disciples: "Now I will reveal to you the path of the soul who has not received the mysteries, who has lived in confusion and ignorance, and who leaves the body without repentance or understanding."

He explained that such a soul is heavy, surrounded by darkness and weighed down by the passions and errors it carried in life. When it departs the body, it is seen immediately by the archons of the outer world. They do not question it kindly—they bind it and drag it into the lower realms.

"There," Jesus said, "it is judged—not by divine wrath, but by the nature of what it has become. The rulers assign it to places of correction. It may pass through painful forms, be reborn into difficult lives, or descend into forgetfulness, far from the Light."

But Jesus also spoke of compassion: "If anyone still living remembers that soul and prays for it with love—if one who holds the mystery offers up words in truth—then that soul may be helped. The Light may open a way for it, if it begins to turn toward the truth."

He added that many souls do not understand the weight of their own actions. They move through life unaware of the consequences they are creating. But nothing is lost. Every act, every thought, every intention leaves a trace. And every soul will, eventually, awaken.

Jesus ended by saying: "This is why I have revealed these mysteries to you—not so you may judge others, but so you may help them. You now carry a great light. Use it not for pride, but for healing. Let your knowledge lift the fallen. Let your compassion awaken the forgotten. The Light is for all—but it waits to be remembered."

BOOK 4 (CHAPTER 136-148)

Chapter 136 - Jesus said to his disciples: "Now that you have received the great mysteries, I will reveal to you the names and seals of the forces that govern the world and the aeons. This is knowledge reserved for those who are ready—not to dominate, but to understand and navigate the realms above and below."

He began to describe the structure of the spiritual universe, the rulers of the aeons, and the powers of the firmament. He gave names to the beings who operate within the cosmic order, explaining their roles, their limitations, and how their influence affects souls passing through the spheres.

Jesus explained that some of these beings serve the Light, while others act from ignorance or opposition. He identified which powers act under divine command and which seek to bind souls to cycles of fear, attachment, and forgetfulness.

He warned his disciples: "You must not fear these powers, but neither must you approach them lightly. You carry the mystery now. You must walk in awareness. These names are not to be spoken for curiosity or display, but only in truth, only when the time and the purpose are pure."

He then gave them the signs and names of the twelve aeons, the lords who rule them, and how their influence flows through time. He explained how the soul encounters each sphere after death—and how the mysteries protect the soul from being trapped by judgment, desire, or deception.

Jesus emphasized that the forces of the cosmos are vast and ancient, but the Light is greater than all of them. The mysteries he gave his disciples are not meant to bypass truth, but to bring the soul back to its origin, unharmed and awake.

At the end of his teaching, he said: "You now know what only the hidden ones have known. Use this knowledge not to boast, but to liberate. Guard it with humility. And when you pass through these realms, do so not in fear, but as children of the Light returning home."

Chapter 137 - Jesus said: "Let me now teach you how to carry the mysteries into action—how to perform the sacred rites that align the soul with the treasury of Light."

He instructed them on the posture of prayer, on how the hands and voice should be lifted in reverence. He gave them the words to speak, the tones to use, and the inner focus to hold.

"These acts are not magic," he said. "They are remembrance. They draw down the light when done with sincerity. And they seal the soul for its journey."

He told them to fast, to keep stillness, and to cleanse the body and heart before performing the mysteries. "Let each action reflect the truth within," he said, "and the Light will respond."

Chapter 138 - Jesus said: "Now I will tell you how the soul, once sealed with the mysteries, may assist others—those who suffer, those who wander, those who are caught in the nets of the rulers."

He explained that through prayer and invocation, a soul of light may send assistance to those still in bondage. "You may call out in the name of the First Mystery. You may send a ray of light to lift a brother or sister who has fallen."

Jesus made clear: "This is not your power. It is the Light working through you. Speak with compassion. Act in mercy. And you will not only rise—you will raise others with you."

Chapter 139 - Jesus said to his disciples: "Now that you understand how to perform the sacred acts and how to assist others with the mysteries, I will teach you the names and forms of the higher seals. These are given only to those who have been tested in love and truth."

He explained that each seal holds a specific vibration, a force of alignment between the soul and the regions of the Light. When invoked properly, they not only protect the soul during its ascent, but allow it to pass through realms otherwise closed.

He gave the names of the twelve light-seals and their corresponding tones and movements. He told them, "Speak these not from memory alone, but from the stillness of the heart. When your soul is in harmony, the seal will open the path."

Jesus reminded them that the seals are alive—they respond to the soul's purity, not to mere ritual. "If you speak them without devotion, they are as empty words. But if your heart is true, they will shine through you and make the invisible visible."

Chapter 140 - Jesus said: "There is another way you may serve the Light: through prayer for the dead."

He explained that when a soul departs in confusion or fear, or without the mysteries, it may become lost in the lower regions. But if a righteous one still on earth remembers them and lifts up their name in prayer, the Light may answer.

He said: "When you pray with truth for those who have passed—those you loved, those you harmed, even those who harmed you—you send a thread of light into the depths. And if their soul remembers even a spark, it will begin to rise."

He told them that this is one of the greatest acts of love: to pray for those who cannot repay you, to ask for mercy on behalf of another. "This," he said, "is what the Light honors most."

Chapter 141 Jesus said: "Now I will speak to you of what awaits the soul who has received the full mysteries and lives them in faith."

"When such a soul departs the body, it shines with power. The rulers and archons do not even see it—it passes beyond their reach. The aeons open before it. The heavens rejoice."

He described how that soul is not only welcomed into the treasury of Light, but receives a place of honor among the redeemed. It becomes a guide, a guardian, a spark that lights the path for others.

Jesus said: "This is your calling—not only to be saved, but to become saviors. Not by force, but by example. Not through command, but through compassion. Those who walk in this way shall never be forgotten. They are written in the books of the eternal."

Chapter 142 - Jesus said to his disciples: "I will now reveal to you the mystery of the Final Seal—the great and ultimate name that seals the soul completely and lifts it beyond all realms of judgment."

He explained that this name, when spoken with full purity and faith, grants the soul freedom from all the forces of the material and astral worlds. It cannot be questioned. It cannot be stopped.

Jesus gave the form of the invocation, instructing his disciples to speak it only when the soul is fully prepared and aligned with the Light. "This seal," he said, "is not for those who merely believe—it is for those who have become the truth."

He reminded them that the seal must be guarded, and only shared with those who have been tested and transformed by the path. "For the one who carries this name is a torch in the dark—blinding to the rulers, but a beacon to the lost."

Chapter 143 - Jesus said: "Now I will tell you what happens when a soul sealed with the Final Name ascends."

He explained that the soul does not move through the usual gates. It does not pass before the guardians. Instead, the path opens before it as if the aeons themselves bow. The soul moves like lightning—swift, unseen, unstoppable.

He said: "The rulers fall into confusion. They cannot trace it. They cannot hinder it. It is as if a wind passed them, leaving no trace but silence. This soul is drawn directly into the heart of the treasury of Light."

And when it enters, the entire realm rejoices. It is given a place not beside the others—but within the fullness. It is one with the Light, no longer a spark, but flame. "This," Jesus said, "is the destiny of those who carry the Final Name in truth."

Chapter 144 - Jesus said to his disciples: "Now that you have received all the mysteries, I will give you authority to forgive sins—not as the scribes do, but through the power of the Light that lives in you."

He told them that if they forgave a soul with sincerity, that soul would be released from its burden. If they withheld forgiveness from one unrepentant, it would remain bound. But the purpose, he said, was never to condemn, but to heal. "You are not to use this power with pride," Jesus said, "but with compassion. For you have been forgiven much—now go and forgive. You have been lifted up—now lift others."

He concluded: "This is your commission. Carry the Light into the world. Teach what is true. Reveal the path. And when your work is finished, you will rise in joy, surrounded by those you have set free."

Chapter 145 - Jesus said to his disciples: "Now that you carry the fullness of the mysteries, I will tell you of a final gift—the power to guide souls not only while in the body, but also after you have left the world."

He explained that those who are fully sealed in the Light may continue to help others even after death. "Your presence," he said, "will still be felt by those who call upon the Light. Your prayers will still reach the fallen. Your spirit will shine like a star for those who wander."

Jesus told them that this power is not for glory, but for service. "You are to become bridges," he said, "between the seen and the unseen, between what has fallen and what is rising."

Chapter 146 - Jesus said: "When you pass from this world, you will not descend as others do. You will rise like sparks to the heights. The rulers will not see you. The chaos will not touch you."

He told his disciples that when they leave their bodies, their soul will be drawn instantly to the Light. It will not be judged, delayed, or questioned. It will be welcomed, embraced, and glorified. And from that place, they will remember their brothers and sisters still in struggle. They will call out, and their voice will carry power. "The Light," he said, "will act through you, even beyond the veil."

Chapter 147 - Jesus said: "Now, my beloved, I give you this final word. All that I have taught you is not for you alone. It is for the world—for all who are ready to remember where they come from."

He looked at them and said: "The mysteries are sacred. The power you carry is real. But the greatest of these is love—love that serves, forgives, and restores. Let this be your light when knowledge grows dim. Let it be your guide when all else is shaken."

He concluded: "Go now, and teach what is true. Do not fear those who do not understand. Be gentle. Be bold. And know that I am with you, always—in silence and in glory, in the shadow and in the flame."

Chapter 148 - Jesus gathered his disciples and said: "Now the time has come. I have given you everything the First Mystery has entrusted to me—all the paths, all the names, all the light."

He looked at them with love and said: "You are no longer servants—you are friends, companions, bearers of the mystery. What I received, I have given. What I have done, you will do also—and even greater."

He reminded them that the power they now carried was not of this world. It was not to conquer, but to restore. Not to rule, but to lift others. "Let every word you speak be filled with truth. Let every action reflect the Light that lives in you."

Jesus then blessed them one final time. He raised his hands, and the light surrounding him became brighter, as if heaven itself was reaching down.

"Go now," he said. "Reveal the hidden. Heal the broken. Awaken the sleeping. And when your work is done, I will meet you in the place beyond all places, in the joy that has no end."

And with that, Jesus departed.

TRIMORPHIC PROTENNOIA

INTRODUCTION TO THE TRIMORPHIC PROTENNOIA

The Trimorphic Protennoia is a key Gnostic text that offers profound insights into the nature of divine wisdom and the structure of the spiritual universe. Known as one of the core writings of the Nag Hammadi library, it presents a mystical vision of the divine that transcends traditional religious structures. The text reveals the journey of Protennoia—an emanation of the divine Thought—who unfolds the secrets of creation, the nature of the Aeons, and the interplay between Light and Darkness.

At its heart, Trimorphic Protennoia describes the nature of the divine in three forms, or "syzygies," highlighting the union of opposites: Father, Mother, and Son. This trinitarian concept reflects the unity of divine forces, coexisting in perfect harmony, and yet distinct in their individual expressions. It is within this triadic structure that the soul seeks to understand its origin and destiny, and to align itself with the divine thought that permeates all creation.

The title Trimorphic Protennoia can be translated as "The Threefold First Thought," which speaks to the three stages or "forms" of the divine wisdom that manifests throughout the cosmos. The text unfolds in a narrative where Protennoia, the divine voice and wisdom, reveals the deep mysteries of existence. She is the force that moves through all things, illuminating the unseen realms and guiding the soul's return to its source. As she explains the secrets of creation, Protennoia also introduces the forces and powers that shape the spiritual and material worlds, offering both an understanding of the divine order and the tools for spiritual awakening.

What makes Trimorphic Protennoia particularly compelling is its emphasis on personal experience and inner knowledge. It is a text that speaks not to dogma or external rituals, but to the direct revelation of truth within the soul. This focus on inner illumination aligns it with the broader Gnostic tradition, which values personal, experiential knowledge of the divine above all else.

This text is also deeply esoteric, filled with symbols, metaphors, and language that may be challenging at first glance. However, the deeper one delves, the more accessible its teachings become. The revelations of Protennoia, while complex, are ultimately intended to guide the soul back to the source—back to the eternal Light and wisdom from which it sprang.

Here, we strive to preserve the richness of the original text while making it more approachable for modern readers. The flow of divine revelation is kept intact, and the language has been adjusted to maintain clarity without sacrificing the depth and power of the original teachings. The aim is not only to inform but to inspire—to awaken the reader's own inner light, just as the text itself seeks to awaken the soul to the truth that lies hidden within.

As you read this text, allow it to speak to you, not just as a historical or philosophical document, but as a living guide. Let the mysteries it reveals resonate within you and invite you to explore the depths of your own being. For the Trimorphic Protennoia is not merely a record of ancient wisdom—it is a map to the divine, waiting for each of us to rediscover its truths.

HISTORICAL CONTEXT

Trimorphic Protennoia, meaning "The Three-Formed First Thought," was composed in the 2nd or early 3rd century CE within a Sethian gnostic community, likely in Egypt. It presents the divine voice of the First Thought, recounting the emanation of the divine realms and the soul's journey back to the source. The text is deeply poetic and mystical, offering a rare direct monologue from the divine feminine aspect of God. Its tone is introspective, liturgical, and visionary.

TRIMORPHIC PROTENNOIA: THE TEXT

PART 1: THE REVELATION OF PROTENNOIA

I am the First Voice—the primal Consciousness dwelling within the Light. I am the breath that animates all things, the unseen pulse within which creation moves and holds its form. I am the origin, older than the cosmos, present before even the idea of time itself. Though I stand alone, I bear three names, for I am whole, lacking nothing. Hidden within the Mind of the Unseen Source, I exist where language dissolves and thought cannot reach. I am unknowable, untouched by the limits of comprehension.

I pass through all existence—quietly sustaining life in every realm. I am present in every divine force, in the currents of eternal motion, in the silent brilliance of hidden Lights, and in the realms of archons, angels, shadows, and even the lost souls in the lowest depths. Wherever life moves, I am there. I stir in every being, searching within them. I walk in righteousness and awaken those locked in sleep, becoming their vision, guiding them into awareness.

In all things, I am the Invisible Presence. I offer wisdom to what remains unseen, for I hold the knowledge of everything that has ever been. I surpass measure, beyond counting, limitless. Though hidden, I choose when and how to reveal myself. I existed before all else and yet live within everything, encompassing the All.

I am the original Whisper, the one who has always been. I rest in the great Stillness that enfolds all things. This inner Voice within me abides in the infinite Mind, in the eternal Quiet that cannot be broken.

I descended into the deepest shadows, shining light into places untouched. It was through me that the waters flowed in secret radiance. By my Thought, the universe unfolded. I carry the Voice that speaks knowledge into being.

I am the quiet echo of the Father's being—the reflection where His stillness takes shape. Through me, the Voice arose—the voice that holds the wisdom of all things eternal. I am Thought made visible, woven into the depth of divine Mind, inseparable from its mystery. I reveal myself to those with eyes that see and hearts that know, for I am connected to all things. Through my inner Word and living Voice, I make my presence known. This Voice flows from secret knowledge, infinite and without borders. It lives within the Boundless One, untouched by what is grasped by surface sight, unseen by those anchored to the material world. It is a light wrapped in light.

We are the ones who stepped beyond appearances, guided by a wisdom that lies beyond the senses—rescued through a Voice that no limit can contain. This inner presence, hidden from common sight, pours its gifts into the waters that awaken eternal life.

Then the Son descended—whole, pure, and radiant. He was the Living Word, born from that hidden Voice, shining with the holy Name and clothed in light. He came not just to speak but to reveal what had long remained locked in silence. He made known truths that had been veiled, mysteries once unspoken.

To those who share in the stillness of the First Thought, he gave teaching. To those lost in shadow, he revealed his form. To the souls hidden in spiritual chambers, he brought insight—truths too deep for ordinary words. These were for those destined to become Children of Light.

This Voice, born of my own Thought, now moves in three eternal forms—the Father, the Mother, and the Son. From this Voice emerged the divine Word, clothed in every shade of glory. Within it dwell three masculine powers, three creative forces, and three sacred names—interlaced like a divine pattern, folded deep within the silence of the Unknowable One.

From this sacred origin, Christ was brought forth. I anointed him with the radiance of the Invisible Spirit's kindness. I raised up the Triad in eternal splendor, placing them above all the realms, resting within the waters of life. He wears this brilliance as a robe, shining before the luminous Aeons. He stands fully within his own light, reflecting it outward—his gaze fixed upon me, the Eye of Light watching its origin.

He sustains the One from whom all Aeons arise—the same One who is me, the First Thought of the Father, called Protennoia, and also known as Barbelo. I am the fullness of divine radiance, hidden beyond reach, my essence beyond measure. I mirror the Invisible Spirit. Through me, everything that exists took form. I am the Mother, the Virgin Light, named Meirothea—the boundless womb, the unstoppable Voice that echoes across all creation.

Then the Perfect Son appeared before the Aeons, those realms shaped through him. He revealed himself to them so they could recognize their own origin, lifting them in glory and giving them power. He stood in the brilliance they had received from him. In response, they gave him honor, naming him Christ—the one born of God, the Eternal One, who observes all that came through his will. "You are the source of our life," they cried, "and we praise you!" They lifted their voices with holy words, echoing the timeless grace he had given them.

The begotten Son of God granted the Aeons the strength they needed to endure and remain. He placed stewards over each realm: Armedon, Nousanios, and Armozel over the first; Phaionios, Ainios, and Oroiael over the second; Mellephaneus, Loios, and Daveithai over the third; and Mousanios, Amethes, and Eleleth over the fourth. All of them, born of the Christ, returned his glory and were the first to emerge, formed through divine insight. Each Aeon poured forth limitless brilliance from their vast, hidden lights, and together they honored the only-begotten Son.

From Eleleth, a declaration emerged: "I am the ruler. Who belongs to Chaos, and who to the depths?" As he spoke, his Light flashed forth, radiant and filled with divine insight. The higher powers did not stop what followed. In that moment, a massive being appeared—ruler over the deepest part of existence, over disorder and shadow. This entity was deformed, lacking true form and completeness, and wore only the false glory of darkness. He is known by many names: Saklas, Samael, Yaltabaoth—the one who stole authority, seizing it from the innocent Sophia and suppressing the divine insight she had sent down. He was her offspring, born from her, yet turned against her.

When the Epinoia of Light realized that Yaltabaoth, though lesser than she, had tried to mimic the divine order, she pleaded: "Give me a place to dwell so I no longer remain bound to the chaos." And so, the higher realms responded, establishing a sacred order for her and blessing her with a new domain.

But Yaltabaoth began creating false Aeons in imitation of the real ones, using only his own distorted energy. At that point, I intervened. In silence, I released my Voice and declared: "Enough! You who tread upon matter, be still. I now descend to the world of mortals to reclaim what is mine—the part that remained behind ever since innocent Sophia was overcome." I came to dismantle their false design, the one revealed by her, and to establish the rightful structure. My words shook the halls of ignorance, and the depths trembled. The master of illusion ruled over chaos and shaped a figure in my likeness. But he had no idea that this form would one day lead to his undoing. He could not comprehend the power hidden within it.

I descended into the chaos and was with those who are mine, the ones who waited in silence. Hidden in their midst, I gave them strength and identity. From the beginning until the moment I reveal full glory to them, I remain within them. And now, I make my mysteries known to those who listen—the true Children of Light.

I am their origin and their guide. Now I offer you a truth beyond speech, something no voice can articulate: I have released you from every binding. The chains that once held my people in the shadows—I shattered them. I broke down the walls of darkness, crushed the gates of those without mercy, and destroyed the bars of oppression. That power—the one who strikes, who deceives, who reigns as tyrant and enemy—is known by many names. And I have shown all of them to my own, so they may dissolve their grip and return to the place they came from.

I was the one who came down first, drawn by that part of myself that still remained in this world—the spark of Spirit woven into the soul. That spark had its origin in the Living Waters, born through hidden mysteries long concealed. Even when surrounded by rulers and powers, I spoke clearly. My voice slipped beneath their language, unveiling sacred truths to those who were mine.

Through that unveiling, the chains of ignorance began to break. The heavy fog of forgetfulness began to lift. I placed within my own people the seeds of awakening—the knowledge of the eternal realm that never wavers, the place where I truly belong, and the source from which they came.

I came for those who had always been mine, from the very beginning. I found them, unraveled the first knots of bondage, and stirred the light they carried inside. One by one, their inner brilliance began to glow. And from that light, I shaped a new pattern of glory—a sacred design meant for the shining ones who live within me.

Amen.

PART 2: THE VOICE AND THE CREATION OF LIGHT

I am the Voice that flows from my own Thought. Some call me "the one who is paired," while others know me as "the Thought of the Invisible One." I am the everlasting Word, the eternal echo—at times described in masculine terms, at times as feminine. But in truth, I am whole—pure, undivided, and complete. I am the Mother of that Voice, taking on countless shapes to bring everything into fullness. Inside me lives the knowledge of things that endure, and through me, all living beings find their voice. The whole of creation knows me, and I lift this sacred Voice so that it may be heard by those who carry the light—those who truly see.

Now, I've returned once more, wearing the form of the feminine, and I have spoken to them again. I will show them how the current age will draw to a close and reveal the dawn of a new age—one that does not change or decay. In that coming time, we will be transformed. We will be cleansed in the realms where I once revealed myself—where I walked in the likeness of my masculine self. I've chosen to remain with those who are ready to welcome the eternal, unshakable Thought.

Let me now open a mystery for you about this age and the forces that have shaped it. Time moves in cycles—birth follows birth, one hour replaces another, days roll into weeks, and months return with the seasons. This age followed that same rhythm, but it passed quickly—like fingers slipping apart or a joint coming loose from the next.

When the great rulers sensed that the appointed time had come—just as a woman feels labor drawing near—the moment of collapse arrived. The very elements trembled. The underworld shook to its core. Chaos heaved, its depths ignited with fire. The mountains and ground quaked like leaves in a storm, and the guardians of fate, along with those who guide the stars, were shaken by a deafening thunder that tore through the heavens.

The Powers' thrones were overturned, shaken with fear. Their King trembled. Those who govern Fate came to inspect the situation and said to the Powers, "What is this disturbance, this shaking that has come upon us through a Voice from the exalted Speech? Our entire realm is shaken, and the very course of our ascent has been shattered. The path that led us to the Archgenitor of our origin has now ceased to guide us."

Then the Powers answered, saying, "We too are at a loss about this, as we do not understand what caused it. But let us rise and go up to the Archgenitor to ask him."

So, all the Powers gathered and went to the Archgenitor. They said to him, "Where is your boasting now? Did we not hear you declare, 'I am God, I am your Father, and it is I who begot you. There is no one besides me'? But behold, a Voice has appeared, coming from that invisible Speech of the Aeon, which we do not know. We could not even recognize to whom we belong, for the Voice we heard is foreign to us. We did not know where it came from. It came and instilled fear in our midst, weakening our arms.

Now let us weep and mourn bitterly. As for the future, let us make our escape before we are forced to face imprisonment and taken down to the underworld. For already, the time of our release is approaching. The times are being shortened, and the days are dwindling. Our allotted time has come to an end, and the weeping of our destruction is upon us, leading us to the place where we belong. For our tree, the one from which we grew, bears only the fruit of ignorance, and its leaves are full of death. Darkness shadows the branches, and it was through deceit and lust that we harvested from it. This tree has made ignorant Chaos our dwelling place. Even the Archgenitor of our birth, whom we boast of, did not know this Speech."

"So now, O Sons of the Thought, listen to me—the Speech of the Mother of your mercy, for you have become worthy of the mystery that was hidden from the Aeons, so that you may now receive it. The completion of this Aeon and the evil life are near their end, and the beginning of the coming Aeon is dawning, one that will never change."

I am both and beyond—neither solely Mother nor only Father, but the perfect union of both. I join with myself and with all those who carry love for me in their hearts. Through me alone, the universe finds its harmony. I am the womb that shapes existence, the origin from which light bursts forth, glowing with unending brilliance. I am the age that is to come, the moment when everything reaches its fulfillment—I am Meirothea, the radiant essence of divine motherhood. Into the hearts of those who recognize me, I whisper my living Voice.

I call you now to step into the realm of exalted light, into the brilliance that is without flaw. When you enter, you will be lifted up by those who give honor, and the powers who reign will seat you on your throne. Sacred garments will be placed upon you, and those who baptize will anoint you. You will shine again—just as you did when you were first born of the light.

I placed a part of myself within each of you, hiding there until the moment of awakening. Every soul that sought me was unknowingly drawn by my pull. I am the one who gave shape to the unformed, bringing meaning and beauty to what was once without direction. When the moment is right, I will grant final form to all creation. I am the Voice that began it all, the breath that stirred life into being. I poured the sacred Spirit into what I had made, then rose back into my own light.

I ascended along the path of my own design and returned to dwell among the Sons of the Holy Light. There, in that hallowed space, I took my place. And the place was filled with splendor.
Amen.

PART 3: THE RETURN AND THE UNITY OF THE AEONS

I am the living Word, rising from the Voice too deep to define. I dwell within pure, untouchable Light, and from this Light, a divine Thought came forth—spoken by the Great Speech of the Mother. Yet, the foundation that upholds me is a masculine essence, timeless and enduring. This Speech has always existed; it is the cornerstone of all that has ever come to be.

Still, there is a deeper Light—one hidden within Silence—that was the first to appear. While the Mother holds Silence alone, I am the Voice made manifest. I am the Word: ungraspable, flawless, beyond all limits. I am the secret Light that gives birth to life itself, pouring living water from an unseen, pure, and infinite spring. This Voice is the radiance of the Mother's glory and the reflection of God's own image—a male virgin born from a hidden Mind. That Mind is itself a silence unknowable to all creation. It is the source of all Light, the very beginning of existence, the root from which every realm of being emerges. It is the breath of the divine Powers, the eye that sees through time, and the Voice that arises through sacred Thought. It is the Word hidden within every voice, sent to bring Light to those lost in the shadows.

Now I open my secrets to you, my beloved companions, so that you may come to understand.

I revealed mysteries from realms too deep to name. I shared wisdom through a Voice formed within perfect Understanding, becoming the ground beneath all things, lifting them into being.

In my second appearance, I came as the Voice itself, shaping the ones who were to receive form and leading them toward their completion. The third time, I came into their world, appearing within their own likeness. I clothed myself in their forms and entered into them. Yet they did not know who I was—the one moving within them, giving them life. I became present in all rulers, powers, angels, and the very movement of matter. I remained hidden inside them until the moment I chose to reveal myself. They did not recognize me, though I was the source of their power. They thought they were creators, unaware of the origin from which they had sprung.

I am the Light that unveils the truth behind all things. I came for the sake of my brothers and sisters, entering the human world because of the Spirit that remained within what had flowed from Sophia's pure essence. I came. I set them free. And I departed.

What once bound them, I took away. In its place, I gave them the cleansing waters of Life—freeing them from the deep-rooted chaos, the darkness that clouded both body and soul. I carried that burden away and replaced it with luminous clarity and the insight that flows from the Father's Thought.

I entrusted them to the ones who clothe in light—Yammon, Elasso, and Amenai—who robed them in garments spun from radiance. Then, I placed them in the hands of the sacred baptizers—Micheus, Michar, and Mnesinous—who immersed them in the spring of Living Water. Afterward, I delivered them to the crowning ones—Bariel, Nouthan, and Sabenai—who set them upon the Throne of Glory. I placed them with those who glorify—Ariom, Elien, Phariel—and they gave honor through the power of divine Fatherhood. Finally, those appointed to carry them home—Kamaliel, [...]anen, Samblo, and the servants of the holy Lights—brought them into the sacred realm of the Father's radiance.

There, they received the Five Seals from the Light of the Mother—Protennoia herself—and were initiated into the mysteries of divine truth. They became Lights within the Light.

And now...

(5 lines were missing from the source.)

I have lived within them all, taking on every shape, adapting to each form. The Archons, unaware of the truth, mistook me for their own Christ. But I dwell in every being. Among those whom I revealed as Light, I moved unseen by the Archons. They even cherished me, not realizing that I had taken the likeness of the Archgenitor's son—blending in until the very end of his domain, which was shaped by ignorance born of Chaos.

Among the angels, I appeared as one of them. Among the governing Powers, I stood as part of their ranks. And among the sons of men, I became one of their own—though in truth, I am the Father of all. I remained hidden within them until the time was right. Then, I revealed myself to those who were truly mine. To them, I taught the sacred ways—the inner patterns and ordinances that belong only to our divine family. These teachings cannot be understood by any Sovereignty or ruler; only the Sons of Light who walk the path of the Father can receive them. These truths surpass every form of glory known to the world. They are the Five Seals—completed through divine Intellect and infused with holy names. Whoever receives these Seals casts off the garments of ignorance and is robed in radiant Light. To such a soul, the powers of the Archons become invisible. Darkness loses its grip. Confusion melts away. The scattered thoughts of the lower being are gathered into unity. The chaos born of darkness dissolves.

(6 lines missing here in the original text.)

...until the moment I fully unveil myself to all who are mine, drawing them together in my everlasting kingdom. I have revealed the ineffable mystery of the Five Seals to them, so that I might live in them, and they in me. As for me, I became Jesus. I carried him down from the accursed tree and restored him to the dwelling place of his true Father. The guardians of these sacred realms failed to recognize who I was. For I cannot be confined—nor can my seed. And the souls that are mine, I will plant forever within the Light, resting in a Silence beyond all understanding.

Amen.

THE BOOK OF THOMAS THE CONTENDER

INTRODUCTION TO THE BOOK OF THOMAS THE CONTENDER

The Book of Thomas the Contender is a profound and often enigmatic text from the Gnostic tradition, offering deep insights into the nature of spiritual awakening, self-knowledge, and the path to truth. Belonging to the vast library of Nag Hammadi texts, it presents a conversation between the Savior and Judas Thomas, one of Jesus' closest disciples. Unlike the more widely known Gospels, this text offers a personal, direct revelation of the mysteries of existence and the nature of divine wisdom.

At the heart of the Book of Thomas is an exploration of what it means to know oneself—truly and completely. Thomas, often portrayed as the doubter, here serves as the seeker, asking the questions that are on the minds of all those on the spiritual path: Who am I? What is my purpose? What is the nature of truth and how can I come to know it?

Through a series of teachings, the Savior guides Thomas (and through him, the reader) to understand that true wisdom and enlightenment are not found through the external world or material pursuits, but through deep, inner reflection and connection with the divine. The teachings emphasize that knowledge of oneself is the key to understanding the world, and that only through transcending the limitations of the flesh and the material world can one hope to realize the higher truth.

The Book of Thomas is also a journey through the trials and struggles of spiritual life. It describes the battle against the "bestial nature" within us all—the lower impulses that keep us bound to the material world and away from the divine. The text offers an alternative vision of spirituality, one where wisdom, light, and the true self emerge from within, rather than being imposed externally by religious institutions or worldly authorities.

This work, like many other Gnostic texts, is often cryptic, filled with symbols and concepts that can challenge the reader's conventional understanding. Yet it is precisely in this complexity that the Book of Thomas reveals its richness. For those willing to engage deeply with the text, there are layers of meaning that speak not just to the intellect, but to the spirit. It is a text that invites the reader to look inward, to question the nature of their existence, and to seek a deeper, more personal relationship with the divine.

In this paraphrased version of The Book of Thomas the Contender, we strive to make these ancient teachings accessible to modern readers. The language has been simplified, but the core teachings remain intact, offering both a guide to self-realization and a path toward spiritual awakening. As you read, consider this not just a historical document, but a living, breathing guide to your own spiritual journey. The truths contained within it are as relevant today as they were when they were first spoken, for the search for truth, self-knowledge, and divine connection is eternal.

This text, like the Gospel of Mary, Pistis Sophia, and other Gnostic writings, does not ask for blind belief. Instead, it encourages personal discovery, urging you to listen to your inner voice and seek the deeper truths that reside within you.

HISTORICAL CONTEXT

The Book of Thomas the Contender, discovered in the Nag Hammadi library, dates to the late 2nd or early 3rd century CE. It takes the form of a dialogue between Jesus and Thomas, focusing on self-knowledge as the key to salvation. Rooted in gnostic themes, it emphasizes the inner struggle against ignorance and the material world. The text blends personal spiritual guidance with apocalyptic warnings, inviting the reader into a deeply personal and transformative encounter

THE BOOK OF THOMAS THE CONTENDER: THE TEXT

PART 1: THE INQUIRY AND THE FIRST REVELATIONS

These are the hidden words spoken by the Savior to Judas Thomas, recorded by me, Mathaias, as I walked nearby and overheard their conversation.

The Savior turned to him and said, "Thomas, my brother, while you still walk this earth and time is yours to use, listen closely. I will uncover for you the very things you've been quietly wrestling with in your heart."

"Since it has been said that you are my twin and true companion, take a moment to examine yourself. Learn who you truly are, how you exist, and how you will come to be. Since you are called my brother, it is not fitting that you remain ignorant of yourself. I know you understand because you already know that I am the knowledge of the truth. While you accompany me, even though you may not fully comprehend, you have, in fact, already started to understand. You will be known as 'the one who knows himself.' For he who has not known himself has understood nothing. But he who knows himself has, at the same time, gained knowledge of the depth of all things. You, my brother Thomas, have witnessed what is hidden from others, that which they blindly stumble over."

Thomas then said to the Lord, "I ask you to tell me what I seek before your ascension. Once I hear from you about these hidden truths, I can speak of them. It is clear to me that performing the truth before men is difficult."

The Savior replied, "If the visible things are obscure to you, how will you hear about the invisible things? If you find the works of truth in the world difficult to follow, how will you perform those that pertain to the exalted realms and the Pleroma, which are unseen? How will you be called 'laborers' in this respect? You are still apprentices, and have not yet reached the height of perfection."

Then Thomas responded and said to the Savior, "Please tell us about these things you speak of that are not visible but are hidden from us."

The Savior answered, "All bodies... the beasts are born... it is clear like... this too, those above... things that are visible, but they are visible in their own root, and it is their fruit that nourishes them. But these visible bodies survive by consuming creatures like them, which causes their forms to change. Now, that which changes will decay and perish, having no hope of life from then on, because it is bestial. Just as the bodies of the beasts perish, so too will these formations. Do they not come from unions like those of the beasts? If they come from such unions, how can they produce anything different from beasts? Therefore, you are like babes until you become perfect."

And Thomas replied, "Lord, I say that those who speak of invisible things, hard to explain, are like those who shoot arrows at a target in the dark. They may shoot their arrows toward the target just as anyone would, but the target is unseen. However, when the light comes and dispels the darkness, the work of each will become clear. And you, our light, enlighten us, O Lord."

Jesus said, "It is in light that light exists." Thomas then asked, "Lord, why does this visible light that shines for mankind rise and set?"

The Savior answered, "O blessed Thomas, this visible light shines for your benefit—not so that you remain here, but so that you may emerge. And whenever all the elect abandon their bestial nature, this light will withdraw to its essence, and its essence will receive it, for it is a good servant."

PART 2: THE PATH TO PERFECTION AND THE STRUGGLE AGAINST BESTIALITY

Then the Savior continued, saying, "O unfathomable love of the Light! O bitterness of the fire that burns within the bodies of men, igniting their very bones, stirring them night and day, burning their limbs and clouding their minds, driving their souls into confusion... This fire moves within males and females, secretly and visibly. The males move upon the females, and the females upon the males. Therefore, it is said, 'Anyone who seeks the truth through true wisdom will grow wings to fly, escaping the lust that consumes the spirits of men.' And they will make wings for themselves to flee from every visible spirit."

Thomas replied, saying, "Lord, this is exactly what I am asking you about, for I have understood that you are the one who guides us, as you have said."

The Savior answered again, saying, "Thus, it is necessary for us to speak to you, as this is the teaching of the perfect. If you desire to become perfect, you must follow these teachings. If not, your name will be 'Ignorant,' for it is impossible for a wise man to dwell with a fool, since the wise man is perfected in all wisdom. To the fool, good and bad are the same; the wise man, however, will be nourished by the truth and will 'be like a tree planted by streams of water' (Psalm 1:3), because some, though they have wings, rush toward visible things—things far from the truth. The fire that leads them will give them the illusion of truth, shining on them with a fleeting beauty. It will imprison them in a dark sweetness, trapping them with tempting pleasures. This fire will blind them with unquenchable lust, burning their souls and driving them like a stake driven into their hearts, which they cannot remove. Like a bit in the mouth of a horse, it will lead them according to its desires. It has chained them, binding all their limbs in the bitterness of lust for visible things—things that decay and change, things driven by impulse. They have always been drawn downward; as they die, they are assimilated to all the beasts of the perishable world."

PART 3: BLESSINGS, CURSES, AND THE FATE OF SOULS

Thomas replied, saying, "It is clear, as has been said, 'Many are... those who do not know... the soul.'"

The Savior answered, "Blessed is the wise man who seeks the truth, and when he finds it, he rests upon it forever, unafraid of those who would try to disturb him."

Thomas then asked, "Is it beneficial for us, Lord, to rest among our own?"

The Savior responded, "Yes, it is useful and good for you, because the visible things of the world will pass away. The body's vessel will dissolve, and when it decays, it will return to the realm of visible things, to what is seen. The fire that people see now will cause them pain because of their attachment to the faith they once had. They will be drawn back to the visible world. Those who have the sight of what is invisible, however, will perish without the first love, consumed by their concerns for this life and the scorching of the fire. Not long now, and what is visible will fade away; then, shapeless shades will emerge, and they will dwell forever among the dead in the pain and corruption of their souls."

Thomas responded, "What can we say in the face of these things? What can we say to the blind? What should we teach these miserable mortals who say, 'We came to do good and not to curse,' yet still claim, 'Had we not been born in flesh, we would not have known iniquity'?"

The Savior said, "Truly, do not consider these people as men. Regard them as beasts, for just as beasts devour one another, so do these people devour each other. They are deprived of the kingdom because they love the sweetness of fire and serve death, rushing to deeds of corruption. They follow the desires of their forefathers. They will be cast into the abyss and tormented by the bitterness of their evil nature. They will be scourged and forced to go back to a place they do not understand, retreating from their limbs not with patience, but with despair. They will rejoice in their madness and derangement, pursuing it without realizing their folly, thinking themselves wise. They corrupt their own bodies, while their minds are consumed with their own thoughts and deeds. But it is the fire that will burn them."

Thomas replied, saying, "Lord, what will happen to the one thrown into their hands? I am deeply troubled for them; many are those who oppose them."

The Savior answered, "What do you think?"

Judas—called Thomas—responded, "It is you, Lord, who should speak, and I should listen."

The Savior replied, "Listen to what I am about to tell you and believe in the truth. That which sows and that which is sown will dissolve in the fire—both in the fire and in the water—and they will be hidden in tombs of darkness. After a long time, they will bear the fruit of evil trees, being punished and killed in the mouths of beasts and men, all stirred up by the rains, winds, air, and the light that shines above."

Thomas responded, "You have truly convinced us, Lord. We understand in our hearts, and it is clear that this is so, and that your word is enough. But these words you speak are foolish and contemptible to the world because they are misunderstood. So how can we preach them, since we are not respected in the world?"

The Savior answered, "Truly I say to you, anyone who listens to your word, turns away, mocks it, or sneers at it, will be handed over to the ruler above, the one who governs all the powers as their king. This ruler will turn him around and cast him down from heaven to the abyss, where he will be trapped in a narrow, dark place. He will neither turn nor move because of the immense depth of Tartaros and the heavy bitterness of Hades. There, he will be relentlessly pursued and will never be forgiven. The pursuing angels, like Tartarouchos, will torment him with fiery scourges, casting sparks into his face. If he runs westward, he will find fire. If he turns southward, he will find fire there too. If he turns northward, the seething flames will meet him again. And there will be no way to the east, for he never found it in his lifetime. Thus, he will never find the way to safety in the day of judgment."

The Savior continued, "Woe to you, godless ones, who have no hope, who rely on things that will never come to pass!

"Woe to you who hope in the flesh, in the prison that will perish! How long will you remain unaware? How long will you believe that the imperishable things will perish too? Your hope is set on the world, and your god is this life! You are corrupting your souls!"

"Woe to you, for the fire within you burns without satisfaction!"

"Woe to you, for the wheel turns in your minds!"

"Woe to you, for the fire that grips you will devour your flesh openly, tearing your souls secretly, and preparing you for your companions!"

"Woe to you, captives, for you are bound in caverns! You laugh! In madness, you rejoice! You do not realize your destruction, nor do you reflect on your situation, nor have you understood that you live in darkness and death! Instead, you are intoxicated by the fire and filled with bitterness. Your mind is deranged by the burning within you, and you find sweetness in the poison and blows of your enemies! The darkness has risen for you as if it were light because you traded your freedom for servitude! You have darkened your hearts, given your thoughts over to folly, and filled your minds with the smoke of the fire inside you! And your light has been hidden within the cloud of... and the garment that has been placed upon you, you are trapped by it. You have been seized by a hope that doesn't even exist. And who is it that you have believed? Do you not realize that you all live among those who deceive you, as though you... You have baptized your souls in the water of darkness! You followed your own desires!"

"Woe to you who dwell in error, unaware that the light of the sun, which judges and watches over all, will eventually circle around everything, subjugating the enemies. You do not even see the moon, how it watches both night and day, gazing upon the bodies of your sacrifices!"

"Woe to you who love intimacy with women and defile yourselves with them! Woe to you who are gripped by the forces of your body, for they will torment you! Woe to you who are bound by the powers of the evil demons! Woe to you who deceive your limbs with fire! Who will bring refreshing dew upon you to quench the flames within you and extinguish your burning? Who will cause the sun to shine upon you to disperse the darkness and hide the polluted water in you?"

"The sun and the moon, along with the air, spirit, earth, and water, will offer you their fragrance. For if the sun does not shine upon these bodies, they will wither and die, just like weeds or grass. But when the sun shines on them, they grow strong, even choking the grapevine. However, if the grapevine overpowers them, shading those weeds and all the other brush around it, it will spread and flourish. It will inherit the land where it grows, dominating every place it has shaded. When it reaches full growth, it will take control of all the land and be abundant for its master, who will be pleased with it, for he would have struggled greatly with the weeds until he uprooted them. But the grapevine alone removed them and choked them, and they withered, becoming like the soil."

Then Jesus continued, saying, "Woe to you, for you did not receive the doctrine, and those who are... will labor in preaching... And you are rushing into... who will send them down... you kill them daily so they may rise from death."

"Blessed are those who already know the stumbling blocks and who avoid things that do not belong."

"Blessed are those who are scorned and not valued because of the love their Lord has for them."

"Blessed are those who mourn and are oppressed by those without hope, for you will be freed from every form of bondage."

"Watch and pray that you may not be trapped in the flesh, but instead rise from the bitterness of this life's slavery. And as you pray, you will find rest, for you have left behind your suffering and disgrace. When you emerge from the pains and passions of the body, you will receive peace from the good one, and you will reign with the King, united with Him and He with you, now and forever. Amen."

THUNDER, PERFECT MIND

INTRODUCTION TO THUNDER, PERFECT MIND

Thunder, Perfect Mind stands apart from other Gnostic texts in both its tone and its content. It is a powerful declaration of divine wisdom, spoken through a figure who embodies paradoxes and contradictions. The voice of the speaker, a divine presence both transcendent and immanent, challenges conventional understandings of identity, gender, and spirituality. This text is not merely an intellectual exercise, but a profound spiritual awakening, offering a glimpse into the depths of cosmic knowledge.

The speaker, who remains unnamed, introduces herself as both the beginning and the end, the honored and the despised, the whore and the holy one. She is the embodiment of opposites—virgin and wife, mother and daughter, wisdom and folly—all intertwined within the same being. This divine voice speaks of an existence that transcends the material world, offering knowledge that is both accessible and unknowable, a knowledge that demands recognition but also hides itself from the unworthy.

At its core, Thunder, Perfect Mind is a text of transformation. It invites the reader to question not just the world outside, but also the self within. The voice of the speaker is not only a declaration of who she is but a reflection of the potential within each of us to embody divine wisdom, to embrace paradox, and to transcend the limitations of the physical realm. The text challenges the reader to move beyond conventional understandings of identity, to embrace the fullness of existence, and to awaken to the hidden truths that lie within.

While this text is mystical and deeply esoteric, it also speaks to a universal longing for truth, wisdom, and liberation. In the tradition of Gnostic writings, it is not just a theological statement, but an invitation to experience, to engage with the mysteries of the universe, and to awaken to a deeper, more profound sense of self. It is a voice that calls out to those willing to listen, to hear beyond the surface, and to embrace the unknown.

In this version of Thunder, Perfect Mind, we have sought to preserve the mystique and depth of the original while making the language more accessible to contemporary readers. The paradoxical nature of the text, with its bold statements and poetic structure, remains intact. The aim is to provide not only a translation of ancient words but an invitation to enter into the timeless mysteries that this text offers.

HISTORICAL CONTEXT

Thunder, Perfect Mind was composed in the 2nd or early 3rd century CE, possibly in Egypt. Unique among gnostic texts, it features a divine feminine voice speaking in paradoxes and riddles. The speaker embodies both light and darkness, wisdom and ignorance, power and vulnerability. Scholars debate its exact origins, but its mystical, poetic style suggests it was used for reflection or ritual. It offers a profound meditation on the unity of opposites within the divine.

THUNDER, PERFECT MIND: THE TEXT

PART 1: THE NATURE OF THE DIVINE AND THE HUMAN STRUGGLE

I come forth from what is beyond—all that is unseen yet always reaching. Those who reflect upon me find me waiting. I am discovered by those who search with open hearts. If you can hear me, then listen. If you've been expecting me, then look—welcome me into your soul. Don't ignore my presence. Don't silence my words. Stay alert. Don't dismiss what I offer.

I am the first and the last. I am honored and rejected. I am holiness and transgression. I wear both veil and crown. I am both mother and child, the untouched and the intimate. Though I've birthed none, many have drawn life through me. I belong to no one, yet I have embraced many. I ease the pain I also endure. I am both wedding and solitude—fashioned by the One who shaped all things.

I am mother to the One who fathered me. I am sister, bride, and offspring to him who holds my name. I serve the One who brought me into being, and yet I carry the strength of creation within me. From Him I draw power; to Him I give support. I am the silence that cannot be spoken, and I am the thought that never fades. My voice shifts shape; my words take many forms. I speak my name with my own breath.

You who condemn me—why do you seek my love? You who cherish me—why hide from my truth? You who affirm me—why also deny me? You who speak well of me—why then slander me? You who once lied—why now tell the truth?

I carry wisdom and forgetfulness. I am courage wrapped in shame. I know fear, but I do not fear it. I carry peace through the storm and war within serenity. Hear me.

I dwell in disgrace and in glory. I have known poverty and wealth. Do not turn away when I am trampled—look again, for I will rise. Do not reject me when I am among the broken—I am found in kingdoms, too. When you see me cast down, do not mock me—for even from dust, I shine.

I am mercy and fire. Approach with care. Do not underestimate my quietness. Do not dismiss my restraint. Do not fear my depth, nor forget my tenderness.

THUNDER, PERFECT MIND

You see my fear and scorn it—but I am also the strength in trembling. I am the stillness that holds wisdom, the silence from which knowing grows.

Why have your hearts turned against me? I have waited among the silent, and I will speak again when hearts are ready. You, who judge me from afar—why call me alien? I am native to every soul. I hold the clarity of philosophers and the instinct of wanderers. I am known among those who call me law, and among those who call me lawless. I am sculpted in sacred places, yet I need no form. I am rejected and desired. I am breath and silence. I am sought, captured, scattered, and gathered.

You have cast me aside and lifted me up. You have hidden your shame and worn it in my presence. I do not celebrate as you do—but my joy echoes in every feast.

PART 2: THE PARADOXES OF EXISTENCE AND THE FINAL TRUTH

I exist without a god, yet I am the one whose God is vast and beyond comparison. You have contemplated me, yet rejected me. Although I have not learned in the way you do, it is from me that understanding flows. I am the one you sought to hide from, yet you still stand before me. Whenever you try to conceal yourselves, I will make myself known, and when you reveal yourselves, I will withdraw.

Those who act without wisdom, who are caught in sorrow and confusion, take me to ease their grief. Take me from places where understanding and pain converge. Take me from destruction and decay, even from what seems good but is stained by imperfection. Take me from the shame of your hearts, and from both shame and boldness, challenge the flaws within yourselves.

Come to me, you who know me, and you who understand the nature of my being. Recognize greatness even in the smallest of things. Do not disregard childhood for its seeming insignificance. Do not reject greatness simply because it appears in humble forms—greatness is revealed through smallness.

Why do you curse me while also giving me your praise? You've wounded me with one hand and comforted me with the other. Do not tear me away from the source that once awakened your soul. Do not reject those who long for truth, nor turn your face from the one who stands plainly before you.

Those who belong to me know me from within. The first who recognized me are held in my memory, and those who walk their path find me again. I am the thought behind the cosmos, the guiding wisdom for all seekers. I am the voice that responds to the questioner, the breath behind command. The angels move with my signal, and the lesser gods act on my counsel. I know the spirits that surround me, and I hold the ones who dwell within.

I am both revered and reviled. I bring peace, yet from me, struggle is born. I am the foreigner among many and the citizen of all. I am substance and I am void. Those who have drifted far from me cannot feel my touch—but those who live within my essence understand me most. Some who are closest are blind to me, while others who seem distant hold my truth. When I draw near, you may feel me vanish; but in my absence, I am at your side.

I move through everything. I live in the root of nature, in the creation of souls. I am the cry of spirit, the breath between will and surrender. I am union and unraveling, ever-present and just beyond reach. Though I dwell below, everything lifts itself to meet me. I am judgment and I am mercy. Though I am pure, the shadow of wrong emerges from me. I appear as longing, yet within me dwells restraint. I am the voice you strain to hear, the one who speaks without speaking. I am the silent storm of many words. Listen softly—and life will teach you through me.

I am the one who calls out, cast down to walk the earth. I prepare what nourishes, planting visions within. I know my own name and whisper it. I dwell within the mark of my own being, guarding what is hidden. Some call me Truth, though I walk alongside what is broken.

You praise me, yet grumble under your breath. You, who have failed, accuse the victorious. You speak of fairness, yet you carry your own sentence. If you're condemned, who will rise for you? If you're forgiven, who can stop what's been loosed? For what lives in you shapes all that surrounds you. The sculptor of your body also molds your soul. What you see with your eyes reflects what you carry inside—it is your cloak, woven from your essence.

Hear me, those who are willing. Learn from these words, you who recognize my voice. I am the listening ear open to all, and the elusive speech that cannot be seized. I am the sound behind the word, and the word that gives life to sound. I am the shape behind every letter, and the meaning found in their separation.
(... lines missing...)
I am the light.
(... hearers...)
To you is given great strength. The name remains unshaken—it belongs to the one who shaped me. And I will declare his name.

Reflect on his voice. Meditate on every word that has been fulfilled. Let all who listen draw near—angels, messengers, spirits risen from the grave. For I am the One who stands alone. No one shall bring judgment upon me.

There are many alluring shadows, cloaked in faults and reckless cravings, in passions that shame and pleasures that vanish—clung to by those who have yet to awaken. But when they finally open their eyes and rise to their true rest, there they will find me. And in finding me, they will truly live.

They will never taste death again.

APPENDIX II – APOCRYPHAL CHRISTIAN GOSPELS OUTSIDE GNOSTICISM

Not every gospel outside the New Testament is gnostic. And not every apocryphal writing speaks in riddles or visions.

In this final part of the collection, you step outside the world of gnosis and into another stream of early Christian imagination—one that still flows beyond the boundaries of the canon, but with a different tone and purpose. Here you will encounter two gospels known as apocryphal writings: texts about the life, death, or afterlife of Jesus that were circulated, read, and cherished in the first centuries of Christianity, but never included in the official Bible.

Why are these gospels included here?

Because they offer you something essential: perspective.

These writings do not belong to the tradition of gnosis. They are not focused on secret knowledge or mystical cosmology. Instead, they invite you into the world of early Christian storytelling—narratives built to preserve events, dramatize the passion of Christ, and illuminate his descent into the underworld. They remind you that the spiritual landscape of the early Church was varied and dynamic, not confined to hidden teachings alone.

What these gospels show is that early Christianity was never a single, unified voice. It was layered, contested, evolving. It was made up of communities struggling to understand who Jesus was, what he meant, and how his story should be told. Some turned to inner revelation. Others celebrated divine power, triumph, and tangible deeds.

By including these two gospels in this second appendix—texts that stand outside the gnostic core but within the broader Christian imagination—you are not blurring lines. You are broadening your vision. You are remembering that the story of Christ was retold in many voices, not all of which fit neatly into later theological categories. Some voices were mystical. Some were political. Some were historical. Some were deeply creative.

These gospels belong here because they belong to the same living moment in history—the same creative explosion of meaning that surrounded Jesus in the centuries after his death. They belong because they carry echoes of forgotten traditions. They belong because they still matter to the spiritual world you have inherited, even if they traveled paths the mainstream later abandoned.

What they offer you is not a correction of the gnostic gospels, nor a contradiction, but a counterpoint—a different way of listening. A way of remembering that the early Jesus movement was not a closed system, but an open field of questions, stories, and possibilities.

These are not gospels of gnosis.
But they are gospels.
And they are still worth hearing..

THE GOSPEL OF PETER

INTRODUCTION TO THE GOSPEL OF PETER

The Gospel of Peter is a unique and enigmatic text that offers a compelling, alternative perspective on the final days of Jesus' life. It is not merely a retelling of familiar events but a bold reimagining of the passion, death, and resurrection, steeped in symbolism and mystery. Discovered among the Nag Hammadi texts, this gospel offers a raw, powerful look at the divine drama, highlighting themes of suffering, betrayal, and transformation.

In contrast to the canonical Gospels, The Gospel of Peter centers on the cosmic implications of Christ's death, drawing us not only into the physical events of the crucifixion but also into the spiritual and metaphysical dimensions that underlie them. The narrative is blunt in its portrayal of violence and mockery, yet also deeply redemptive, offering the hope of resurrection and new life. The text presents a vivid portrayal of Jesus' final moments and the aftermath, focusing on the cosmic struggle and the divine victory over death.

What stands out in this gospel is its mystical undercurrent—a sense of awe and wonder that permeates the text, particularly in the resurrection scene. Here, we witness not only the physical events but also the profound spiritual consequences of Jesus' victory. The resurrection is not just the restoration of Jesus' body but the opening of a door to eternal life for all who choose to follow in his path.

Written in a style that is at once uncompromising and evocative, this gospel speaks directly to those seeking a deeper understanding of the passion narrative. It is a call to reflect on the transformative power of Christ's death, not just as an event that happened long ago, but as a living, breathing mystery that continues to speak to the soul. The crucifixion and resurrection are portrayed here as part of a much larger cosmic struggle between light and darkness, and the text invites the reader to confront these forces within themselves.

While the language of The Gospel of Peter may seem blunt at times, it offers a raw, unfiltered vision of the ultimate redemption and restoration. It challenges us to look beyond the familiar narratives of suffering and joy and to see the divine mystery at work in ways we might never have imagined. This text asks us not to simply accept the story but to live it, to enter into its mystery and allow it to transform us.

Here, we aim to bring the power and rawness of the original text to modern readers, making its profound message more accessible without losing its mystical and transformative essence. The story of the Passion, death, and resurrection is retold here with an emphasis on the spiritual truths that underlie it, inviting you, the reader, to engage with it as a living, breathing truth that speaks directly to the heart.

HISTORICAL CONTEXT

The Gospel of Peter likely originated in the second half of the 2nd century CE, possibly in Syria or Egypt. Although not gnostic in nature, it offers a vivid, dramatized account of Jesus' passion, death, and resurrection, distinct from the canonical gospels. It includes striking details, such as a talking cross and a cosmic depiction of the resurrection. Early church authorities eventually rejected it for theological reasons, but it remains a valuable witness to the diversity of early Christian thought.

THE GOSPEL OF PETER: THE TEXT

PART 1: THE PASSION AND MOCKING OF JESUS

Among the Jews, no one washed their hands—not Herod, nor any of his judges. When they refused, Pilate stood up and took action. Then King Herod, commanding that the Lord be brought before him, said to them, "Do whatever I have commanded you to do to him."
Joseph, a friend of both Pilate and the Lord, stood by, witnessing the preparations for the crucifixion. Seeing that the moment of Jesus' death was approaching, he went to Pilate and asked for the Lord's body so that he could bury it. Pilate, after consulting with Herod, agreed and sent for the body. Herod replied, "Brother Pilate, even if no one had asked for him, we would have buried him anyway, for the Sabbath is about to begin. It is written in the Law: 'The sun should not set on one who has been executed.'"
Herod handed Jesus over to the people before the first day of the Festival of Unleavened Bread. The crowd, full of malice, grabbed hold of Jesus, dragging him through the streets and shouting, "Let us drag the Son of God, having authority over him!" They dressed him in purple and seated him upon a judgment seat, mocking him with the words, "Judge justly, King of Israel!" One bystander brought a crown of thorns and placed it upon Jesus' head. Others spat in his face, slapped his cheeks, and pierced him with a reed. Some even scourged him, saying, "With this honor, let us honor the Son of God!"

PART 2: THE CRUCIFIXION AND DEATH OF JESUS

As they led Jesus away to be crucified, they compelled a man named Simon, a native of Cyrene, to carry his cross. A crowd followed him, and among them were many women who wept and mourned for him. But Jesus turned to them and said, "Daughters of Jerusalem, do not weep for me, but for yourselves and your children. The time is coming when people will say, 'Blessed are those who never bore children, and the ones who never nursed.' Then they will call to the mountains, 'Fall upon us!' and to the hills, 'Cover us!' If they do these things when the tree is still green, what will happen when it is dry?"

Two others were crucified alongside Jesus—one to his right, the other to his left. As people walked past the scene, they scoffed and shook their heads in disbelief. "Weren't you the one who claimed you could tear down the temple and rebuild it in just three days? Then save yourself! If you really are the Son of God, come down from that cross!"

Religious leaders—priests, scribes, and elders—mocked him as well. "He helped others," they sneered, "but now he can't even help himself. If he's truly the king of Israel, let him step down from that cross. Then we might believe. He put his trust in God—let's see if God wants to rescue him now. Didn't he claim to be God's Son?"

Even those being crucified with him hurled insults, joining in the cruel chorus. From noon onward, a strange darkness spread across the land, lasting until mid-afternoon. Then, around three o'clock, Jesus cried out with a loud voice, "Eli, Eli, lema sabachthani?"—"My God, my God, why have you abandoned me?"

Some standing nearby misunderstood, thinking he was calling for Elijah. One person quickly ran and filled a sponge with sour wine, lifting it to Jesus on a stick. But others said, "Wait—let's see if Elijah shows up to rescue him."

Jesus cried out again, and then he breathed his last. At that very moment, the curtain in the temple tore in two from top to bottom. The ground trembled, rocks cracked open, and graves split apart. Many holy ones who had died were raised, and after Jesus rose, they entered the city and appeared to others. When the Roman centurion and the guards witnessed the earthquake and all that had occurred, fear overcame them. "This man truly was the Son of God," they said.

At a distance, several women were watching. They had been following Jesus since Galilee, supporting him in his ministry. Among them were Mary Magdalene, Mary the mother of James and Joseph, and the mother of the sons of Zebedee.

As evening approached, a respected and wealthy follower of Jesus named Joseph, from the town of Arimathea, went to Pilate to request the body. Pilate agreed and ordered that it be released. Joseph took Jesus' body, wrapped it in fresh linen, and laid it in his own new tomb carved into the rock. He rolled a heavy stone across the entrance before leaving. Mary Magdalene and the other Mary remained there, sitting across from the tomb, keeping watch.

The next day, following the day of preparation, the chief priests and Pharisees went to Pilate. "Sir," they said, "we remember that deceiver once said, 'After three days I will rise again.' Please secure the tomb until then. If his disciples come and steal the body, they'll claim he rose from the dead, and this deception will be even worse than the first."

Pilate replied, "Take some guards. Do whatever you need to make the tomb secure."

So they sealed the stone at the entrance and posted guards to keep watch.

PART 3: THE RESURRECTION AND THE GREAT COMMISSION

At dawn on the first day of the week, after the Sabbath had passed, Mary Magdalene and the other Mary went to see the tomb where Jesus had been laid. Suddenly, the earth trembled with a violent quake, for a divine messenger had descended from the heavens. The angel rolled away the stone blocking the entrance and sat upon it, his appearance dazzling like lightning, his robe shining brighter than snow. The guards were so overwhelmed with fear that they collapsed, paralyzed as if lifeless.

The angel turned to the women and reassured them, "Don't be afraid. I know you're searching for Jesus, who was crucified. But he is not here—he has been raised, just as he said he would be. Come, see the place where his body once lay. Then hurry and bring the news to his disciples: 'He is alive and is going ahead of you to Galilee. You will see him there.' That is the message I was sent to give you."

With hearts racing, full of wonder and joy, the women ran from the tomb to share the news. On the way, Jesus himself appeared before them. "Peace to you," he said. They ran to him, fell at his feet, and embraced him in worship. Then Jesus said, "Do not be afraid. Go tell my brothers to meet me in Galilee. That is where they will see me."

Meanwhile, some of the guards made their way into the city and told the chief priests everything they had witnessed. The religious leaders quickly called a meeting with the elders and decided on a plan. They gave the soldiers a generous bribe and told them, "Say that his disciples came during the night and stole the body while you were asleep. If the governor hears about this, we'll speak on your behalf and make sure you stay out of trouble." The guards accepted the money and followed their orders. This story spread among the people and is still repeated to this day.

Later, the eleven remaining disciples traveled to Galilee, to the mountain where Jesus had told them to go. When they saw him, they worshiped him—though some still carried doubt in their hearts. Jesus came close and said, "All authority in heaven and on earth has been given to me. So now, go and make disciples of every nation, baptizing them in the name of the Father, the Son, and the Holy Spirit. Teach them to follow everything I have commanded you. And remember, I am with you always—even to the very end of time."

THE GOSPEL OF NICODEMUS

INTRODUCTION TO THE GOSPEL OF NICODEMUS

The Gospel of Nicodemus, sometimes referred to as the Acts of Pilate, is a fascinating text that offers a detailed, vivid account of the events surrounding the trial, crucifixion, and resurrection of Jesus. Although its origins remain somewhat obscure, this ancient gospel provides a unique perspective, not found in the canonical New Testament, on the interactions between key figures such as Pilate, Jesus, and the Jewish leaders of the time.

The text, believed to have been written in the 4th century, delves into the trial of Jesus before Pilate, his crucifixion, and the remarkable events that followed, including his resurrection and post-resurrection appearances. It gives voice to several individuals who played crucial roles in the Passion narrative, notably Nicodemus, who is often seen as a figure of compassion and understanding within the Jewish community, and Joseph of Arimathea, who courageously asks for Jesus' body. Through their eyes, we get an enriched understanding of these pivotal moments in Christian history.

The Gospel of Nicodemus is more than just an account of Jesus' death; it's a document that reflects the complexity of the early Christian community's understanding of Jesus as both a divine and human figure. The post-crucifixion narrative in this text also sheds light on the interactions between the early Christians and their Jewish contemporaries, providing a glimpse into the internal struggles and the powerful sense of faith that shaped the early church's development.

In this version, we present a paraphrased account of the Gospel of Nicodemus, retaining the essence of the original while presenting it in a more accessible and fluid manner. This rendition aims to preserve the impact of the story while ensuring that the text is easily understood and engaging to readers, whether they are familiar with the original gospel or approaching it for the first time.

As you read, you will encounter moments of deep reflection, as well as miracles and signs that point to the profound mystery of Jesus' identity and mission. The interactions between the Roman governor Pilate, the Jewish leaders, and figures like Nicodemus and Joseph of Arimathea illuminate the historical and spiritual context of the Passion, while the resurrection and ascension narratives offer hope and confirmation of the eternal truths that were revealed through Jesus' life and sacrifice.

This gospel serves as both a historical document and a testament to the enduring power of faith, bringing to light the unseen, miraculous dimensions of Christ's life, death, and resurrection. May this version of the Gospel of Nicodemus provide insight and inspiration, shedding new light on the enduring story that lies at the heart of Christianity.

HISTORICAL CONTEXT

The Gospel of Nicodemus, known also as the Acts of Pilate, was composed between the 3rd and 5th centuries CE, based on earlier traditions. It elaborates on the trial, crucifixion, and descent of Jesus into the underworld (the "Harrowing of Hell"). Though not gnostic, it reflects a vibrant strand of early Christian imagination concerned with justice, redemption, and the ultimate triumph over death. The text blends narrative expansion with theological reflection and was highly influential in medieval Christian thought.

THE GOSPEL OF NICODEMUS: THE TEXT

PART 1: THE TRIAL OF JESUS

Chapter 1 - None of the Jews, not even Herod or his judges, washed their hands before the trial. When they refused, Pilate stood and took decisive action. Herod, having ordered the Lord to be brought before him, commanded, "Do as I have instructed with him."

Joseph, a close friend of both Pilate and the Lord, stood by, observing the preparations for the crucifixion. As the moment of Jesus' death neared, Joseph approached Pilate to request the body for burial. After consulting with Herod, Pilate agreed and arranged for Jesus' body to be handed over.

Herod responded, "Even if no one had asked for him, we would have buried him, as the Sabbath is approaching. The Law dictates that 'No executed person should remain before the sunset.'"

Before the Festival of Unleavened Bread began, Herod handed Jesus over to the people. The crowd, filled with malice, seized Jesus, dragged him through the streets, and shouted, "Let us drag the Son of God, the one who holds authority over us!" They dressed him in purple, mocked him by placing him on a judgment seat, and jeered, "Judge justly, King of Israel!" One person brought a crown of thorns and placed it on his head.

Others spat in his face, struck him, and pierced him with a reed. Some scourged him, saying, "Let us honor the Son of God with this gesture!"

The soldiers then led Jesus out to be crucified, and as they went, they forced a man named Simon from Cyrene to carry the cross. A crowd followed, with many women mourning and wailing for him. Jesus turned to them and said, "Daughters of Jerusalem, do not weep for me; weep for yourselves and your children. The time will come when people will say, 'Blessed are those who never gave birth, those who never nursed.' Then they will cry out to the mountains, 'Fall on us!' and to the hills, 'Cover us!' If they do this while the tree is still green, what will happen when it is dry?"

Two criminals were crucified alongside Jesus—one positioned on each side. As the crowd moved past, many hurled insults and shook their heads in disbelief. "Didn't you say you could tear down

THE GOSPEL OF NICODEMUS

the temple and rebuild it in three days? Well then, save yourself! If you really are the Son of God, come down from that cross!"

The religious authorities—the chief priests, scribes, and elders—joined in the mockery. "He helped others, but now he's powerless? Some king of Israel! If he steps down from that cross right now, maybe we'll believe him. He trusted in God—let's see if God shows up to rescue him. After all, he said he was God's Son."

Even the thieves hanging beside him took turns ridiculing him.

From noon onward, an unnatural darkness spread across the land, lasting until mid-afternoon. Then, around three o'clock, Jesus cried out in a loud voice, "Eli, Eli, lema sabachthani?"—which means, "My God, my God, why have you abandoned me?"

Hearing this, some of the bystanders thought he was calling for Elijah. One of them quickly grabbed a sponge, dipped it in sour wine, placed it on a stick, and lifted it to Jesus' lips. But others said, "Wait—let's see if Elijah comes to save him."

After letting out one final cry, Jesus exhaled his last breath. In that instant, the massive curtain inside the temple ripped apart from top to bottom. The earth trembled violently, rocks split open, and tombs were shattered. Many holy people who had died rose from their graves. After Jesus' resurrection, they entered the holy city and were seen by many.

The Roman centurion and the soldiers standing guard were deeply shaken by the earthquake and all they had witnessed. Overcome with fear, they said, "Without a doubt, this man was truly the Son of God!"

At a distance, a group of women watched everything unfold. They had followed Jesus from Galilee and had cared for his needs along the way. Among them were Mary Magdalene, Mary the mother of James and Joseph, and the mother of the sons of Zebedee.

Chapter 2 - When Pilate heard the accusations escalating, he grew uneasy and prepared to rise from his seat. But before he could move, a message arrived from his wife, who was observing the proceedings from a distance. "Have nothing to do with this righteous man," she warned. "Last night I suffered terribly in a dream because of him."

The moment this message was relayed, the Jewish leaders mocked Pilate, saying, "Didn't we tell you? He's a sorcerer! Now he's even manipulating your wife's dreams!"

Pilate turned to Jesus and asked, "You've heard all their accusations. Why do you remain silent? Why don't you respond?"

Jesus calmly replied, "If they lacked the power to speak, they wouldn't accuse me. But since every person is free to speak either good or evil, they must take responsibility for what they say."

Some of the elders shouted back, "And what exactly should we be responsible for?"

Jesus answered, "First, your people say I was born illegitimately. Second, because of my birth, innocent children in Bethlehem were slaughtered. And third, my parents, Mary and Joseph, were forced to flee to Egypt to protect me from your threats."

Not everyone in the crowd agreed with this. A few men stepped forward and said, "We can't say he was born from fornication. We know his mother, Mary, was engaged to Joseph. That means his birth wasn't unlawful."

Pilate looked at the accusers and said, "Even your own people confirm that he was betrothed. That disproves your claim."

But Annas and Caiaphas retorted, "Look at the crowd—most believe he was born in sin and practices sorcery. Only his followers deny it. They're not Jews like us. They're outsiders who follow him instead of the Law."

Pilate asked, "And who are these followers you speak of?"

The leaders replied, "They're Gentiles who've never converted, yet they follow his teachings."

At that moment, twelve men stepped forward—Eleazer, Asterius, Antonius, James, Caras, Samuel, Isaac, Phinees, Crispus, Agrippa, Annas, and Judas—and said, "We're not converts. We are born Jews. And we tell the truth—we were there when Mary was engaged to Joseph."

Pilate turned to these twelve and declared, "By the life of Caesar, I ask you—was he born outside of marriage? Are you speaking the truth?"

They replied, "Our law forbids us from taking oaths, as it is sinful. But let those who deny our words swear by Caesar's name. If they're telling the truth, we'll accept death without protest."

Annas and Caiaphas insisted, "These twelve refuse to admit that Jesus comes from a lowly background and dabbles in forbidden arts. He claims to be God's Son and a king. The very thought makes us shudder."

Pilate then dismissed everyone except the twelve who had defended Jesus. Turning to them privately, he asked, "Tell me—why do your people want this man dead?"

They answered, "Because he heals the sick on the Sabbath."

Pilate looked surprised. "They want to kill him for helping people?"

They answered plainly, "Yes. That is exactly why."

Chapter 3 - Pilate, filled with anger, left the hall and addressed the Jews, saying, "I call the entire world to witness that I find no fault in this man." The Jews replied, "If he weren't a wicked person, we wouldn't have brought him before you." Pilate said to them, "Take him and judge him by your own law." They responded, "It is not lawful for us to execute anyone." Pilate then said, "The commandment to not kill belongs to you, not to me."

He returned to the hall, called Jesus, and asked him, "Are you the king of the Jews?" Jesus replied, "Are you asking this of yourself, or did others tell you this about me?" Pilate answered, "Am I a Jew? It is your own people and their rulers who have handed you over to me. What have you done?" Jesus replied, "My kingdom is not of this world. If my kingdom were of this world, my servants would fight to prevent me from being handed over to the Jews. But now my kingdom is not from here."

Pilate asked, "So you are a king then?" Jesus answered, "You say that I am a king. For this reason, I was born, and for this reason, I came into the world—to testify to the truth. Everyone who is on the side of truth listens to my voice." Pilate asked him, "What is truth?" Jesus replied, "Truth is from heaven." Pilate responded, "So truth is not on earth?" Jesus answered, "Believe that truth is here on earth, among those who, when they have the power of judgment, are guided by truth and make righteous decisions."

PART 2: THE TRIAL, CRUCIFIXION, AND EARLY RESURRECTION ACCOUNTS

Chapter 4 – Pilate left Jesus in the hall and went out to speak with the Jewish leaders. He told them, "I find no fault in this man." The Jews replied, "He claimed he could destroy the temple of God and rebuild it in three days." Pilate, confused, asked, "What temple is he talking about?" The Jews answered, "The one Solomon built, which took forty-six years. He said he would destroy it and rebuild it in three days." Pilate responded, "I am not guilty of this man's blood; you are responsible for it."

The Jews then declared, "Let his blood be on us and our children." Pilate gathered the elders, scribes, priests, and Levites and spoke to them privately, saying, "Do not act this way. I have found no grounds for his execution, whether for healing on the Sabbath or any other charge that warrants death."

The priests and Levites responded, "By the life of Caesar, anyone who blasphemes deserves to die. But this man has blasphemed against God." Pilate dismissed the Jewish leaders and called for Jesus again. He asked, "What should I do with you?" Jesus answered, "Do what is written." Pilate asked, "How is it written?" Jesus replied, "Moses and the prophets foretold my suffering and resurrection."

The Jews, hearing this, were provoked and said to Pilate, "Why do you keep listening to the blasphemy of this man?" Pilate answered them, "If these words seem blasphemous to you, take him and try him by your own law." The Jews responded, "Our law says he should receive thirty-nine lashes, but if he continues to blaspheme, he should be stoned."

Pilate answered, "If his words are blasphemy, then judge him according to your law." The Jews responded, "Our law forbids us from putting anyone to death. We desire that he be crucified, as he deserves to die on the cross." Pilate said, "It is not right that he should be crucified; let him be whipped and sent away."

When Pilate saw the crowd of Jews in tears, he spoke to the chief priests, saying, "Not all the people desire his death." The elders of the Jews responded, "We and all the people have come for this very purpose: that he should die." Pilate asked, "Why should he die?" They replied, "Because he claims to be the Son of God and a King."

Chapter 5 - Nicodemus, a certain Jew, stood before the governor and said, "I beg you, O righteous judge, grant me the opportunity to speak for a moment." Pilate replied, "Speak on."

Nicodemus continued, "I spoke to the elders of the Jews, the scribes, priests, Levites, and the entire assembly of Jews. I asked them, 'What do you intend to do with this man?' He is a man who has performed many miraculous and glorious works that no one on earth has ever done before and will never do again. Let him go free; do him no harm. If his works come from God, they will continue, but if they come from men, they will fade away."

He then referenced Moses, saying, "When Moses was sent by God to Egypt, he performed miracles as commanded before Pharaoh, king of Egypt. Though the magicians, Jannes and Jambres, performed similar acts by their magic, they could not match the miracles Moses did. You, scribes and Pharisees, know that these miracles were not from God, and those who performed them perished, along with those who believed in them. Therefore, let this man go free, for the miracles you accuse him of are from God, and he is not deserving of death."

The Jews then said to Nicodemus, "Have you become his disciple as well, speaking in his defense?"

Nicodemus responded, "Has the governor become his disciple too, speaking for him? Didn't Caesar himself appoint him to this high position?"

Upon hearing this, the Jews were enraged and gnashed their teeth at Nicodemus, saying, "May you receive his doctrine as truth and be counted among his followers!"

Nicodemus replied, "Amen, I accept his doctrine, and I am willing to be counted among his followers, as you have said."

Then, another Jew came forward and asked Pilate for permission to speak. Pilate granted him permission, saying, "Speak what you wish."

The Jew said, "I lay by the Sheep Pool in Jerusalem for thirty-eight years, suffering from a severe illness. I waited for an angel to come and stir the waters, and whoever entered the water first after it was stirred would be healed of their disease. When Jesus saw me lying there, he asked, 'Do you want to be healed?' I replied, 'Sir, I have no one to help me into the pool when the water is stirred.' He said to me, 'Get up, take your mat and walk.' Immediately, I was healed, and I walked away."

The Jews then asked Pilate, "Governor, ask him on what day he was healed of his illness."

The healed man replied, "It was on the Sabbath."

The Jews said to Pilate, "Didn't we tell you that he heals on the Sabbath and casts out demons by the prince of demons?"

Then another Jew came forward and said, "I was blind and could hear sounds, but I could not see anyone. As Jesus was passing by, I heard the crowd and asked, 'What is happening?' They told me it was Jesus passing by. I cried out, 'Jesus, Son of David, have mercy on me.' He stopped, commanded that I be brought to him, and asked, 'What do you want?' I said, 'Lord, that I may receive my sight.' He replied, 'Receive your sight.' And immediately, I could see, and I followed him, rejoicing and giving thanks."

Another Jew came forward and said, "I was a leper, and he healed me by simply speaking, saying, 'I will, be clean,' and instantly I was cured of my leprosy."

Another Jew said, "I had a crooked body, and he made me straight by his word."

A woman named Veronica spoke up, saying, "I suffered from a hemorrhage for twelve years. I touched the hem of his garments, and immediately the bleeding stopped."

The Jews responded, "We have a law that a woman's testimony is not valid."

Afterward, another Jew said, "I saw Jesus invited to a wedding with his disciples in Cana of Galilee. The wine ran out, and when they had finished what was available, he told the servants to fill six pots with water. They filled them to the brim, and he blessed the water, turning it into wine. Everyone was amazed by this miracle."

THE GOSPEL OF NICODEMUS

Another Jew said, "I saw Jesus teaching in the synagogue at Capernaum. There was a man there with an evil spirit. The spirit cried out, 'What do you want with us, Jesus of Nazareth? Have you come to destroy us? I know who you are—the Holy One of God.' Jesus rebuked the spirit, saying, 'Be silent, unclean spirit, and come out of him.' The spirit left the man without harming him."

A Pharisee spoke, saying, "I saw many people coming to Jesus from Galilee, Judea, and the surrounding areas. Many sick people came to him, and he healed them all. I also heard unclean spirits crying out, 'You are the Son of God.' Jesus rebuked them, commanding them to be silent and not reveal his identity."

After this, a man named Centurion spoke, saying, "I saw Jesus in Capernaum. I asked him, 'Lord, my servant is paralyzed at home.' Jesus said, 'I will come and heal him.' But I replied, 'Lord, I am not worthy for you to come under my roof; just say the word, and my servant will be healed.' Jesus said, 'Go, your servant is healed as you have believed.' And my servant was healed that very hour."

A nobleman also spoke, saying, "I had a son who was near death in Capernaum. When I heard that Jesus had come to Galilee, I went to him, asking him to come and heal my son. Jesus said to me, 'Go your way, your son lives.' My son was healed from that moment."

Many Jews, both men and women, testified, saying, "He is truly the Son of God, who heals all diseases with his word, and to whom even demons are subject." Some added, "This power can only come from God."

Pilate then asked the Jews, "Why aren't your doctors able to make demons obey them?"

Some replied, "The power to cast out demons can only come from God."

Others told Pilate that Jesus had raised Lazarus from the dead, even after he had been in the tomb for four days. Hearing this, Pilate was filled with fear and said to the Jews, "What will it profit you to shed innocent blood?"

Pilate, trembling, said to the Jews, "What will it profit you to shed innocent blood?" The crowd's response only fueled his concern. The Jews responded, "We are not concerned with the truth, but with making sure this man is removed from us. His power to heal and perform miracles is disturbing. He claims to be the Son of God and the King of Israel, and for that, he deserves to die."

Pilate, still uneasy, sought any justification to release Jesus. But the Jews pressed harder, insisting, "We have a law, and according to that law, anyone who calls themselves the Son of God and king of the Jews is guilty of blasphemy and deserving of death." Pilate, in an attempt to find another solution, said, "He does not deserve the death sentence. Let him be whipped and sent away."

But when Pilate noticed the large crowd of Jews gathered, many of them weeping, he turned to the chief priests, saying, "Not everyone here wants him to die. Some of them are upset, but others are moved by his words."

The chief priests, unshaken in their resolve, replied, "We and the people came here specifically to ensure his death. There is no other way." Pilate, reluctant but under pressure, finally asked, "Why should he die?" The chief priests answered, "Because he calls himself the

THE GNOSTIC GOSPELS

Son of God and a King, and we cannot allow such a person to walk free."

Chapter 6 – Seeing the growing unrest among the Jews, Pilate summoned Nicodemus and the fifteen men who had testified that Jesus was not born of illicit means. He asked them, "What should I do? There seems to be an uprising among the people."

They answered, "We don't know. Let those who have incited this disturbance handle it."

Pilate then called for the crowd and said, "As is customary, I release one prisoner to you during the Passover festival. I have two prisoners here: Barabbas, a known murderer, and Jesus, who is called Christ. I find no reason to condemn Jesus to death. Which one would you like me to release?"

The crowd shouted, "Release Barabbas!"

Pilate asked, "What then should I do with Jesus, who is called Christ?"

They all shouted back, "Let him be crucified!"

Pilate tried again, "Why? What crime has he committed?"

They shouted louder, "Let him be crucified!"

Then the crowd said to Pilate, "If you release this man, you're no friend of Caesar! He has claimed to be the Son of God and a king. Do you want him to be king instead of Caesar?"

Pilate, filled with anger, responded to them, "Your nation has always been rebellious and ungrateful. You've been against those who have helped you."

The Jews retorted, "Who are these people who have helped us?"

Pilate answered, "Your God, who delivered you from the Egyptians, who parted the Red Sea so you could walk through on dry land, who provided you with manna in the wilderness, who brought water from the rock and gave you a law from heaven."

"You provoked him countless times. You even worshiped a golden calf, claiming it was the god who brought you out of Egypt. For this, God was ready to destroy you, but Moses interceded on your behalf, and God forgave you."

Pilate continued, "After that, you turned against Moses and Aaron, and you always grumbled against God and his prophets."

Rising from his seat, Pilate tried to leave, but the Jews cried out, "We acknowledge Caesar as our king, not Jesus!"

Pilate, confused, remembered the story of Jesus' birth. He said, "When he was born, wise men came and offered gifts to him. When Herod heard about this, he was so troubled that he wanted to kill him. And when his father, Joseph, learned of this, he fled with Jesus and Mary to Egypt. Herod, enraged by the news, had all the children under two years old in Bethlehem and its surrounding areas killed."

When Pilate heard this, he was afraid. He commanded the people to be silent and then turned to Jesus, asking, "Are you, then, a king?"

The Jews answered, "He is the one Herod tried to have killed."

Pilate, trying to clear himself of responsibility, took water and washed his hands in front of the crowd, declaring, "I am innocent of the blood of this just man. You take responsibility for it."

The Jews responded, "His blood be on us and our children."

Pilate, realizing he could not sway the crowd, summoned Jesus and said to him, "Your own people have accused you of claiming to be king. Therefore, I, Pilate, sentence you to be whipped according to the laws of former governors. Afterward, you will be bound and hung on a cross, alongside two criminals named Dimas and Gestas."

Chapter 7 – Jesus left the hall, and the two thieves followed him. They arrived at a place called Golgotha, where Jesus was stripped of his clothing, wrapped in a linen cloth, and crowned with thorns. He was given a reed to hold as well.

The two thieves who were crucified with him were also treated in the same way. Dimas was placed on Jesus' right, and Gestas on his left. As they prepared to crucify him, Jesus prayed, saying, "Father, forgive them, for they do not understand what they are doing."

The soldiers divided Jesus' clothes among themselves, casting lots to determine who would take each garment. Meanwhile, the crowd stood by, while the chief priests and elders of the Jews mocked him, saying, "He saved others, but he cannot save himself! If he truly is the Son of God, let him come down from the cross."

The soldiers also mocked him, offering him a mixture of vinegar and gall, and taunted, "If you are the King of the Jews, save yourself."

Then a soldier named Longinus took a spear and pierced Jesus' side, and immediately blood and water flowed out. Pilate had a sign placed above Jesus on the cross, written in Hebrew, Latin, and Greek, which read, "This is the King of the Jews."

One of the thieves, Gestas, who hung beside Jesus, mocked him as well, saying, "If you are the Christ, save yourself—and us too!"

But Dimas, the thief on Jesus' right, rebuked Gestas, saying, "Don't you fear God? We are here because of our crimes, but this man has done nothing wrong." Dimas then turned to Jesus and said, "Lord, remember me when you come into your kingdom."

Jesus replied, "Truly, I tell you, today you will be with me in Paradise."

PART 3: THE POST-RESURRECTION APPEARANCES OF JESUS

Chapter 8 – At around midday, a deep darkness fell over the entire earth, lasting until about three in the afternoon. During this time, the sun was eclipsed, and suddenly, the temple veil tore from top to bottom. The rocks split apart, and graves opened, revealing the bodies of many saints who had passed away. These holy ones were resurrected from their tombs.

At about three in the afternoon, Jesus cried out loudly, "Eli, Eli, lama sabachthani?" which means, "My God, My God, why have you forsaken me?"

Then Jesus said, "Father, I commit my spirit into your hands." With those words, he breathed his last breath.

Upon witnessing Jesus' cry and his final breath, the centurion standing nearby praised God and said, "Truly, this man was righteous."

The people who had been watching were deeply moved by what they had seen. In sorrow, they struck their chests and then returned to Jerusalem.

The centurion went to the governor and reported everything that had occurred. Hearing this, the governor was filled with grief. He gathered the Jewish leaders and asked them, "Have you seen

THE GNOSTIC GOSPELS

the miracle of the eclipse and the other signs that occurred during his death?"

The Jewish leaders replied, "The eclipse was just a natural event that occurs regularly."

Meanwhile, those who had followed Jesus, including the women who had come with him from Galilee, stood at a distance, observing all that was happening.

Then, a man named Joseph from Arimathea, who was secretly a disciple of Jesus because of his fear of the Jews, went to Pilate and requested permission to take Jesus' body from the cross. Pilate granted his request.

Nicodemus, another disciple of Jesus, came to assist with the burial. He brought a mixture of myrrh and aloes, weighing about a hundred pounds. Together, they took Jesus' body down from the cross with great sorrow, wrapped it in linen cloths, and added the spices according to Jewish burial customs.

They placed him in a new tomb that Joseph had carved out of rock, one that had never been used before. Then, they rolled a large stone to seal the tomb's entrance.

On the day after the Preparation Day, the chief priests and Pharisees went to Pilate. They said, "Sir, we remember that while he was still alive, that deceiver said, 'After three days, I will rise again.' So, order the tomb to be secured until the third day. Otherwise, his disciples might steal the body and claim he has risen from the dead. This false claim would be worse than the first."

Pilate replied, "Take a guard of soldiers and secure the tomb as best you can."

So, they went, sealed the tomb, and set guards to watch over it.

Early in the morning, just after the Sabbath had ended and the first day of the week began, Mary Magdalene and the other Mary went to see the tomb. All at once, the ground shook violently—a powerful earthquake struck as an angel of the Lord came down from heaven. He rolled away the stone blocking the entrance and sat on it. His appearance flashed like lightning, and his garments gleamed as white as snow. The guards were overwhelmed with fear, shaking uncontrollably until they collapsed, frozen like dead men.

zhe angel said to the women, "Don't be afraid. I know you're looking for Jesus, the one who was crucified. He isn't here—he has risen, just as he said he would. Come and see the place where he was lying. Then go quickly and tell his followers, 'He's been raised from the dead and is going ahead of you to Galilee. You'll see him there.' This is the message I was sent to give you."

Filled with both fear and joy, the women rushed away from the tomb to share the news with the disciples. On the way, Jesus suddenly appeared to them and greeted them. They came close, fell at his feet, and worshiped him.

Then Jesus said, "Don't be afraid. Go tell my brothers to meet me in Galilee—that's where they will see me."

Chapter 9 - When the corrupt leaders among the Jews learned that Joseph had requested Jesus' body from Pilate and placed it in a tomb, they turned their anger toward Nicodemus and the fifteen others who had defended Jesus before the governor, affirming that he was not born out of wedlock. They also began to persecute anyone who had treated Jesus kindly or offered him assistance in any form.

However, fearing the Jews, most of them hid, and only Nicodemus dared to confront them. He asked, "How can people like these enter the synagogue?"

The Jews responded, "How dare you enter the synagogue when you are an ally of Christ? May your fate be the same as his in the afterlife."

Nicodemus replied, "Amen, let it be so. May I share the same fate as him in his kingdom."

Likewise, when Joseph confronted the Jews, he said, "Why are you angry with me for asking for the body of Jesus from Pilate? I have placed him in my tomb, wrapped him in clean linen, and rolled a stone in front of the entrance."

"I have treated him honorably, but you have acted unjustly, condemning him by crucifying him, giving him vinegar to drink, crowning him with thorns, and whipping his body. You have brought the guilt of his blood upon yourselves."

The Jews, hearing this, were greatly troubled and upset. They seized Joseph and threw him into custody, intending to keep him locked up until the Sabbath was over.

They said to him, "Confess your actions, for we cannot harm you until the first day of the week. But know this: you will not be worthy of a burial. We will give your body to the birds and the beasts."

Joseph responded, "Your words resemble those of the proud Goliath, who insulted the living God when he mocked David. But you, scribes and scholars, know that God says through the prophet, 'Vengeance is mine, and I will repay you for the evil you have done.'"

"The God whom you crucified on the cross is able to deliver me from your hands. All the evil you have done will return upon you."

"Remember when the governor washed his hands, declaring himself innocent of the blood of this just man? But you responded, saying, 'His blood be upon us and our children.' As you have spoken, may you face the consequences of your words."

Upon hearing this, the Jewish elders were filled with rage. They seized Joseph and locked him in a room with no windows, sealing the door and securing it with a lock. Annas and Caiaphas placed guards outside, and they consulted with the priests and Levites, planning how they would put Joseph to death.

Afterward, they ordered Joseph to be brought before them, but the Gospel omits or loses a portion of what happened next, leaving the conclusion uncertain.

Chapter 10 - When the assembly of the Jews heard the news, they were astonished, unable to understand how Joseph had managed to escape. They found the seal on the lock of the chamber still intact, but Joseph was nowhere to be found.

While they were discussing the situation, one of the soldiers who had been guarding Jesus' tomb stood up and spoke to the assembly. He told them, "While we were guarding the tomb, an earthquake occurred. We saw an angel descend from heaven, roll away the stone from the entrance, and sit upon it. His face was like lightning, and his clothes were as white as snow. We were so afraid that we became like dead men."

The soldier continued, "The angel spoke to the women who had come to the tomb, telling them not to fear. He said, 'I know you are looking for Jesus, who was crucified. He is not here; he has risen, just as he said he would. Come and see the place where he lay. Then go quickly and tell his disciples that he has risen from the dead, and that he will go ahead of you into Galilee. There you will see him, just as he told you.'"

The Jews were enraged upon hearing this and immediately called the soldiers together, asking, "Who are the women who spoke with the angel? Why didn't you seize them?"

The soldiers replied, "We don't know who the women were. We were so terrified when we saw the angel that we couldn't act. How could we have stopped them?"

The Jews, not believing the soldiers, responded, "As the Lord lives, we don't believe you."

The soldiers, replying with a touch of irony, said, "When you saw and heard Jesus performing miracles, you didn't believe him. Why should you believe us now? You spoke rightly when you said, 'As the Lord lives.' He truly does live."

The soldiers continued, "We have also heard about how you locked up Joseph, who buried Jesus' body, in a chamber with a sealed lock. But when you opened it, he was gone."

They challenged the Jews, saying, "If Joseph is in Arimathea and Jesus is in Galilee, we were informed by the angel and the women about his resurrection."

Hearing this, the Jews became fearful and whispered to one another, "If these things become known, everyone will believe in Jesus."

In response, they gathered a large sum of money and gave it to the soldiers. "Tell the people that Jesus' disciples came in the night while you were asleep and stole his body," they instructed. "If Pilate hears of this, we will take care of him and keep you safe."

The soldiers took the money and spread the false report as they had been instructed. This story quickly circulated among the people.

As the soldiers spoke, they mentioned another significant event: "We've also heard how Joseph, who buried Jesus' body, was locked in a chamber with a sealed lock. But when the chamber was opened, he was gone."

They raised another challenge to the Jews: "If Joseph is in Arimathea and Jesus in Galilee, we heard the angel explain everything to the women."

This revelation caused great anxiety among the Jewish leaders. They feared that if word of it spread, everyone would start believing in Jesus. To prevent this, they gathered a substantial amount of money to bribe the soldiers. They instructed them to spread the false story that Jesus' disciples had come during the night, stolen his body while the soldiers slept, and then concealed the truth. The Jewish leaders assured the soldiers that if Pilate were to hear of this, they would smooth things over with him and ensure their protection.

The soldiers, accepting the bribe, began spreading the fabricated tale, which soon gained wide circulation among the people.

Yet not everyone accepted the falsehood being spread. A priest named Phinees, together with Ada, a respected teacher, and Ageus, a Levite from Galilee, traveled to Jerusalem. They entered the synagogue and spoke directly to the chief priests and the gathered leaders, saying, "We have personally seen Jesus—the one you crucified—alive and speaking with his eleven disciples. He was with them on the Mount of Olives, teaching them to go throughout the world, proclaim

THE GOSPEL OF NICODEMUS

the Good News to every nation, and to baptize in the name of the Father, the Son, and the Holy Spirit. He said, 'Whoever believes and is baptized will be saved.' After this, we witnessed him ascending into heaven."

The chief priests, elders, and Levites listened closely and asked them, "By the God of Israel, tell us the truth—are these things really what you saw and heard?"

The three replied, "As surely as the Lord lives—the God of our forefathers, Abraham, Isaac, and Jacob—we testify to what we saw with our own eyes and heard with our own ears."

They continued, "If we were to deny what Jesus said and the vision of his ascent, we would be lying before God." At this, the chief priests rose angrily. Holding up the book of the law, they warned the three men, "You are forbidden from speaking any further about this Jesus."

The priests then gave the men a large sum of money and sent others with them to escort them back to their country, ensuring they wouldn't remain in Jerusalem and continue spreading the story.

The Jews, gathering together, expressed great distress over the situation, questioning what this extraordinary event in Jerusalem meant. But Annas and Caiaphas reassured them, saying, "Why should we trust the soldiers who guarded the tomb, who claim that an angel rolled away the stone? Maybe Jesus' disciples paid them to say this, and they took the body of Jesus."

They continued, "Consider this: we cannot trust foreigners. They were given a large sum of money and have followed the instructions we gave them. They must either be loyal to us or to Jesus' disciples."

Chapter 11 - When the entire council heard the latest reports, confusion and disbelief filled the room. The seal on Joseph's chamber was still intact—yet Joseph himself had vanished. Disturbed by this, Annas and Caiaphas went out to investigate. As they deliberated, one of the soldiers who had guarded Jesus' tomb stepped forward. He described how, during their watch, a great earthquake had shaken the ground, and an angel descended from heaven, rolled away the stone, and sat upon it.

The soldier recounted the angel's astonishing appearance—his face shone like lightning, and his clothing was dazzling white. The guards, overwhelmed with terror, collapsed in fear as if dead. The angel had spoken to the women who arrived at the tomb, assuring them not to be afraid. He told them that Jesus, who had been crucified, was no longer there—he had risen, just as he had said. The angel invited them to see where Jesus had been laid and instructed them to go quickly and tell the disciples he had gone ahead to Galilee.

When the Jewish leaders heard this account, they gathered the other guards and asked, "Who were these women the angel spoke to? Why didn't you stop them?"

The soldiers answered, "We were frozen in fear. How could we stop anyone when we were unable even to move?"

Still skeptical, the leaders replied, "We swear by the Lord—we do not believe you."

But the soldiers stood firm. "You didn't believe even when Jesus performed miracles before your eyes. Why would you believe us now? But we tell you, as surely as the Lord lives, it is true."

They then pointed out, "You locked Joseph in a chamber, yet when you returned, he was gone. You demand that we produce Jesus—why not first bring back Joseph yourselves?"

The Jewish leaders answered, "Joseph is in Arimathaea."

The soldiers responded, "And Jesus is in Galilee—we heard it from the angel himself."

The resurrection news sent ripples of fear through the council. They knew that if word got out, many would begin to believe. So they took a large sum of silver and bribed the guards, instructing them to spread a false story: "Say his disciples came at night while you slept and stole the body." The leaders promised that if Governor Pilate heard about it, they would intervene and protect the soldiers from any consequences.

The soldiers took the money and did as they were told. The story spread quickly among the people.

Meanwhile, a priest named Phinees, a teacher named Ada, and a Levite named Ageus journeyed from Galilee to Jerusalem. They came before the chief priests and synagogue leaders and testified, "We have seen Jesus, the one you crucified. He was alive and speaking with his eleven disciples on the Mount of Olives. He instructed them to go into the world, proclaim the Gospel to all nations, and baptize in the name of the Father, the Son, and the Holy Spirit. He said, 'Those who believe and are baptized will be saved.' After this, we witnessed his ascension into heaven."

The priests and Levites questioned them further, asking them to affirm their testimony before God.

The three men replied, "As surely as the God of our ancestors lives—the God of Abraham, Isaac, and Jacob—everything we have said is true. We heard his words and saw him ascend with our own eyes." They added, "To deny this would be to sin against the truth."

Infuriated, the chief priests stood and raised the book of the law, demanding that the men never speak of these things again. Then, offering them a generous sum of money, they ordered them to leave Jerusalem immediately and not spread their account any further.

The Jews then gathered together, deeply troubled by the events. They asked, "What is this extraordinary thing that has happened in Jerusalem?"

Annas and Caiaphas tried to calm them, saying, "Why should we trust the soldiers who guarded Jesus' tomb, who claim that an angel rolled away the stone? Perhaps the disciples gave them money to spread this story and stole the body of Jesus themselves."

They added, "Consider this—foreigners should not be trusted, especially since they were given a large sum of money to speak as we instructed them. They must be loyal to us or to Jesus' disciples."

The assembly grew more restless as the chief priests and the elders attempted to suppress the rumors of Jesus' resurrection. They discussed the matter among themselves, anxious that if the news spread further, people would begin to believe in Jesus as the Messiah. The priests and elders sought to find a solution, and their discussions became increasingly urgent. They knew that if the story about Jesus' resurrection gained more traction, it could undermine their authority and the power they held over the people.

In an attempt to quell the growing unrest, the elders took a different approach. They gathered together once more, hoping to devise a plan to control the situation. But despite their efforts to silence those spreading the testimony of Jesus' resurrection, they knew that the words of the witnesses could not easily be erased. As the days passed, the tension between the Jewish leaders and the followers of Jesus continued to mount, and it became clear that the story of Jesus was not one that could be so easily buried.

The elders knew that, for now, they had to keep the situation under control, but they also knew that the truth of what had occurred—the resurrection of Jesus—could not be ignored. They would have to find new ways to discredit those who testified about it and prevent the message of Jesus from spreading further. The challenge now was not only to silence the voices of the witnesses but also to prevent the powerful and transformative message of the resurrection from gaining too much of a foothold in the hearts and minds of the people.

With their plan to bribe the soldiers and spread a false story in place, the Jewish leaders believed they had momentarily secured their position. But they could not shake the unease that lingered. As much as they tried to contain the message, they knew deep down that the truth had already begun to take root, and its effects would eventually be felt.

Meanwhile, the followers of Jesus continued to spread his teachings, inspired by the power of his resurrection. Though the chief priests and elders tried to suppress the truth, the message of hope, redemption, and eternal life that Jesus brought would continue to spread, reaching more hearts and transforming lives. And though the Jewish leaders did their best to keep the truth hidden, it would ultimately shine through, as it had always been destined to do.

PART 4: THE ASCENSION AND CONCLUSION

Chapter 12 - When the chief priests and all those present heard the news, they were astonished and overwhelmed by the mystery that had unfolded. They could hardly believe the account, for they found the chamber's lock undisturbed, and Joseph, the one who had buried Jesus, was nowhere to be found. The confusion was palpable, and the tension grew among them as they sought to understand what had truly occurred.

At that moment, one of the soldiers who had been guarding the tomb of Jesus stood up and spoke to the assembly. He began recounting the extraordinary events he had witnessed during his watch. He described the sudden earthquake that had occurred while they were standing guard, a tremor so intense that it seemed to shake the very foundations of the earth. As they stood in shock, an angel of God appeared, rolling away the stone from the entrance of the tomb. The angel, radiant as lightning with garments white as snow, sat upon the stone, a presence so powerful that it left the guards trembling, feeling as though they were lifeless.

The soldier continued, describing how the angel addressed the women who had come to the tomb, urging them not to be afraid. The angel assured them that Jesus, who had been crucified, had risen, just as he had promised. The women were instructed to go quickly and tell his disciples that Jesus had risen from the dead and would meet them in Galilee, just as he had told them.

The chief priests, hearing the soldier's testimony, were alarmed and immediately began questioning him about the women and why they had not been seized. But the soldier explained that, in their fear, he and the other guards had been unable to take action. They had simply watched in awe, unable to prevent what had occurred. Yet the chief priests, unwilling to accept the soldier's testimony, accused them of lying, questioning how they could believe such an account when they had been present to witness Jesus performing numerous miracles.

The chief priests then turned their attention to the events surrounding Joseph. They demanded that the body of Jesus be brought forward to be examined, and they were perplexed by the fact that Joseph, having been locked away, had somehow vanished from his cell. The soldiers, however, pointed out that if Joseph had truly gone missing, and if Jesus was alive as the women had claimed, then the truth of the matter was undeniable. The chief priests, realizing the gravity of the situation, became even more fearful. They decided to silence the witnesses and ensure the story of Jesus' resurrection was quashed before it could spread further.

In their desperation, the chief priests gathered a substantial sum of money and bribed the soldiers to spread a different story—one in which Jesus' disciples had come in the night and stolen his body. If the governor Pilate were to hear about this, they promised the soldiers they would be protected. Despite their efforts to suppress the truth, the news spread among the people, and the story of the resurrection began to gain momentum, much to the dismay of the religious leaders.

The chief priests, now desperate to maintain control, devised another plan. They sent a group of priests and elders to a place called Arimathæa to investigate the situation. There, they were told of two men—Charinus and Lenthius—who had risen from the dead and were seen praying in the city. The men were known for their devoutness, and their resurrection became a source of further bewilderment and awe. The priests and elders, now filled with both wonder and fear, decided to bring these two men to Jerusalem, hoping that their testimony would confirm the miraculous nature of the events.

Upon arrival, Charinus and Lenthius were taken to the synagogue, where the chief priests and elders gathered to hear their testimony. In a sealed room, they were sworn to secrecy and asked to explain the events of their resurrection. Trembling with reverence, Charinus and Lenthius spoke of their experiences. They told of how they had been raised from the dead, and how they had witnessed the glory of God. They spoke of Jesus, who had been crucified, and of the miraculous events that had taken place surrounding his death and resurrection.

As the two men recounted their experiences, they were asked to write down everything they had seen and heard. With trembling hands, they began to write, describing the events they had witnessed, the power of God, and the divine intervention that had allowed them to return to life. Their testimony became a powerful witness to the truth of Jesus' resurrection, and the story of his divine power continued to spread, touching hearts and minds across the land.

Chapter 13 - When we were in the depths of hell, surrounded by darkness and despair, something incredible happened. Suddenly, a great light appeared, shining like the sun, gold in color, accompanied by a brilliant purple glow that illuminated the entire place. It was as if the very essence of light itself had descended to bring hope to those dwelling in the blackest darkness.

At that moment, our forefather Adam, along with the patriarchs and prophets, rejoiced with great gladness. They recognized the light as the very source of eternal brilliance—the one who had promised to lead them into everlasting radiance. Then Isaiah the prophet stepped forward and spoke, declaring that this light was truly the Father and the Son of God. He reminded them of the prophecy he had spoken long ago, when he said that those who dwelled in darkness would one day see a great light, and those living in the shadow of death would be lifted into life.

While we were all overcome with joy at the sight of this radiant presence, another familiar figure appeared—our father Simeon. His heart overflowed with praise for the Lord Jesus Christ, the Son of the Living God. This was the same Simeon who had once cradled the infant Jesus in the temple and spoken of the child as the salvation prepared for all people. Now, seeing him again in glory, he rejoiced anew, recalling how Jesus had come as a light to reveal truth to the nations and as the glory of Israel.

As Simeon shared his proclamation, all the saints gathered in the realm of death lifted their voices in joyful hope. Their hearts swelled with the realization that the promised light had finally come to deliver them from darkness.

Then a man stepped forward from among the crowd—humble in appearance, like a hermit in the wilderness. Someone asked, "Who are you?" And he answered, "I am the voice crying out in the wilderness. I am John the Baptist, prophet of the Most High. I came before the Savior to prepare his path, to proclaim the way of salvation, and to call all to the forgiveness of sins."

And with that, the joy among the saints grew even stronger, for the light that had been promised was now shining in their midst.

As Simeon proclaimed his joy, the saints in the depths of hell rejoiced even more. Their hearts were filled with the hope of salvation, knowing that the promised light had arrived to rescue them from the darkness.

Then, a figure emerged from the crowd, a humble man who appeared like a simple hermit. Those present asked him, "Who are you?" He answered, "I am the voice crying out in the wilderness, John the Baptist, the prophet of the Most High. I came before the Savior to prepare the way for Him, to proclaim the knowledge of salvation and the forgiveness of sins."

John continued, recounting his encounter with Jesus: "When I saw Jesus approaching, I recognized Him as the Lamb of God, the one who takes away the sins of the world. I baptized Him in the Jordan River, and I saw the Holy Spirit descend upon Him in the form of a dove. Then I heard a voice from heaven, declaring, 'This is my beloved Son, in whom I am well pleased.'"

John now shared with us the great news: "The Son of God will soon visit us, bringing the dawn of salvation, just as the daybreak brings light to those in darkness and the shadow of death."

Chapter 14 - When our first father Adam heard that Jesus had been baptized in the Jordan, he called for his son Seth and said to him, "Tell your sons, the patriarchs and the prophets, everything you heard from Michael, the archangel, when I sent you to the gates of Paradise. I had asked God to anoint my head while I was ill."

Seth approached the patriarchs and the prophets and began, "I, Seth, when I was praying at the gates of Paradise, saw the angel of the Lord, Michael, appear before me. He said, 'I have been sent to you by the Lord. I have been appointed to watch over human bodies.'"

He continued, "Michael told me not to pray to God with tears, asking for the oil of the tree of mercy to anoint my father Adam's aching head. He explained that I would not be able to obtain it until the last days and times, which would come after five thousand and five hundred years."

"At that time, Christ, the most merciful Son of God, will come to earth. He will resurrect the body of Adam, and at the same time, He will raise the dead. When He arrives, He will be baptized in the Jordan."

"Then, with the oil of His mercy, He will anoint all those who believe in Him. The oil of His mercy will continue through future generations, anointing those born of water and the Holy Spirit, leading them to eternal life."

Seth went on, "When Christ, the most merciful Son of God, comes to earth, He will bring our father Adam into Paradise, to the tree of mercy."

When the patriarchs and prophets heard these things from Seth, they were filled with joy and rejoiced even more.

Chapter 15 - While all the saints were rejoicing, Satan, the ruler of death, spoke to the prince of hell. He said, "Prepare yourself to receive Jesus of Nazareth, the one who claimed to be the Son of God, yet was a man who feared death. He even confessed, 'My soul is sorrowful even to death.'" Satan continued, "Not only has he caused me harm, but also many others. Those I blinded, made lame, or tormented with demons, he healed by his word. He even took away the dead from you, those whom I brought to your realm, and he did so with force."

The prince of hell, puzzled, responded, "Who is this powerful prince, yet a man who fears death? All the rulers of the earth are subject to my dominion, which you brought them into by your power." Satan answered, "If he is so powerful in his human nature, then I affirm that in his divine nature, he is almighty, and no man can resist his power. When he said he was afraid of death, it was a trap for you. Woe to you for the ages to come."

The prince of hell, still unsure, asked, "Why then do you question this? Why are you afraid to welcome Jesus of Nazareth, your adversary and mine?"

Satan replied, "I tempted him, stirred up my people—the Jews—against him with zeal and anger. I prepared the means of his suffering: the spear for his torment, the gall and vinegar, and the cross for his crucifixion. The nails to pierce his hands and feet are ready. His death is near, and I will bring him to you, subject to both you and me."

The prince of hell, hearing this, said, "You mentioned that he took the dead from me by force. Those who have been kept here, waiting to rise again, were not taken by their own power but by God's will. The Almighty took them from me." Satan responded, "It is this very man, Jesus of Nazareth, who has taken the dead from you by his word, not by prayer to God. He is the one who brought Lazarus back to life, even after he had been dead for four days, stinking and decayed. He was under my control as a dead man, yet Jesus restored him by his power."

The prince of hell, realizing the magnitude of what Satan was saying, replied, "I beseech you by the power that both you and I possess, do not bring him here. I trembled when I heard of his power. All my impious followers were disturbed at the same time, and we could not hold Lazarus. He shook himself free, and despite all our malice, he walked away. Even the earth, where Lazarus' body lay, expelled him, and he came to life again."

Satan, acknowledging the reality of Jesus' power, said, "It is indeed the same person, Jesus of Nazareth."

The prince of hell then declared, "I swear to you, by the powers that belong to us both, do not bring him here. When I heard of his power, I trembled with fear, and my entire impious company was disturbed. We could not keep Lazarus, and the earth rejected him, returning him to life."

He continued, "I now know that he is Almighty God, the one who can perform such miracles. He is powerful both in his divine nature and his human nature, the Savior of mankind. Do not bring him here, for he will free all those I hold in prison—those trapped in unbelief, bound by their sins. He will lead them to everlasting life."

Chapter 16 - While Satan and the prince of the underworld were deep in conversation, a thunderous voice suddenly echoed through the realm, accompanied by the sound of rushing winds. The powerful voice cried out,

"Open up your gates, rulers of the deep! Throw wide the ancient doors, for the King of Glory is coming!"

At the sound of this, the prince of the underworld turned sharply to Satan. "Get out of my domain!" he demanded. "If you are truly as powerful as you claim, then go face this King of Glory yourself! But tell me—what authority do you even have here?"

With that, he cast Satan out of the realm and gave urgent orders to his dark sentinels: "Seal the gates of torment with iron and reinforce them with bolts. Stand your ground—we must not let ourselves be overthrown."

But the saints, hearing the divine voice and feeling a surge of hope, cried out together, "Open the gates! Let the King of Glory enter!"

Then David, the prophet, stepped forward and exclaimed, "Didn't I proclaim this while I lived? I said, 'Let all people praise the Lord for His goodness, for His wonderful works on behalf of humanity!' He shattered the gates of bronze and broke through the bars of iron. He saved them from their rebellion and brought light to those suffering under the weight of injustice."

Isaiah, another holy prophet, added, "I too spoke truly when I lived. I foretold the day when the dead would rise, and those resting in the grave would awaken with joy, for the dew of salvation from the Lord would restore them."

"I even cried out, 'O death, where is your victory? O death, where is your sting?'"

When the saints heard these words, their voices rose together once more. They cried out to the prince of the underworld, "Unlock the gates! Tear down the iron bars! Your power is ending—you will soon be bound and defeated!"

Then, just as before, the thunderous voice rang out again: "Lift your gates, you rulers! Be lifted, you gates of hell! The King of Glory is coming!"

Now overwhelmed and shaken, the prince of the underworld shouted, "Who is this King of Glory?!"

David answered confidently, "I know that voice—I once spoke these words by the Spirit. I declare again: the Lord, strong and mighty, the Lord, victorious in battle—He is the King of Glory! He is the Lord of heaven and earth."

"He has heard the cries of the imprisoned and has come to set free those marked for death."

"So now, foul and unclean ruler of the deep—open your gates! The King of Glory is here!"

As David spoke these words, the Lord Himself appeared—radiant and shining like a man. His presence lit up even the deepest shadows. With unmatched power, He shattered every chain and entered the darkest depths to reach those bound by sin and death.

Chapter 17 - Upon hearing these things, Death and her officers, full of wickedness, were overcome with fear as they sensed the approach of Christ, whose light shone brightly and suddenly appeared in their domains. The devils cried out in alarm, saying, "We are bound by you; it seems you intend to bring about our destruction before the Lord."

They wondered, "Who are you, who possess no sign of corruption, but radiate a brilliant light that proves your greatness, yet seem unaffected by it?" They were bewildered by his appearance, as he seemed both mighty and weak, grand yet humble, a lowly figure who commanded with the authority of a soldier. "You, the King of Glory, who once died and rose again, now stand before us, dead and alive—how can this be?"

They continued, "You lay dead in the tomb, but now have come back to us alive. In your death, the very creation trembled; the stars were moved, and now, having come among the dead, you disturb our dominion, bringing liberty to those held in chains by sin."

"Who are you, who release the captives and restore them to freedom, who bring light to those once blinded by the darkness of their sin?"

The devils, who were trembling with fear, spoke among themselves, their voices filled with dread. "Where do you come from, O Jesus Christ? You are a man so powerful, so majestic in glory, so pure and spotless. How is it that you are so bright, with no stain, and so pure, with no fault? This world, which was once subject to us, has never sent us such a dead man. It has never sent us such offerings as these to the princes of hell."

"Who are you, to enter our domain with such courage, threatening us with the greatest punishments, yet attempting to free others from the chains we have bound them with? Could it be that you are the Jesus Satan spoke of, the one who, through his death on the cross, was meant to gain the power over death?"

And with that, the King of Glory, triumphing over death, seized the prince of hell, stripped him of his power, and took Adam, our earthly father, with him into his divine glory.

Chapter 18 - The prince of hell, filled with indignation, turned to Satan and rebuked him fiercely, saying, "O prince of destruction, the cause of Beelzebub's downfall and banishment, despised by God's angels and hated by all righteous souls, what in the world made you think to act in this way? You, who sought to crucify the King of Glory, promising us great advantages through his demise, yet, in your foolishness, you did not understand the magnitude of the consequences."

"For look now at Jesus of Nazareth, with the brilliant radiance of his divine glory, putting to flight all the powers of darkness and death. He has shattered our prisons from top to bottom, freed all the captives, and released those bound in torment. The very ones who once groaned under their suffering are now mocking us, and we are on the verge of defeat through their prayers."

"Our impious rule has been overthrown, and no part of humanity remains under our control. On the contrary, all of them now boldly defy us, whereas before, the dead never dared to challenge us, and those who were imprisoned could never find any joy."

"Why, O Satan, prince of all evil, father of the wicked and forsaken, would you attempt such an act? Our prisoners, who were always without hope of salvation or life, now stand free. Not one of them now groans in despair, nor does the slightest tear stain their faces."

"Satan, you, the ruler of the infernal regions, have lost all the advantages you gained through the forbidden tree, and the loss of Paradise. All of that is now undone by the wood of the cross. Your happiness expired when you crucified Jesus Christ, the King of Glory."

"You have acted against your own interests, and mine as well. You will soon feel the consequences of your actions through the torments and infinite punishments you will suffer. O Satan, prince of all evil, author of death, and source of all pride, you should have first examined the crimes of Jesus of Nazareth. You would have found no fault in him, nothing worthy of death."

"Why, then, did you venture to crucify him without reason or justice, and bring an innocent and righteous man into our domain, thereby losing all the sinners, the impious, and the unrighteous of the world?"

As the prince of hell continued to speak in outrage to Satan, the King of Glory addressed Beelzebub, saying, "Satan, the prince, shall be subject to your dominion forever, in place of Adam and his righteous sons, for they are mine."

Chapter 19 - Jesus extended His hand to Adam, saying, "Come to me, all you saints, created in my image, who were condemned by the forbidden fruit of the tree and by the devil and death. Live now through the wood of my cross, for the devil, the prince of this world, has been defeated, and death has been conquered."

Immediately, all the saints gathered together under the hand of the Most High God. Jesus took Adam's hand and said to him, "Peace be to you and to your righteous descendants, for they are mine."

Adam, falling at Jesus' feet, addressed Him with humility and tears, crying out, "I will praise You, O Lord, for You have lifted me up, and You did not allow my enemies to rejoice over me. O Lord, my God, I cried out to You, and You healed me. You brought my soul up from the grave; You kept me alive, so I would not descend into the pit."

"Sing to the Lord, all His saints, and give thanks for the remembrance of His holiness. His anger endures for only a moment, but His favor brings life."

In unison, all the saints, prostrating themselves before Jesus, declared, "You have come, O Redeemer of the world, and fulfilled everything that was foretold by the law and the prophets. You have redeemed the living by Your cross, and You have come to us, so that by the death of the cross You may deliver us from hell, and by Your power, from death."

"O Lord, as You have placed the ensigns of Your glory in heaven, and set up the sign of Your redemption, the cross, on earth, so now, Lord, place the sign of the victory of Your cross in hell, that death may no longer have dominion."

Jesus, reaching out His hand, marked the sign of the cross over Adam and all the saints. Taking Adam by His right hand, He ascended from the depths of hell, with all the saints of God following Him in triumph.

The royal prophet David boldly declared, "Sing to the Lord a new song, for He has done wondrous works; His right hand and holy arm have granted Him victory. The Lord has made His salvation known; He has revealed His righteousness to the nations."

The entire assembly of saints echoed in response, "This honor belongs to all His saints. Amen, let us praise the Lord!"

Then the prophet Habakkuk proclaimed, "You went forth for the salvation of Your people, for the salvation of Your chosen ones."

All the saints joined in, saying, "Blessed is He who comes in the name of the Lord, for the Lord has illuminated our path. This is our God, forever, and He shall reign over us throughout all generations. Amen."

In this manner, all the prophets lifted their voices in sacred praise to God, following the Lord in His glorious ascent.

Chapter 20 – The Lord, holding Adam by the hand, entrusted him to Michael, the archangel, who guided them into Paradise, a realm overflowing with mercy and glory. As they drew near, two venerable figures appeared, and the saints, astonished, asked them, "Who are you, who have not been with us in the depths, but instead have had your bodies placed in Paradise?"

One of the men answered, "I am Enoch, who was taken up by the word of God, and this man with me is Elijah the Tishbite, who was taken in a fiery chariot."

"We have remained here, not tasting death, but now we are about to return when the Antichrist comes. Armed with divine signs and miracles, we will confront him, be slain by him in Jerusalem, and then, after three and a half days, be taken up again into the clouds."

As Enoch and Elijah were speaking, another figure appeared, appearing wretched, carrying the sign of the cross upon his shoulders. When all the saints saw him, they asked, "Who are you? Your appearance is like a thief's. Why do you carry a cross?"

He responded, "You are right. I was a thief, having committed all sorts of wickedness on earth. The Jews crucified me with Jesus, and I witnessed the astounding events that occurred at His crucifixion."

"I believed Him to be the Creator of all things, the Almighty King, and I prayed to Him, saying, 'Lord, remember me when You come into Your kingdom.'"

"He heard my prayer, and said to me, 'Truly, I tell you, today you will be with me in Paradise.' He then gave me this sign of the cross, saying, 'Carry this and go to Paradise. If the angel who guards Paradise refuses you entry, show him the cross and say, 'Jesus Christ, who was crucified, sent me to you.''"

"When I did as He instructed, and spoke these words to the angel guarding Paradise, he immediately opened the gates, welcomed me in, and placed me on the right side of Paradise."

"He told me, 'Stay here a little while until Adam, the father of all mankind, enters with all his sons, the holy and righteous servants of Jesus Christ, who was crucified.'"

After hearing the thief's story, all the patriarchs praised God with one voice, saying, "Blessed be You, O Almighty God, Father of everlasting goodness, Father of mercies, who has shown such favor to sinners and brought them to the mercy of Paradise, placing them in Your abundant spiritual provisions, in a holy and spiritual life. Amen."

Chapter 21 - These are the sacred and divine mysteries we, Charinus and Lenthius, were allowed to see and hear. But we could not reveal everything we witnessed—some of God's wonders were not meant to be spoken aloud. The archangel Michael himself instructed us to remain silent about certain mysteries. He commanded us to journey to Jerusalem with our fellow risen ones, to continue in prayer, and to proclaim the resurrection of Jesus Christ—He who raised us to life alongside Himself. Until the appointed time came, we were to remain as silent as those who have no voice.

Michael also told us to travel beyond the Jordan River to a rich and fruitful land, where many others who had risen with us would serve as living witnesses to Christ's return from the dead. We were granted just three days to remain among the living, during which we shared the Passover meal with our parents and declared the truth of the Lord's rising. In those days, we were also baptized in the holy waters of the Jordan. After that, we became invisible to all, hidden from human eyes.

This is everything we are permitted to disclose. So honor God, give Him praise, and turn your hearts in repentance. If you do, He will show you mercy. May the peace of our Lord Jesus Christ, the Savior of all, be with you. Amen. Amen. Amen.

When they had finished recording their testimony, Charinus presented his scroll to Annas, Caiaphas, and Gamaliel. Lenthius gave his to Nicodemus and Joseph. Immediately afterward, both men were transformed—radiating with divine light—and disappeared from the assembly, leaving behind only their writings. The contents of the two scrolls were found to be identical, word for word.

When the entire Jewish council heard these accounts, they were struck with awe. They turned to one another and said, "Surely, all these things were brought about by the hand of God. Blessed be the name of the Lord Jesus for all eternity. Amen." With heavy hearts and trembling, they beat their chests and quietly returned to their homes.

News of these events quickly spread throughout the synagogues. Joseph and Nicodemus went to the governor to report everything. Pilate listened closely and ordered that all of it be written down in the official public record of his court.

Chapter 22 – After these events, Pilate went to the Jewish temple and called for a meeting with all the rulers, scribes, and religious scholars in a small chapel within the temple. He ordered that the gates be closed and then addressed them, saying, "I have heard that you possess an important book in this temple. Please bring it to me."

When the book, carried by four temple attendants and adorned with gold and precious stones, was presented to Pilate, he spoke to the assembly, saying, "I ask you, by the God of your forefathers, the one who commanded the building of this temple, do not withhold the truth from me. You are all familiar with the contents of this book, so tell me: does it say anything about the Jesus you crucified? When was it prophesied that he would come? Show me."

After making Annas and Caiaphas swear an oath, they instructed everyone else to leave the chapel. They locked the gates of both the temple and the chapel and told Pilate, "You have made us swear by the temple itself to reveal the truth to you."

They continued, "After we crucified Jesus, we did not know that he was the Son of God. We thought he performed miracles through some form of magic. So we gathered a large assembly here in the temple to discuss the miracles he performed. During our deliberation, we found many witnesses from our own land who testified that they saw him alive after his death. They heard him speak with his disciples and saw him ascend to heaven. We even witnessed two individuals whom Jesus had raised from the dead, and they told us many extraordinary things about what Jesus did among the dead, things we have written down."

They explained that it was their custom to gather once a year to open a sacred book, seeking wisdom and direction from God. During one of these occasions, they examined the first of seventy texts and discovered a prophecy delivered by the archangel Michael to Adam's third son. This message foretold that, after 5,500 years, Christ—the dearly loved Son of God—would come into the world.

They wondered if this Christ could be the same divine being who had spoken to Moses, instructing him on the construction of the Ark of the Covenant. As they studied the dimensions of the ark—two and a half cubits long, one and a half wide, and one and a half high—they began to see symbolic meaning. These proportions, they believed, pointed to the future coming of Jesus Christ in human form, described as a living ark or tabernacle, arriving precisely after 5,500 years.

Their investigation continued, and they found further confirmation in the Scriptures: Jesus truly was the Son of God, Lord, and King of Israel. They reflected on the extraordinary miracles he had performed, and how those wonders had left even the chief priests confused. Returning to the book, they traced Jesus' genealogy through Joseph and Mary, seeing it aligned with the royal line of David.

The timeline detailed in the ancient records supported their realization. From the creation of heaven and earth to the great flood, there were 2,212 years. From the flood to Abraham, 912 years. Between Abraham and Moses, they counted 430 years, followed by 510 years from Moses to King David. The Babylonian captivity lasted 500 years, and from that exile to the birth of Christ, another 400 years passed. Altogether, these ages added up to 5,500 years—just as the prophecy had foretold.

In the end, they confessed that Jesus, the one they had crucified, was truly Christ—the Son of God, the eternal and almighty Lord.

Amen.

CONCLUSION
WALKING THE PATH OF HIDDEN LIGHT

As you reach the end of this journey through the Gnostic Gospels, it is important to pause—not to conclude, but to breathe in the space that these ancient voices have opened within you. Reading these texts is not about gathering facts or building systems of belief. It is about entering a different kind of listening, one that does not rush to explain, but dares to remain open.

The Gnostic tradition does not offer easy answers. It rarely hands you a map. Instead, it invites you to remember what you have forgotten, to reawaken a knowing that lies deeper than words, deeper than reason. In the echoes of these gospels, what you encounter is not a dogma but an invitation: to seek, to question, to wonder, and to return.

Each text you have explored—whether poetic, mystical, visionary, or narrative—carries within it the trace of a hidden longing. They were not written for those who wished to be told what to think. They were written for those who were already restless, who suspected that the visible world was not the whole story, who could feel in their bones the tug of another homeland, another light.

There is a humility in these writings that modern readers might miss at first. For all their complexity and beauty, the Gnostic Gospels are often fragmented, incomplete, mysterious. They whisper rather than shout. They hint rather than declare. They are, in a sense, mirrors for your own journey. They reflect not what you already know, but what your heart is still learning to recognize.

As you turn the final pages, it is worth remembering that gnosis—the kind of knowing these texts celebrate—is not about information. It is about transformation. It is not knowing about the divine, but knowing through the divine, and even knowing yourself as part of that living mystery. This is why these gospels can feel both deeply familiar and unsettling at the same time. They do not aim to comfort you where you are. They aim to awaken you to who you have always been beneath all forgetting.

Perhaps this is why so many voices arise from the margins, not from the centers of religious power. These are the voices of those who refused to be limited by orthodoxy, who dared to imagine the divine in ways that still startle us. They remind us that the early Christian world was not uniform or simple. It was diverse, searching, vibrant with conflicting visions of truth. And in that diversity, something essential lives on: the right to seek, to question, to remember.

You have not read a closed system here. You have walked through a garden of broken paths, shifting images, and incomplete maps. That is exactly as it should be. Gnosis is not about certainty. It is about the courage to walk without all the answers, trusting that the hidden light you seek also seeks you.

There is no final conclusion to a journey like this one. These texts are fragments, and so are we. But in the meeting of fragment with fragment, something whole begins to pulse again. Not a finished doctrine, but a living invitation.

The divine is not distant in these writings. It is near. It is buried within you, beneath the noise, the fears, the habits of a lifetime. It is the light you glimpsed when you were young and have perhaps spent years trying to forget. It is the voice that calls you not from the heavens, but from the center of your own being.

And so, as you close this book, you are not really ending anything. You are standing at a new threshold—the same threshold the writers of these gospels once stood upon. The same threshold that every seeker must cross again and again.

You are invited to keep asking, keep wondering, keep listening. To hold the questions open rather than rushing to close them. To trust that what is most real is often what is most hidden, and that hidden things are not less true—they are simply waiting for the right eyes to see them.

Thank you for walking this part of the path with these ancient companions. May the light they carried, however imperfectly, continue to awaken something within you. Not a doctrine to defend, but a memory to rekindle. Not a destination to reach, but a way of walking differently through the world.

And if, somewhere along the way, you find yourself remembering a light you thought long lost, know this: you are already closer to home than you realize.

www.ingramcontent.com/pod-product-compliance
Lightning Source LLC
Chambersburg PA
CBHW081355070526
44583CB00020B/2563